A FLINT PUNK ROCK MEMOIR

by John P. Ribner

This memoir is a highly subjective work of creative nonfiction. It's based on my memories of events that took place over 30+ years. Every recollection is colored by my perception, biases, and opinions. Also, some conversations are recreations instead of word-for-word transcriptions. The names of most major characters and some incidents were changed to preserve their identities. This is also true of their identifying characteristics, occupations, and places of residence. Lastly, the actual names of a few people mentioned in this book were used with permission.

This book is dedicated to all the kids who came of age in their local punk rock scene.

I'm talking about the dissenters, dropouts, and the freaks.

And I'm looking at you, individualists, and all the kooks, loners, and losers too.

As for the misfits, oddballs, and outsiders, this is for you, too.

It's even for the wackos and weirdos who lived life on the outside looking in.

Most importantly, it's for all the brave souls who've journeyed through the darkness to find themselves.

Foreword

From the first time I heard my favorite punk rock band, I dreamed of becoming a famous singer/songwriter.

I've nurtured that burning passion since I was 15 years old, but I was grounded and realistic about it. I just wanted to take over the music scene in my hometown of Flint, Michigan. From there, I would conquer the world. Too bad all my bands ended in disaster.

Failing to achieve my biggest dream isn't something I can just walk away from. For years, I've longed for some sort of closure on that part of my life. Since I can't get it from a sold-out farewell tour, I wrote this book. It sounded like a great idea, but I needed to know if my readers were interested in a memoir of my punk rock days.

To answer that question, I did what any independent author would do. I reached out to my readers on Facebook and told them about my idea and their responses were overwhelmingly positive. That's what inspired me to go forward with this crazy idea. Their continued support and messages asking, "Is it done yet?" pushed me to finish the words you're reading now.

While my Facebook friends were supportive, other people don't want me to write this book. They're members of my family. If that sounds surprising, then you don't know the Flint Ribners. I call my childhood home "Trauma Central" for a reason. It's always been a hotbed of negativity, and my family was particularly nasty when it came to my music.

I only told one family member that I was writing this book. I'd just finished a small chunk of it, and my excitement got the better of me. I called him and gave him a quick rundown on it. I'll never forget his response.

"Nobody cares about your stupid band!" he snarled.

I felt that familiar feeling of white-hot rage surge through my veins. It's the reaction I usually get when we talk. Since he's family, he knows all the right buttons to push. I didn't blow up like I'd done thousands of times before because I didn't want to give him that satisfaction.

By keeping my cool, I was able to take a step back and see why he said such a nasty thing to me. This book is about my time in Flint's punk rock scene, and he hated my music. That's why he shit all over my enthusiasm for it. Instead of arguing with him, I calmly asked him why he said that to me.

"You're almost 50 years old," he replied.

"So?"

"You need to grow up!"

"What's that supposed to mean?"

He told me that people only want to read about bands that made it big. According to him, I was just some loser who never made it out of my parents' garage. That was bullshit because he knew I'd played shows all over Michigan, and I recorded a few CDs. While that doesn't make me famous, I did accomplish more than he gave me credit for.

My family member was right about one thing, though. I didn't accomplish everything I wanted to do in music. It was quite the opposite. My dreams detonated like a rocket and scattered the smoldering remnants all over Flint. And that's exactly why I should tell my story.

I said, "Failure is the greatest teacher... "

"...Then you must be genius by now," he said.

"Real funny."

"I'm not joking," he said. "This is stupid."

"So, I'm not allowed to write about my life?" I asked.

"If you like wasting your time," he replied.

"Now you sound like my dad."

"Well, he was right."

"Oh really?"

"Yeah! You wasted your life then, and you're wasting it now."

As calmly as possible, I said, "Fuck you very much."

"I'm just trying to help you," he said.

"Whatever..."

"...So, you're gonna be hard-headed like you always are."

"You could say that."

"Don't come crying to me when it blows up in your face," he said.

"I won't."

That's where we left it, but I know I haven't heard the last from him. He'll read this book, and he'll be pissed because I discussed my dysfunctional family in it. I can't talk about my time in Flint's punk scene without doing that because the two subjects are so intertwined. That dirty laundry needs to be washed and hung out to dry so I can heal from it.

That's why I wrote this book.

At this point, I think an introduction is in order.

My name is John P. Ribner and, through no fault of my own, I was born to John and Dolly Ribner of Flint, Michigan. As their oldest child, they expected me to be a carbon copy of themselves. Things didn't quite work out that way.

The older I got, the more I wanted to be my own person. The more I did that, the more they tried to cram this square peg into a round hole. All that push and pull between us turned our split-level home on Jennings Road into a red-hot warzone.

Like so many other angry, abused, and misunderstood kids in the 1980s, punk rock became my refuge. The day I came home with a mohawk was the day Mom and Dad knew they couldn't snuff out my burning desire to be me. They fought fire with fire instead.

The two of them launched into an attack that went way beyond the typical parental scolding. They circled me like dragons as they rained searing flames of anger down upon my ego. Mom demanded that I sit through that blazing onslaught like a good little soldier or take a beating from my dad. I chose a comfy spot on the couch and dutifully awaited my incineration.

The old man was the first to step up to the plate and swing. He called me an "imbecile," "moron," and other things that questioned my intelligence. He also said I lacked the basic mental faculties needed to survive. He ended his half of the sermon by saying, "You're not my son. You're nothing to me!" That was hardly a news flash.

Mom's narrative also scorched me to the bone. Her face twisted into a look of pure disgust as she called me a "selfish rotten son of a bitch." She was too angry to see the irony in that. When I tried to defend myself against her verbal attacks, she said, "No woman is going to want you!" I didn't realize it then, but she instilled a fear of rejection inside me. She also conditioned me to think that love is abuse.

I wish I could say that "Operation Dragon Fire" was a one-time

3

thing. Too bad those search-and-destroy missions defined my childhood. It robbed me of my self-esteem and left me feeling unsafe, unwanted, and unloved. The worst part about it was that I started to believe all the hurtful things Mom and Dad said to me.

As bad as things were with my parents, there were some good times too. Those happened when I was a little kid. My parents were schoolteachers and my mom started teaching me the basics long before I was old enough for Kindergarten. For example, I learned my letters and numbers before I was five. This was a glowing testament to my parents' greatness.

When their friends came over, my parents trotted me out like I was a trained monkey. I recited the alphabet, spelled short words, and even did a little math. I also did impressions of my dad's New York accent. Those little performances were always a hit, and the adults lavished me with attention. I basked in that short-lived glory and grew to miss it as I got older.

By the time I was in high school, the praise and acceptance from my parents were long gone. My penchant for punk was an embarrassment to them, so they cut me off from everything but my most basic needs. Like many of Flint's lost and forgotten kids, I started to look for a surrogate family. This search eventually led me to the Capitol Theatre.

I was drawn to that once-ornate movie house because it was the center of the city's punk scene during the Reagan era. Each weekend, hundreds of kids went there to hear brutal, three-chord opuses of teen angst. While music attracted them, a sense of community kept them coming back.

Unlike everyone else, I didn't go to the Capitol to make friends. I went down there to perform with my band. That sets the stage for this memoir. It tells the story of an attention-seeking kid with poor social skills who sought validation from kids with issues of their own.

What could possibly go wrong?

PART ONE

1986-1990

1.
It's All Glenn Danzig's Fault

Hearing The Misfits for the first time was a life-changing experience for me.

That tiny spark ignited a blazing passion to become a singer/songwriter. While The Misfits are my favorite punk band, they weren't my first. Skateboarding was my "gateway drug" to a music addiction that introduced me to Glenn Danzig's influential punk band from Lodi, New Jersey.

One fateful day in 1985, I saw a group of skaters shredding the parking lot at the Genesee Valley Mall. Back then, I wasn't a jock, stoner, or popular kid; I was just some no-name nerd creeping through high school life. I knew that skateboarding, with its counterculture mentality and look, would become my new identity.

The next day, I walked into Roller Wheels Skate Shop on Richfield Road. I felt like I was entering a strange and fascinating new world. A bunch of skateboards hung on the walls in a dazzling display of colors and graphics. Of all the eye-catching choices, I picked the Madrid John Lucero. Its image of a sinister jester stoked the flames that burned inside the bubbling cauldron of my teenage psyche.

I also bought an issue of *Thrasher* magazine. It was the No. 1 skateboard magazine of the 1980s. In addition to news from the world of pro skating, the writers reviewed punk bands like Black Flag, Septic Death, and the Circle Jerks. Just like skating, those bands inspired me to be rebellious.

The summer of 1985 was all about shredding the asphalt parking lots on West Pierson Road and listening to punk rock. My fun ended way too soon, and I had to return to Hamady High School. It was named after Michael J. Hamady, one of the founders of the Hamady Brothers grocery stores. That iconic business made a huge impact on Flint's culture. Long after it closed in 1991, people still call grocery bags

"Hamady sacks."

My experience at Hamady High School wasn't as memorable or enduring.

The school was ground zero for mullets, heavy metal, and drug addiction. The dirty rogues who lived on the dirt roads of my neighborhood, aka Mayfair, were a closed-minded bunch. A skateboarding punk rocker was something their simple minds couldn't comprehend.

When I rode my skateboard to school in the fall, those losers called me a "pussy" and a "skater fag." It was exactly what I expected. The crowned princes of Mulletavia were shocked when I pushed back on their bullshit. The pride I had in my new identity was something worth fighting for. They soon realized that messing with me was more trouble than it was worth.

In the middle of the school year, another kid who was into skateboarding transferred to Hamady. Cameron Leon was a tall, thin dude with a long, sandy-blonde mullet that ran down the middle of his back. I immediately wrote him off as another burnout headed for the juvenile detention center on Pasadena Avenue.

I changed my mind about Cam the day he wore a Mr. Zogs Sex Wax T-shirt to school. Mr. Zog's is a surfing product but the shirts were popular with skateboarders too. No Mayfair metalhead would have been caught dead wearing one. I thought Cam's fashion choice was a risky one, but none of his stoner friends bothered him about it. He had a natural way of charming people, even those idiotic longhairs he called friends.

I thought Cam and I might get along, but I wasn't brave enough to say, "What's up?" I decided to bait him into talking to me by wearing my Zorlac Double Cut T-shirt to school. If he skated, he'd probably say something to me. Just like I predicted, he took one look at my shirt and asked me how long I'd been skating. That was enough to get me talking.

As friendships go, Cam and I were an odd couple. I was shy, naïve, and sheltered while he was Eddie Haskell with a mullet. His smooth, fast-talking ways inspired me to call him "Cam the Scam." It stuck, at least between us.

It was good to finally have a friend who was into the same things I was. Too bad it didn't last long. Cam moved back in with his mom before the end of the school year. That left me relatively alone deep inside enemy territory. I did the only thing I could do, which was retreat deep inside myself while I was in school, and do my thing after the bell rang.

The following summer was another solo adventure in skateboarding and punk rock. To kick it off, I decided to get a new skateboard. I took a trip to Roller Wheels and bought a Fogtown Beast. I also picked up a copy of the June 1986 issue of *Thrasher*. Little did I know it would change my life forever.

The cover had a picture of a guy with black hair running down the front of his face. He was steeped in shadows and he glared at the viewer from behind a stone gargoyle. A one-word barker read, "Danzig." I thought he was another pro skater until I read that he was Glenn Danzig, former singer of The Misfits.

I flipped to Danzig's interview on page 63. It was the first time I'd heard about The Misfits and they had already broken up by then. The interview focused on his new band, Samhain.

The more I read, the more my 15-year-old self was enamored with him. What impressed me most was the fact that he wrote all the lyrics and music for both his bands. I also dug his uncompromising commitment to his musical vision.

I read that interview over and over until the ink from *Thrasher's* pulpy pages stained my fingertips. At that point, there was only one thing to do. I had to hear The Misfits and Samhain. One warm summer day, I hopped on my bike and rode 12 miles through some sketchy neighborhoods. My destination was Rock-a-Rolla Records on Miller Road.

When I got there, I told the long-haired dude behind the counter that I wanted some Misfits vinyl. Little did I know he was Scott Carlson, the singer and bassist for Repulsion. In the mid-1980s, he – along with Matt Olivo, Aaron Freeman, and Dave "The Grave" Hollingshead – brought Flint's punk scene to national attention with the "grindcore" sound they created.

There I was face to face with one of Flint's biggest icons, but I didn't even know it. For his part, Scott seemed rather unimpressed with me. To him, I was just another kid wearing a studded army surplus vest with hand-painted skulls on it. Good thing he was kind enough to help me find what I was looking for.

Since the *Thrasher* article quoted the chorus from the song "Astro

Zombies," I wanted the record with that song. Too bad the legendary *Walk Among Us* album was out of print back then. I took my chances on the *Evilive* EP, which had a live version of "Astro Zombies" on it.

I clenched that sacred slab of vinyl like it was gold as I pedaled my way back home. When I got there, I set the needle down on the groove that marked the third song on side A. Anticipation shot through me as the record crackled.

Within seconds, The Misfits' sound filled my bedroom. That brutally raw live recording gave me a great idea of Danzig's approach to punk. He blended catchy melodies with lyrics that referenced old horror movies. It was backed by a sound that had all the hooks of 1950s rock with a hard-driving punk edge.

By the time "Astro Zombies" came to an end, The Misfits became my favorite band. Two days after my first trip to Rock-a-Rolla, I headed back there. Scott Carlson sold me *Die, Die My Darling*, *Earth A.D./Wolf's Blood*, and *Legacy of Brutality* that summer.

While all the albums were great, *Legacy of Brutality* was my favorite. Danzig's deep crooning on the Elvis-inspired "American Nightmare" gave me chills. "Some Kinda Hate," "Spinal Remains," and "Hybrid Moments" also received some heavy rotation on my turntable. I was hooked and there was no turning back.

Listening to the sonic frenzy of The Misfits' caused a vision to bubble up from my subconscious. In it, I stood center stage, singing punk songs that I'd written. This was more than just some idle fantasy; I was determined to make it happen. I knew it with absolute certainty.

I also knew I couldn't have a band if I started my junior year at Hamady.

The school wasn't exactly a breeding ground for up-and-coming punk rock talent. There was only one thing to do; I had to switch schools. That wouldn't be easy. My family's roots were firmly planted on the 20 acres of property on North Jennings Road. That land had been in my mother's family for generations. There was no way they were going to uproot so I could transfer to another school district.

My only option was to transfer to Luke M. Powers Catholic High School. It was the biggest and only Catholic school in Genesee County. Since it was a private school, I wouldn't have to change districts to go there.

Transferring to Powers presented some problems. Much to my mother's deep dismay, I was a horrible Catholic. Secondly, the school would be crawling with detestable preppie scum. I was willing to bet that there would be some skater types there too. I could recruit my future band from this presumed pool of punk rock potential.

Convincing Mom and Dad to let me go to Powers wouldn't be easy. At that school, Jesus was Lord and Savior, but cash was king. Mom and Dad weren't going to bankroll my further adventures down the punk rock rabbit hole. This meant I'd have to pull off something I call the "Great Con Job of 1986."

I knew that the way to my parents' wallets was through their egos. Since they were proud of being successful schoolteachers, I'd use that as leverage. I knew exactly how to do it, too. To make it work, I put on my most convincing look of wide-eyed innocence and told them I wanted to transfer to Powers.

"No!" my dad snapped, in his thick, New York accent.

"Why not?"

"I'm not going to pay more money for you to fail!"

"I'm not failing…"

"…Bullshit!"

"C'mon…"

"I said no!"

"What do you think, Mom?" I asked.

She said, "I asked you if you wanted to go there two years ago but you said 'no.'"

"That was then, this is now," I said.

"What changed?"

I told her what I thought she wanted to hear. It was something about wanting a better education than what Hamady had to offer, blah blah blah. There was some truth to that. Hamady was a joke. The district had to move the fifth, sixth, and seventh graders into the high school just to keep it from closing.

Mom said, "Are you going to be serious about this?"

"Yes!" I replied.

Dad shouted, "I can't believe you're considering it!"

"Why shouldn't I?" Mom said.

"He's just gonna screw around," Dad replied.

"No I won't!"

"Bullshit!"

10

Dad was a dead end, so I turned back to Mom for a lifeline. She reminded me of my bad habit of starting strong at the beginning of a school year, then falling off the rails. She wasn't wrong so I didn't try to deny it. I just promised her that things would be different at Powers.

"He's lying!" Dad shouted.

"You never give me a chance," I whined.

"You never tell the truth," Dad growled.

Mom told him to let me talk and I explained how serious I'd be at my new school. Mom was thrilled with the idea that I'd be getting an education rooted in the Catholic faith. Dad said I had ulterior motives, but he couldn't figure out what those were. In his moment of doubt, he reverted to his go-to response and said, "No!"

Big John put his foot down, but I knew it was an empty gesture. My impassioned plea worked its magic on Mom. With her on board, she pressured the old man until he crumbled like he always did. For all his big talk about being a "strong man" and a "trailblazer," his wife ran the show. I'd known that since I was a kid, and I worked that angle every chance I got.

The Great Con Job of 1986 was a success, but I felt a little sleazy about it. If my parents were expecting an honor roll performance, they made a horrible investment. Despite being the son of two teachers, I never cared about school. I was a lazy kid who was too easily distracted every time I opened a textbook.

I found a way to fight my feelings of guilt, though. I told myself that it was all Glenn Danzig's fault. If he wouldn't have been such a great singer/songwriter, I wouldn't have wanted to start a band. And if I didn't want to do that, there would be no reason for me to transfer.

I did want to start a band, though. I wanted it more than I had ever wanted anything up to that point in my life. Like it or not, switching schools was my best chance at making it happen. If I didn't take my shot, I would regret it for the rest of my life.

As the last days of summer came to an end, I was excited to start school.

2.
Might As Well Jump

I committed social suicide when I transferred to Powers as a junior. Those kids grew up together and had formed their social alliances. With none of that to fall back, I walked in there as a stranger. I was on my own from bell to bell.

The school's academic policies didn't do me any favors. Powers considered my transfer credits inferior to their esteemed curriculum. As a result, they stuck me in remedial classes with sophomores and even some freshmen. The guidance counselor warned me about this when I enrolled, but I didn't think it would be a big deal.

I wasn't ready for all the teasing I got from those spoiled little brats. The underclassmen were ruthless. On any given day, one of them would ask me if I was a junior. I would say that I was, and they'd say things like, "Oh! You got held back."

Everybody else thought it was hilarious, but it got old with me. I didn't mind being the "new kid," but I wasn't going to let them call me the "dumb kid." That led to several exchanges just in my first few weeks.

Lunch was the worst part of the day. Since I didn't make any friends, I sat at a table by myself. People laughed and said things just loud enough for me to hear, of course. To avoid embarrassment, I started sneaking into the auditorium and eating lunch there. My Phantom of the Opera routine spared me from being teased, but it wasn't going to help me build my band.

After a month, I was ready to pack it in and go back to Hamady. Fortunately, I befriended two punk rock girls in a remedial Algebra class. The kindness in their eyes shined through the curtains of bangs that shielded them from the cruelties of teenage life. To me, they were the "Sisters of Mercy" because they were the only people who showed me any.

12

The Sisters shared some much-needed items for my Flint punk rock starter kit. The first thing they told me was to get my music at Wyatt Earp Records. I'd passed that place on Corunna Road a few times, but I thought it was a country and western record store. It was ground zero for punk rock music in Flint.

Doug Earp was the owner of the store and a descendent of the famous Western lawman. Wyatt Earp Records had the biggest selection of punk, post-punk, and new wave music in the county. Doug also helped fund the punk shows held at the Capitol Theatre.

Speaking of the Capitol, I told the Sisters that I wanted to start a band. They said they'd introduce me to Scott Repperton. He booked most of the shows, and they said he could make or break a band. That's why it was best to stay on his good side. I told them I needed a band before I had to worry about impressing "Big Daddy" Repperton.

The Sisters only knew two musicians at Powers, and those dudes already had a band. I knew who they were talking about because I'd passed them in the halls. One of them had an overgrown Dutch boy haircut and wore dad glasses. The other one was tall, skinny, and had a sunken face that accentuated every angle of his skull.

Chubby Ramone and Skeletor's hardcore-punk crossover band mixed the best parts of Poison Idea and Voivod. This bond, and their shared social anxieties, made them inseparable. I didn't have a snowball's chance in Hell of recruiting them for my project.

I eventually met someone I thought I could work with. He was in one of my classes, and I could tell he was a musician because he had a Zildjian medallion on his keychain. Zildjian was a brand of cymbals favored by many of the decade's most-popular drummers. Only a serious rocker would have something like that.

While I needed a drummer, I wasn't sure about this guy. It was the Van Halen logo on his Trapper Keeper that had me spooked. The Van Halen fans at Hamady used to call me a "pussy" and a "skater fag" because I was into punk. Needless to say, I didn't care for the band or its fans.

Despite my misgivings, I screwed up the courage to say hello. He turned and looked at me, probably for the first time, and said hello. I nodded toward his keychain and asked him if he played the drums. He said, "Who wants to know?" I extended my hand and introduced

13

myself. He shook it and said his name was Wallace Griggsley, "but everyone calls me Wally."

We talked about music as we worked together on a class project. He went on and on about the Van Halen brothers' virtuosity. I dropped hints about wanting to meet musicians, and he asked me if I wanted to start a band. I was glad he did because it saved me from having to bring it up. That could have been awkward.

I told him I did want to start a band, and he asked me what kind of music I liked. If he was a typical Van Halen fan, I couldn't just say, "I'm into punk." The genre's three-chord simplicity and anti-commercial message were the opposite of everything Van Halen stood for. I told him that my ideal band would have that classic three-chord rock sound with edgy lyrics.

"You mean like punk?" he said.

"Something like that," I replied.

I braced myself for the rejection that was sure to follow. I was surprised when Wally said he might be interested in trying something new. He said he wanted to hear my influences, so I told him I'd make him a mixtape of my favorite Misfits songs. It was the first thing I did when I got home that day.

The next day, I gave Wally the tape and he said he'd listen to it. I didn't mention it when I saw him in class the day after that because I didn't want to look desperate. Later that week, he told me he heard the tape and would have no problem playing something like that.

"Great!" I said. "All I have to do now is find a guitarist and bassist."

"I might be able to help with that," he replied.

Wally invited me to have lunch with him and his friends. His table was populated with an eclectic group of glee club singers, marching band members, and HAM radio operators. In other words, they were nerds.

Everyone in the lunchroom was staring at me while I sat with them. Well, it felt that way, at least. A tiny voice inside my head kept urging me to dash for the auditorium, but I kept my ass planted in that seat instead. I switched schools to put a band together, and Wally was my ticket to making that happen.

As I got to know them, I felt disappointed in myself. I always talked a big game about how wrong it is to judge people by the way they look. I thought I was above all that. Hanging with Wally and company taught me that I was just as judgmental as everyone else at that status-obsessed school.

Wally introduced me to my future bandmates. The first was a guy named Charles Watkins. He was a skinny, hyperactive dude who spoke in a machine-gun staccato pattern. I was told that "Chaz the Spaz" played a mean guitar, and he was into the Dead Kennedys and the Sex Pistols. That meant we had something in common.

The next guy I met was Tim McNamara. At six feet, three inches tall, he came by his nickname "Tiny" quite naturally. His most noticeable trait was that he had one blue eye and one hazel eye. More importantly, he was an experienced bass guitar player who idolized Geezer Butler of Black Sabbath.

Of everyone at the table, I really clicked with Tiny. It was his cavalier sense of humor that did it. It matched mine quite well.

After a couple of weeks, Wally said it was time for me to put up or shut up. I had to produce some song lyrics, a band name, and a direction for the project.

I said, "No problem."

I pulled out my notebook of lyrics and passed them around the table. Each of the guys flipped through them. While the guys liked my songs, not all of them were crazy about my choice of band names.

I wanted to call the group Wolf Charm, which I got from an occult encyclopedia. The ancient Germanic people hung severed wolf heads on their doors to ward off evil. Wally and Chaz said it reminded them of Lucky Charms cereal.

I said, "Well, I only got one more idea."

"What's that?" Wally asked.

"Death Symbol," I replied.

"Death Symbol?"

"Yeah!"

"How'd you come up with that?"

I told Wally and the guys that my Mom was looking at all the skulls I drew on my folder. She asked me why I did that, and I said that I liked skulls. She said, "But that's a death symbol." The guys said they liked it and, just like that, Death Symbol became the name of my first band.

The next order of business was to schedule a practice. I suggested a weekend sleepover at my house. I wasn't sure if my parents would go for it, but I didn't mention that to the guys. I planned to ask Mom first, which would veto Dad's no-vote.

My plan to have a band practice sleepover at my house worked. How could it not? I used the same formula as I did for the Great Con Job of 1986. Dad said "no" right off the cuff, but Mom said I could. When I told they guys that we could jam at my house, Chaz and Tiny looked at Wally.

Wally said, "It looks like we're having our first practice."

Tiny, Chaz, and I all cheered. It drew some funny looks from some preppies at the table behind us. I heard one of them mumble "nerds" under his breath, but I was too excited to care. I was on my way to living my punk rock dreams.

I transferred to Powers to form a band, and in less than a month, I did. It was a cause for celebration. I wanted to buy Poison Idea's *Kings of Punk* album, and that was the perfect excuse to check out Wyatt Earp Records. Somehow I knew that it was going to be my Flint punk rock coming-of-age moment.

I drove down Linden Road then turned a right on Corunna Road. I went another half mile or so until I saw the tiny record shack on my left. I pulled into the gravel lot and parked a few feet from the door. Iggy Pop's "Billy is a Runaway" was blaring from inside the building.

Walking inside that building was like crossing a threshold. I thought that I'd entered a punk rock paradise because I did. I saw a huge corkboard on my left. It was plastered with photocopied flyers for hall shows and musicians-wanted ads. To my right was the counter with a man behind it. He was talking to a couple of punk girls.

As I went further into the store, I got a full view of the dude. He was probably in his 40s and looked like Gary Shandling in a flannel shirt. He looked at me and said, "Can I help you find something?" in a slow drawl. My voice cracked a little when I said, "Poison Idea," and the girls giggled. The guy pointed to the rows of records and said, "Right there in the P-section."

I heard one of the girls say, "pee section," and they giggled again. The whole thing embarrassed me, but I tried my best not to let it show. I just made a beeline toward the records and started flipping through the stacks. I cruised past The Pixies, The Plimsouls, and The Pogues before I found what I was looking for.

16

When I got to the counter, the guy rang up the record. He then motioned to a wooden cassette rack behind him. There, I saw names including Dissonance, Guilty Bystanders, and Smiling Sacrifice photocopied onto cassette liners.

The guy said, "You should check out some of these local bands."

I suddenly felt uncomfortable and embarrassed, and I knew right away what was wrong with me. I got used to being the only punk at Hamady High School. That made me a neighborhood novelty. At Wyatt Earp's, I was just one of many punks around town. And it felt like I was the only one who hadn't recorded a tape or played a show.

I was overwhelmed with emotions that was so intense that my face became hot. I silently swore that I would never buy a tape from any of those local bands. To the guy behind the counter, I said, "Maybe next time."

I paid for my record and went to leave. Before I could, he thrust a hand as wide a garden spade toward me and introduced himself. He was Doug Earp, the owner. I shook his hand and told him my name.

He said, "Glad to meet ya, J.P."

"Glad to meet you too," I replied.

"Come back anytime."

"Thanks," I said.

When I walked outside, I heard something crunch beneath my shoe. I looked down and saw a cassette case, tape, and liner notes. I picked it up and discovered that it was Repulsion's *Slaughter of the Innocent*. I might not have wanted to pay for a local band's tape, but I was more than willing to grab one that someone dropped.

When I played that tape, I was blown away! I was thrashing away to the pounding intensity of "The Stench of Burning Death," "Eaten Alive," and all the other songs. I could see why everyone worshiped Repulsion. I also was reminded that I hadn't done anything in music yet, which made me feel the same way I did at Wyatt Earp's.

Repulsion was going to be a tough act to follow. I was sure those other local bands were, too. That meant a lot was riding on our upcoming practice. I planned to give it my all, and I hoped the guys would too. It was the only way Death Symbol would be the best punk group to crawl out of the shadows of General Motors' smokestacks.

3.
I Was an Overnight Sensation

I paced back and forth as I waited for the guys to show up. I was excited and terrified about what could happen. On the one hand, I couldn't wait to have my first experience singing in a band. On the other hand, I was afraid my parents might embarrass me in front of my friends.

It's sad that I had to be concerned about that. Most kids didn't have to worry about their parents humiliating them. That's because most parents did everything to boost their kids' self-esteem. John and Dolly weren't like most parents.

They took a cruel delight in tearing me down in front of a crowd, especially when that crowd was my friends. By the time I was 16, I'd lost count of how many times they shredded me like that. I didn't want that shameful spectacle to ruin Death Symbol's first practice.

I had good reason to believe that my parents might attack me in front of the guys. While Mom said yes to my band practice, Dad was less than supportive. His exact words were, "I don't want that faggot bullshit in my house!" That was his go-to term for anything that I liked.

The old man was a former high school and college jock still clinging to his bygone glory days. He didn't understand what it was like to be an awkward, insecure kid fumbling his way through high school in the 1980s. I was lucky that Mom was into the arts, which is why she vetoed all of Dad's hissing and spitting over my band practice.

A pair of headlights cut a ghostly swath through the mists that gathered outside.

I ran to the window and saw Wally's Chevy Econoline van in the driveway. I helped them load their gear inside then watched them set up. As I did, I realized that Wally and the guys were experienced musicians

18

while I just sang Misfits songs in the shower.

In a matter of minutes, I would have to step up to the microphone and prove I had what it takes to be a frontman. Nagging doubts chattered inside my mind. What if I'm not good enough? What if I sing out of tune? My insecurities quickly grew into a monster that threatened to devour me.

Tiny was the first to get set up. He plugged in his black Fender Musicmaster bass and tuned up. Chaz took a bit longer to attach his various effects pedals, tune his guitar, and dial up the perfect tone. Wally had a big drum set, so he was the last to get ready. After what seemed like forever, he finally secured the last Zildjian cymbal to its stand.

I said, "We ready to go?"

"After the photoshoot," Wally replied.

"What photoshoot?" I asked.

"The one we're doing now," was his stern reply.

To avoid our sonic assault, Mom and Dad went out for dinner and a movie. They told me that we had to stop playing when they got home. I wanted to play right away because I knew Mom and Dad wouldn't be gone all night.

I started to explain that to Wally when Tiny pulled me aside. He said it was best to let Wally have his way with "the small details." I could tell by his tone that Tiny feared Wally on some level. I decided to follow his lead until I got a better handle on the situation.

I took the guys on a quick tour of the house to find the best place for the shots. We decided on the cinder block wall in the garage because it looked like the wall of a dungeon. With the black and white film, the pictures would look like some of the old Misfits photos from the early '80s.

I was the first to get photographed. As I stood in front of the wall, I crossed my arms in front of me. With my left hand, I extended my index and pinky fingers, and with my right hand, I extended my middle and ring fingers. I tilted down and let my hair fall in front of my face. I thought it made me look wicked.

Wally said, "What are you doing?"

"What?"

"Your hands," he said.

"I thought it would look cool."

"You'll cut that out if you want to have your band practice," he snapped.

19

His outburst caught me off guard and I froze. I couldn't understand why he was giving me an attitude over a stupid picture. Before I could say anything, he accused me of making Satanic hand gestures. He also said that he wasn't going to "allow" that in the band.

I said, "It wasn't Satanic."

"Oh really?" he replied.

"Yeah," I said.

"Well, if you do it again, I'm quitting!"

I looked at Tiny and Chaz for some help, but they just stared at their shoes. I turned back to Wally but didn't say anything to him. I needed him to make this band thing happen so I couldn't risk upsetting him. As much as I hated it, I stood there and let him disrespect me in my own home.

I said, "Just take the picture."

"Lose the attitude," he replied.

"Whatever."

I felt like such a fool. I was so worried that my parents would humiliate me that I never thought a threat could come from within my band. I also realized that I didn't know Wally all that well before I joined a band with him. That knowledge came a little too late to do me any good.

He finally took the damn picture, minus my offensive hand gestures, of course. He then snapped photos of Tiny and Chaz, then handed the camera to Tiny to take his picture. That ended our family-friendly photo session.

When we were finally ready to play some music, Wally took charge like he did earlier. He wanted to make sure we went through the arrangements as slowly as possible to make sure everything was just right. As we did, it caused plenty of discussion between the three musicians while I sat there in silence.

Wally wrote everything down on a dry erase board he brought with him. He agonized over every chord change and transition. Those must have been more of those "little details" that Tiny mentioned. After what seemed like an eternity, we were finally ready to play our first song as a band.

Wally counted off the "one-two-three-four" on his drumsticks and the guys exploded out of the gate with the music to "Haunted House."

I came in a bit shaky in the first verse. By the time we hit the chorus, I felt comfortable enough to merge with what the guys threw down.

The more we played my songs, the easier it was for me to sing them. When I finally hit my stride, I felt strong, confident, and invincible. I never experienced those feelings before that night. Through the unbridled power of punk rock, my voice would finally be heard.

We played each of the tunes four or five times before we took a break. I sat there thinking about what I had just experienced. Up until that night, my lyrics were just some scribbling in a notebook. Now, they were actual songs. That feeling of power I had earlier was still buzzing through my body like the feedback from Chaz's guitar amp.

Wally said we should get back to the songs, and I agreed with him. We stepped up to our instruments, and Wally counted off the beat. At the count of four, Death Symbol thundered to life again. So did the feelings and emotions that were swelling inside of me.

As we played, I became consumed by that raging sense of power. It felt like every cell in my body was exploding into an orgasm-like sensation. It was better than any drug could ever be. Caught up in those emotions, I was surprised when my parents came home. It felt like they had just left, but they'd been gone for hours.

I unplugged the mic and started to roll it up. The guys followed suit with their gear. Mom saw that we were putting things away for the night, and she asked us if we were done.

I said, "You told me we had to stop when you got home."

"You're God damn right we did!" Dad barked.

"I want to hear your songs," Mom said.

"Forget it," Dad grumbled.

"Oh, come on, Johnny," she whined.

"It's a waste!" Dad growled.

I said, "We've been playing all night."

"So?" Mom replied.

"We're tired…"

She said, "Oh, come on. Just one song… "

There was a reason I didn't want to play for my mom and dad. The first two tunes were harmless enough, but the third would be a problem. It painted an unflattering picture of life in my childhood home. Secretly, I hoped that Mom would pick up on Dad's hint that he didn't want to listen to us play.

Mom kept needling at us to play a song for her. In the end, I knew Dad would give in to her just like he always did. I also knew this would piss him off because he didn't show any backbone in a room filled with guys. He'd be seething with rage and would find a way to take it out on me like he always did.

Just as I predicted, Dad got sick of listening to Mom. He finally told us to "hurry up and play one song." Seeing that I wasn't going to get out of it, I turned to the guys and said, "Let's do 'Haunted House.'"

I watched my parents' expressions as we went through it. Mom seemed mildly amused while Dad looked like he'd been sucking lemons. He looked even more pissed when Mom begged use to play another song in that nails-on-a-chalkboard whine of hers. I said "fine," and we ran through "Green Blood."

When we finished, Mom said we sounded better than she thought we would. I thanked her, then started to put the mic away. She asked if we had any more songs, and I said we didn't. That's when Wally piped up and said, "Yes we do."

I turned to Wally and whispered, "Shut up!"

"Is that true?" Mom asked.

I said, "No."

"Yes we do!" Wally said. "You should know that, J.P."

"Why's that?" Mom asked.

"Because he wrote it," Wally said.

"Will you play it?" she said.

"We've been playing all night," I replied.

"Please!" Mom whined.

"I got one more in me," Wally said. "How 'bout you guys?"

Chaz and Tiny agreed with him, which was hardly a surprise. I turned around and glared at Wally as he sat there gloating. I wanted to smash his face in, but I knew I wouldn't. I just stood there as Mom kept pleading like a child. Her voice was so damn annoying that I saw why the old man always gave in to her.

I said, "I think Dad wants to go to bed…"

"…Speak for me again and I'll crack your fuckin' skull!" Dad growled.

"Johnny!" Mom hissed.

What was the old man thinking? The time to crack my skull is after company leaves, not while they're still there. There's no sense ruining your reputation over a murder that could be taken care of later.

22

Mom shamed Dad into shutting up then she returned her attention to us. She had a nasty habit of discounting the word "no," especially when I said it. Like a waterfall pounding on rocks, she relentlessly pestered us in that grating voice of hers.

Dad said, "Just play the fucking thing already!"

Fine, I thought. If she wants to hear our last song so badly, she'll get it right between her eyes. I looked over at Wally, and he flashed me that mocking grin. It was so disgusting that I turned away from him and said, "Okay. This one's called 'I Was a Teenage Scapegoat.'"

"Teenage scapegoat?" Mom asked.

It was too late to answer her. Wally counted off the beat, and the gutless wonders jumped into the song. When it was my time to sing, I ripped into it with everything I had.

I was a teenage scapegoat
For my mom and dad
In order for them to be good,
They had to make me bad

Nothing was their fault
They had to be blame-free
So they took their pain and shame
And stuffed it into me...

Like a Christmas turkey...

I was a teenage scapegoat
Yes, I swear it's true
They ripped me with their words
Then beat me black and blue

Nothing was their fault
They had to be blame-free
So they took their pain and shame
And forced it onto me

Scapegoat!
Someone yells at you
Scapegoat!

23

And you're feeling blue
Scapegoat!
Take your misery
Scapegoat!
Put it all on me

I was a teenage scapegoat
It started long ago
I hope this life of mine
Is one you'll never know

You'll always take the fall
So they can be blame-free
And they'll make you suffer
In total misery
You'll see
You'll be
A scapegoat just like me"

After the last note rang out, a tense silence hung in the air. Mom had a look of pure shock on her face. It was the first time she shut up since she came home. Dad frantically bit down on his lower lip. It was the face he always made right before he'd crack me across the face.

My parents were mad because I'd violated their No. 1 rule. No matter how vicious and abusive they were to me, I wasn't allowed to say anything about it. Since I did, I fully expected to take a beating from the old man.

No beating happened, but that was because we had company. Mom pulled Dad out of there, and the two of them toddled off to bed. I got lucky that night, but I knew Dad would make me pay for that song one way or another.

Wally recorded our practice on a boombox radio. The four of us gathered around that device and voted on the best takes of each song. I was surprised "Good King Wally" let me have a say in the process. Once we chose the three best takes, he copied them onto another blank tape. That's when an idea hit me.

I remembered that the Sisters of Mercy told me about *Take No*

Prisoners. It was a local radio show that was broadcast out of a station in the basement of Central High School. The program was hosted by Ben Hamper. (This was before he found fame with his book, *Rivethead: Tales from the Assembly Line*.) He and co-host Jim McDonald played an eclectic mix of punk, reggae, and other alternative music. They also played local punk bands.

I told Wally we should drive the tape to the station to get it played on the air. He and Tiny volunteered to do that while Chaz and I stayed back. Our job was to record anything Ben and Jim might say about Death Symbol. They ended up mentioning our band on the air since it was the first time a local band drove their demo tape to the station during a show.

They played all three of our songs that night. That gave me a rush that was raw, powerful, and it shot through my body like lightning. As I basked in the afterglow, I thought about my future as a punk rock singer. I was convinced that it was my destiny.

When Wally and Tiny got back, there was nothing left to do but go to sleep. We rolled out our sleeping bags and set them out on the same floor we'd jammed on that night. While the guys snored beside me, I found it hard to fall asleep. I was too excited about everything that went down.

Sure, there was some bad stuff that happened. My parents acted up as usual, and Wally showed his nasty side. I wasn't worried about Mom and Dad because they were always going to be that way. As far as Wally was concerned, I figured he'd get over himself after seeing everything our band did in just one night.

As I drifted off to sleep, I was sure that Death Symbol was on its way to becoming the best punk back in Flint.

4.
All Good Things...

"I'm sorry I ruined your band."

I recognized Tiny's voice on the phone, but I didn't understand what he meant. It had been a week since our first practice, and I was still buzzing about everything we did. How could he have "ruined" Death Symbol?

I said, "What are you talking about?"

"Wally quit," he replied.

"What?"

"And he said it's all my fault," he replied.

Once I got over my initial shock, I asked him why Wally did that. He said he didn't know. According to him, Wally just called and said he quit, then told Tiny to break the news to me. That was a cowardly move for a guy who was talking big at my house.

"I'm sorry," Tiny said.

"It's not your fault."

"I know how much this meant to you."

"What went wrong?" I said.

"I asked him to talk to me about it, but he wouldn't."

"Why not?"

"I don't know," he said.

"That's bullshit!"

"That's Wally," he said. "Until he's ready to let something go, there's nothing you can do."

Tiny's words sounded ominous, but I still needed to get to the bottom of this. To do that, I'd have to call Wally. As a neutral party, I figured I could broker a peace deal so Death Symbol could stay together.

Wally's mom answered when I called. She asked who was calling, and I gave her my name. She said, "One moment," in a cold tone. While I waited, I could hear the theme song from *Jeopardy* playing on the TV somewhere in his house. After what seemed like forever, I heard someone pick up the phone.

Wally said, "What do you want?"

His voice had the same cold tone as Mommy Dearest. It pissed me off that he would greet me like that, especially after he quit my band without telling me. I knew I couldn't act on that emotion, though. That wouldn't fix anything.

"What's going on with you and the band?" I asked.

"I quit!"

"Why?" I asked.

"Ask Tiny."

"I did, but he said you wouldn't tell him why."

"Did he tell you about my shirts?"

"No…"

"…Ask him about that."

"Why don't you tell me?" I said.

Wally told me that he lent Tiny some expensive shirts that he got at Chess King. Tiny wanted to wear them to impress some girl. I noticed Wally's voice dripped with venom at the mere mention of the opposite sex. The problem was that Tiny allegedly returned the shirts dirty, wrinkled, and reeking of Hai Karate cologne.

To me, it sounded like Tiny had a couple of good dates. To Wally, it was an affront to his dignity. That wasn't a stretch. Wally had a nasty habit of taking the smallest thing and imagining it was a huge disrespect. What I didn't understand was how this was band business. I said as much to Wally.

"I'm done with him," he replied.

"But he's your friend…"

That set Wally off on a sermon about what a true friend is and isn't. In the end, he had one demand: If I didn't kick Tiny out of the band, Wally would quit. He dropped that on me out of the blue, and I didn't have a lot of time to consider my options.

Sure, I could bow down to Wally's demands to keep him in the band. But how long would that last? He'd already threatened to quit over a picture, so he'd probably do the same thing every time he wanted to get his way. And he was the type who always had to have his way.

There was another reason I didn't want to bow down to Wally's demands. He and Tiny had been friends for a long time, and they'd probably get over this shirt thing. When that happened, I would always be the asshole who kicked Tiny out of the band. Where would that leave me in all this?

"Well?" Wally asked.

The emperor had a tone in his voice because I had kept him waiting. So, my choice was to kick Tiny out of the band or Wally would quit. I wanted to tell him to shove his ultimatum up his ass, but I decided to be diplomatic instead. It was my last-ditch effort to save Death Symbol.

I said, "We have a good thing going here…"

"…Had."

"I don't think you want to throw it all that away over some shirts."

"Think again," he replied.

"So, you're not going to change your mind on this?"

"Nope."

"What if Tiny apologizes?"

"It's too late for that," he said.

"What if he paid for the shirts?"

Wally snorted then said, "He can't afford it."

I asked him how much the shirts cost and he rattled off a price. I'd been holding on to some money I made working for my dad. I stashed it away for a rainy day, and this situation was a tornado warning! I offered to pay for the shirts. If that's what Wally was really upset about, that should solve things.

"That won't work," he said.

"Why not?"

"He won't learn his lesson if you bail him out."

"Learn his lesson?"

"That's right!"

"This is a punk band, not Sunday school," I said.

"It's what I say it is," Wally snapped. "And I say you need to make a choice."

"I'm not gonna kick him out just 'cause you say so… "

"…Good luck with your two-man band!"

He slammed the phone down, leaving me with a humming dial tone in my ear. I thought about the last thing he said. It felt like he was hinting that Chaz was with him on this. Was he bluffing? There was only one way to know for sure.

28

I dialed Chaz's number, and he picked up on the second ring. I asked him if he heard about what happened, and he said he did. I asked him what he thought about that, and he said he wasn't getting in the middle of it. I said I didn't want to, either.

"Then why are you calling me?" he said.

"Because I wanna keep the band together…"

Chaz shouted, "I don't care!" then slammed the phone down. That was the second time someone had did that to me in one night. Despite what he said, Chaz had chosen a side after all.

Death Symbol died one week after its only practice. I guess it's true when they say that "all good things must come to an end."

When I thought about that, a scalding feeling spread through me like a lava flow. It started in my throat then traveled up until the heat engulfed my face. Even my ears felt like they were on fire. I took some deep breaths until those strange effects of my anger went away.

I called Tiny back and broke the bad news. He told me that he and Wally fought like that all the time, and they would probably make up in a few weeks. While that was great for their friendship, it sucked for me. To Tiny's credit, he apologized for everything, but it didn't offer much comfort.

When I hung up with him, I just wanted to escape to my room. Too bad my mom blocked my way. I was so wrapped up in my conversation that I didn't know that she and Dad were standing behind me the whole time. Mom asked me what was wrong, and I told her I didn't want to talk about it. She refused to let up about it, just like the night she bugged us to play our songs.

Finally, Dad growled, "Answer her!"

The threat of my dad's violent temper convinced me to tell them everything that happened. I thought they would be proud that I did the right thing, but I couldn't have been more wrong. For reasons that I wasn't able to fathom at 16, they ripped into me over my "idiotic" decision.

Mom's voice assaulted me in that high-pitched, shrieking tone of hers. She said I was "stupid" because Tiny wasn't really my friend. I asked her how she could know that. Did she have some mystical powers that allowed her to read my friends' intentions like an aura? If so, what did she see in Wally? And Chaz?

Dad screamed at me for daring to question my mom. Then he ripped into me about what an "fucking idiot" I was. He said the world was going to "cut me to ribbons" because I wasn't streetwise. His voice felt like a machete that hacked away at my self-esteem.

I said, "Just leave me alone!"

"No!" he screamed.

"Whatever..."

"Look at you," he said. "You're too damn dumb to learn your lesson."

"What lesson?"

"This is what happens when you act like a big shot!" he said.

That was the pot calling the kettle black! When Dad was with his friends, he always had to be the center of attention. Meanwhile, he expected me to be some quivering coward who was afraid of his own shadow. That's why he thought I should have kissed Wally's fat ass.

I shouted, "I'm not gonna take his shit so you can get off on it!"

Dad's upper teeth clamped down on his lower lip and began furiously chewing at it. I knew what was coming and it was too late to stop it. A looping overhand right crashed into the side of my head. The punch rocked me like I was a bobblehead doll and left my ears ringing.

Mom started yelling at Dad for hitting me. That gave me the chance to turn tail and flee to my room. I slammed the door behind me, closing out the sounds of their shouts. In the privacy of my room, I beat myself up over my mistakes instead of my dad doing it for me.

When the old man said I was an "idiot," he wasn't completely wrong. It was stupid of me to think I could just transfer to a new school and start a band. I was a stranger to Wally and Chaz so why should they care about me or my goals in music? The short answer is that they didn't.

Those two stabbed me in the back, and I'd have to see them five days a week. How would I deal with that? And where would I sit at lunch? I'd rather go back to sneaking into the auditorium instead of breaking bread with those losers.

At school, I experienced a cold war like the one that raged between the US and the Soviet Union. Wally and I glared at each other in the halls and class, but we didn't speak to each other. It was the same with

Chaz. I didn't know why they were so mad at me. They were the ones acting like assholes.

On Friday, the two of them finally broke the icy walls of silence between us. It was at the end of the day, and I was getting my books out of my locker. I caught Wally's large frame and Chaz's lanky body out of the corner of my eye. It was like Laurel and Hardy standing in the hallway.

Chaz said something about how he couldn't wait to hear Take No Prisoners that weekend. He was talking in that voice people use when they want someone to hear them. Wally said something about the show having an "extra special treat." They were trying to rub my nose in something, but I wasn't going to let them get away with that.

"Go fuck yourselves," I growled.

Neither one of them said anything back because they weren't used to anyone standing up to them. I was only cool with them because they were in my band. Now that they took that away from me, there was no reason to be nice. They should have thought that through before shooting off their big mouths.

Even though I knew I shouldn't, I tuned in to Take No Prisoners that weekend. I couldn't help myself. What I heard made me want to kill those two morons. Under a new band name, they recorded the three songs we did and had them played on the show. I felt as violated as the victim of a robbery.

I just knew the rest of my junior year was going to suck. I was stuck at a school where I only had one friend and many enemies. I channeled all that emotional turmoil into a new song. I only hoped I could play with a new band someday.

"Lost in Space"

I'm floating here with no direction
Cut off, alone, and out of place
I reach out to make some connection
But I drift away...

I float along with no direction
Disappear without a trace
I just missed my connection
So I drift away... lost in space

31

Lost in space, outer dimension
Lost in space, not my intention
To be so far from the human race
Lost in space

I speed to earth, disintegration
Disappear without a trace
Burning flames, my cremation
Ashes drift away... lost in space

Lost in space, outer dimension
Lost in space, not my intention
To be so far from the human race
Lost in space
Lost in space
Lost in space
Lost in space

5.
"Handsome Dan"
Saves the Day

Dan O'Hallahan, Dan O'Hallahan... halfway through my junior year, I kept hearing the name Dan O'Hallahan.

He was a kid I knew from Hamady High School. Dan was a happy-go-lucky dude with a blond flattop and sparkling blue eyes that made him a dead ringer for Mark Harmon in *Summer School*. That's why I used to call him "Handsome Dan."

I'd forgotten all about him after I transferred to Powers. I was on a quest to achieve punk rock stardom, after all. During my junior year, some Hamady kids told me that Dan got into skateboarding and playing guitar. They also said he wanted to be in a band, and urged me to give him a call.

I knew I had to call him. What were the odds that there was another skate-punk in my school district? It felt like fate, so the situation called for something more than me saying "Hey. How's it going?" I knew just what to do.

When he answered, I said "Dan O'Hallahan" in a rather grandiose tone.

"This is him," he replied.

"Dan O'Hallahan," I said, in an even more grandiose manner.

"Who is this?"

After an appropriately dramatic pause, I said, "It's none other than J.P. Ribner."

"Hey man!"

Dan sounded just as cheerful as I remembered him from school. As we got caught up, he asked me why I transferred to Powers. I told him everything, including the sad tale of Death Symbol's demise. He said Wally sounded like a "total dick." I agreed.

33

Dan said, "Are you looking to get another band together?"

"I've been kickin' the idea around," I replied.

"Well, I've been playing guitar…"

I asked him who his influences were, and he said The Sex Pistols, Dead Kennedys, and Black Flag. I told him I liked those bands, but The Misfits were my favorite. He said he liked them too, and we discussed our favorite Misfits songs. It didn't take long for the conversation to reach its inevitable conclusion.

Dan said, "So, do you wanna jam sometime?"

"We could do that," I said.

I was glad that he asked me to jam instead of the other way around. I didn't want to come off like I was desperate. I made that mistake with Wally, and he used it against me. I didn't think Dan would do that, but I had no way of knowing for sure.

I said, "I'll probably be around Friday if you wanna get together."

"I'll be there," he replied.

Dan showed up at my house that Friday just like he said he would. He brought his gear with him, and I had some gear of my own.

Since Death Symbol broke up, I bought a bass guitar and amp. I spent many months learning how to play and sing all of my songs. I was so proud of that accomplishment that I called myself the "Lemmy Kilmister of Mayfair." I could only dream of being half as good as Motorhead's iconic and legendary frontman.

Once Dan was ready, I said we should warm up with some songs we both knew. We rocked our way through the Sex Pistols' "Anarchy in the UK." We followed that with "I Wanna be Sedated" by The Ramones.

Even though it was our first time jamming, it felt like we'd been doing it for a while. We just came together so naturally, and our styles were a perfect blend. That meant there was only one thing left to do, and that was to show him my original songs. This was a risk because he could steal my songs, but something told me he wasn't like Wally and Chaz.

It blew my mind how quickly Dan picked up my tunes. Our styles came together again, and everything sounded the way that it should have. We played them over and over until we had them down. By the time his mom came to get him, I knew I'd found a bandmate.

Since our first practice, Dan and I started hanging out on the weekends. We played music and skateboarded in the parking lots up and down Pierson Road. Those sessions usually ended when this redneck security guard in a white van showed up. He'd yell "No skateboardin' on the preh-muh-seez" and we'd flip him off and ride away laughing.

As my friendship with Dan grew, our unique musical sound emerged. It was heavily influenced by our favorite bands from the New York City hardcore scene. We developed a stripped-down punk/metal crossover sound with sarcastic lyrics that took on social issues.

I had all kinds of inspiration back then. One time, I wrote a song about a girl who passed out during an all-school mass at Powers. I don't know if she was claustrophobic or couldn't take the heat of the crowd. Either way, I knew something bad was going to happen when she started to teeter back and forth in the bleachers.

After swaying a few times like a palm tree in a hurricane, she plunged face-first into the bleachers. Her head buried between the wooden planks while her body and legs remained stiff as a board. She was stuck there like a javelin on a track field. That's when her dress hitched up and exposed her granny panties to the entire school.

I busted up laughing and the teachers sitting next to me became furious. I knew I shouldn't laugh at those things, but I couldn't help myself. Whether I was right or wrong, the spectacle didn't last long. A teacher and some civic-minded freshmen got the girl's dress back down, then led her out of the gym.

While most people would have just ignored that whole thing, I felt inspired. When I got back to class, I let the teacher drone on while I scribbled some lyrics into my notebook. I arranged the words until I finally had something I wanted to play.

"You Got Stiff, You Passed Out"

Standing in a group
Like sardines in a tin
100 people crowding you
The air is getting thin
You're afraid to leave
Because everyone will stare
But your body's heating up
Your brain is losing air...

35

As you plunge forward
You will hear me shout
You got stiff, you passed out!

I wrote that song on a Friday, and Dan was coming over after
school. When he got there, I told him about "Javelin Girl," and he
chuckled. When I showed him my lyrics, he busted up laughing. He
also said that was the kind of songs we should be doing. That was the
encouragement I needed after Death Symbol's demise.

Dan shook me out of my dry spell, and I wrote more songs. By the
time we slid into the summer of 1987, we were practicing every
weekend. This productivity attracted attention, and some of it wasn't
good.

My dad hated my music and he wasn't shy about sharing his
opinions. The more we practiced, the more he bitched about it. Since
he couldn't convince me to quit, he said he knew someone who would.
It was some guy he knew who played in cover bands around Flint.

My dad kept saying how this friend of his was going to "put me in
my place." The old man blew a lot of smoke, so I didn't take it
seriously. I just kept jamming with Dan because we had every intention
of putting a band together once we found the right people.

In the summer of 1987, Dan got a hot tip on a drummer. It was
some kid named Jeff who was Dan's cousin's neighbor's girlfriend's
nephew or something. All I knew was that the guy played drums and
was into punk. That was enough to have him over for an audition.

I drove out to the dude's house, which was in the deepest recesses
of Flushing Township. I knocked on the door and the first thing the kid
said was, "Help me load my gear." I thought that was a little pushy, but
I didn't say anything because we needed a drummer.

When we finally got to my house and started jamming, I saw
another side of Jeff. He was a talented drummer who caught on quickly.
As he pounded those skins like a maniac, we attracted the attention of
some neighborhood kids. They were a bunch of heavy metal mullet-
heads from Hamady, but I didn't mind. Having them there was like
playing in front of an audience.

As we were jamming, my dad told me he was going to Walli's. I
didn't think anything of it because he practically lived at that restaurant

on West Pierson Road. It wasn't the food or the gigantic, rotating metallic ball with neon spires that attracted him. He went there to hold court with a group of guys who looked up to him.

I shouted, "One, two, three, four" and the three of us launched into our songs again. When we got to the end of the last one, I hit the low E string on a down-stroke and the note reverberated. Dan and Jeff followed suit to give the song a big ending.

As I stood there basking in our sonic glory, a red sports car pulled into the driveway. It stopped just inches from the garage and the driver's side door flung open. A middle-aged guy got out and walked toward us like a puffed-up peacock. He was bald up top, but he had an ear-to-ear hair doughnut with a long, braided tail in the back. It was the perfect complement to his .38 Special T-shirt and acid-washed jeans.

"You must be P.J.?" he said.

"J.P." I replied.

"I'm Frank Puller."

The dude extended his hand. As we shook, he squeezed down so hard that he practically crushed my palm in his grip. Before I could do anything, he jerked my hand toward him, which yanked me off my feet and made me stumble. As I struggled to regain my balance, he thrust my arm back toward my body then released his grip.

I saw my dad's truck pull into the driveway. When he came into the garage, he told me that Frank was there to talk to me about music and I'd better listen. That's when I realized what was going on. Frank was the dude my dad said would "put me in my place." So, the old man wasn't kidding after all.

"So, you think you can play bass?" Frank said.

"A little…"

"…A little?"

"Yeah," I replied.

"Well you're gonna have to do more than that if you wanna be in a band."

"Okay."

"Let me show you how it's done…"

He reached for my bass, but I didn't give it to him. Dad demanded that I hand it over, so I did. Frank played some funky slaps, chops, and scale runs that produced some "oohs" and "ahs" from the kids in the garage. After a few minutes of this musical dick wagging, he thrust my bass back into my hands.

"If you can't play like that, you don't belong in a band," Frank said.

"He just plays the same note over and over again," Dad shouted.

The old man looked around the garage to see if anyone heard him. He loved having an audience as much as he loved throwing me under the bus to get the attention he craved. A couple of the kids let out a weak giggle at best, but that wasn't the kind of juice Dad was hoping for.

Dad said, "My son thinks he's some kind of leader."

"Well, he won't get far if he can't play his instrument," Frank replied.

"You hear that, Jay?" Dad boomed. "You're not such a big shot now, are you?"

I didn't say anything. Why should I give either of them the satisfaction of knowing that I was pissed? I didn't want Dan and Jeff to see that, either. I was trying to lead my band after all.

"So," Frank said. "What kind of music do you play?"

"Punk," I said.

He snorted then said, "Why the hell would you do that?"

"Yeah!" Dad shouted. "Why the hell are you doing that?"

"Because I like it," I replied.

Frank told me that only losers play punk. That pissed me off but I couldn't do anything about it. My dad had this thing about me respecting elders, even if they were disrespecting me. He would've beaten me down in front of my friends if I talked back to Frank.

Frank turned to my dad and said, "He looks mad."

"I don't care," Dad said. "He needs to hear it!"

Frank turned back to me and said, "Are you mad?"

"Don't worry about it," I answered.

"Do I look worried?" Frank said.

"I don't know…"

"A little punk like you is the least of my worries."

I looked at the old man in some desperate hope that he'd put an end to it. The wicked smile on his face told me that he wasn't going to do a thing. He looked like the devil himself as he stood there, snickering at my discomfort with the situation. He wanted to see me suffer and he was getting off on the whole thing.

Frank said, "I don't know why anyone would be stupid enough to play punk."

"It's not stupid," I said.

"If you really think that, then you don't care about your bandmates," he replied.

"What?"

"There's no money in punk."

"I don't do it for money," I said.

"Then you're wasting their time," he replied, gesturing to my friends.

Dad shouted, "I told you this whole thing's a waste!"

"Whatever," I replied.

Frank said, "You can be a bum if you want to…"

"…I'm not a bum."

"Yes, you are," Frank said. "And you're taking your friends down with you."

I said, "Forget this," and started to walk away from him. Dad shouted, "Don't you turn your back on him!" I recognized the tone in his voice and knew what it implied. Like it or not, I had to sit there and listen to that asshole run me down in front of my friends.

Frank said he'd been playing music for 30 years. He followed that with a lecture about "the way things are done in the music business." He told me that I needed to quit writing songs because bands like April Wine and Lynyrd Skynyrd already had the best tunes. My future, according to him, depended on playing those songs in bars.

I told him to look around the garage. I was the oldest one out of all my friends, and I still had one more year in high school. It would be a while before we could play bars. He said something about me being a "stupid kid" and Dad laughed.

I said, "How about you play what you want, and I'll play what I want."

"I'm done wasting my time on someone who's too stupid to learn!" Frank replied.

I couldn't believe the balls on that guy! I offered him a peaceful way to end our conversation, but he just had to get his digs in. At that point, I was done. I didn't care if my dad knocked my head off. I turned away from Frank and walked over to the other side of the garage.

Frank turned to Dan and said, "Don't you wanna play in a band that makes money?"

"I'm in this band, and I'd like to get back to our practice," Dan replied.

Dan shut him down and the old windbag had it coming. Frank

turned his attention to Jeff the drummer. Frank told Jeff that his time was valuable, and he deserved to get paid for it. When they got done talking, Frank shook Jeff's hand then he walked out of the garage with my dad.

Jeff came up to me and said, "Load my drums."

"What?"

"Load my drums," he said. "I'm ready to go."

"Are you serious right now?" I said.

"Did I stutter?"

"You'll be stuttering when I bust you in the jaw!" I growled.

Dan quickly stepped between us and deescalated the situation. I was glad he did because that wasn't a good time for Jeff to get an attitude with me. I might not have been able to talk back to Frank, but I would have mopped the floor with that kid.

"I need to go home," Jeff said, his voice trembling.

Dan said, "My mom will take him home," Dan replied.

"You're lucky," I said to Jeff. "I was going to make you walk."

Dan asked to use the phone, so I led him into the house. Jeff came with us, clinging to Dan like he was his lifeline. While Dan was talking to his mom, my dad came inside and approached Jeff. I had a funny feeling that this wasn't going to be good.

"Are you going to play in my idiot son's band?" my dad asked.

"No way!" Jeff replied.

"Good!" Dad said. "At least you have some sense."

"Thanks," Jeff said.

"No. Thank you!"

The old man reached into his pocket and pulled out a wad of $20 bills. He peeled off three of those bills and handed them to Jeff. My father stood there as Jeff counted his money, and I knew that look on my father's face. He was expecting a huge "thank you," but Jeff just put the money in his pocket without another word.

"What do you think?" Dad said. "I took care of you, right?"

"I don't know…"

"What do you mean?"

"That guy said I should know my worth," Jeff replied.

"What guy?" Dad said.

"Your friend out there," Jeff replied.

"You mean Frank," Dad said.

"Yeah," Jeff replied. "He told me I'm worth more than 60 bucks."

Damn! Jeff might have been an asshole, but he had a set of balls on him. Dad's expression went from shock to barely concealed rage. He was pissed because he shot his big mouth off, and Jeff called him out on it.

The old man knew there was no way he could go back on his word. I watched with sadistic glee as he pulled out that wad of twenties again and gave Jeff another $60. Just like before, Jeff counted the money and put it in his pocket without so much as a "thank you."

My dad said, "I need to talk to J.P."

Dan and Jeff went back outside, and the old man pounced on me like a tiger. He started shouting at me for being a shitty son for "letting" my friend disrespect him. He looked like a maniac with the veins in his neck bulging with every word.

I said, "What the hell is your problem?"

"That punk didn't even thank me!"

"Take it up with him then."

"I'm talking to you!" he shouted.

"You and Frank created that monster, not me," I said.

"What are you talking about?"

"He's the one who told Jeff he deserved to get paid for his time."

"He never said that!" Dad growled.

"Yeah he did!" I shouted.

"So what?" Dad said. "You still should've said something."

"But you told me to listen to Frank..."

"We're talking about that friend of yours."

"He's not my friend," I said.

Dad said, "He's an ungrateful little punk."

"You were kissing that punk's ass a minute ago..."

Dad's upper teeth clamped down on his lower lip. In less than a second, that clenched fist at his side connected with my mouth. The impact rocked my head back and made me see stars. I still had enough presence of mind to cover my head with my hands, though. I was glad I did because Dad blasted with a barrage of punches.

I would have never thought I could take my dad, but his attack triggered something inside of me. After everything that happened, I wasn't in the mood to take a beating from him. I lunged forward through his punches and shoved him across the living room.

That was the first time I ever got physical with him and the moment seemed frozen in time. Dad stood there with a look of shock on his face while I stood my ground. There was no telling which way that would have gone because my mom came running into the room, hollering at my dad.

As they argued, I ran back out to the garage. I got there just in time to see Dan loading Jeff's drums into his mom's car. I wanted to catch him before he left because I was worried that Dan might ditch me and start a band with Jeff. It was a crazy thought; but, after everything that happened that day, it would have been just my luck.

I said, "I'm sorry my dad fucked everything up."

"Don't worry about it," Dan replied.

"We were so close to gettin' a drummer..."

"...He's not the one for us," Dan said.

"But he was good."

"If he let that guy get into his head like that, he wouldn't have lasted long," Dan replied.

"Good point," I said. "But still..."

"Don't worry about it," he said. "We'll find someone."

"But what if we don't?"

"Don't worry," Dan said. "I'm not going anywhere."

It was like Dan read my mind. I needed him to tell me that he'd stick with me despite the setback we had that day. I was glad that he did. He also gave me hope that there was another drummer out there and we'd find him.

6.
The Summer of '88

I welcomed the summer of 1988 with both arms opened wide.

After two grueling years at Powers, I'd finally graduated and was free of its shackles. For the first time in my life, it felt like the future was wide open, and anything was possible. All I had to do was reach out and grab what I wanted. The only thing I wanted was the punk rock life.

Despite my enthusiasm, things didn't start so great. Dan and I never found a drummer, even though we tried like hell to do so since the previous summer. We ignored that setback and kept jamming and writing songs. As much as I loved that, I was still playing in my parents' garage while people I went to school with were playing shows at the Capitol Theatre.

One day, Dan called me. The first words out of his mouth were, "Dude! I found a bassist!" What we really needed was a drummer, but I was willing to take on a bass player. If we did, I could hand off those duties and focus on my vocals.

I asked Dan who this bass player was, and he said I already knew him. That's weird, I thought. If I knew a bassist who wanted to jam with us, he would have already been in the band. I asked Dan who the mystery musician was, and he said, "Cameron." I zipped through my mental Rolodex but came up blank.

Dan said, "Think about it."

"Cam the Scam?" I asked.

"He said you called him that."

"Yeah, I know him," I said. "But how do you know him?"

Dan said he met Cam at school. I had no idea that Cam moved back in with his dad sometime near the end of the 1987/1988 school year. I wasn't at Hamady then, but Dan was, and Cam found him. That's when he found out Dan and I had a band (sort of) and asked if we needed a bassist.

I said, "I've never heard Cam play."

"Me neither," Dan said. "But I figured he could sit in with us."

"I guess so," I replied.

On Friday, my old friend Cam Leon pulled into the driveway in a brown Chevette. When he got out of the car, he looked the same as I remembered him. He was even wearing that same Mr. Zogs Sex Wax T-shirt he had when we met.

Cam and I got caught up right there in my driveway. Now that he was living with his dad again, he started working at Herriman's Family Restaurant. The place was an institution for us Mount Morris Township kids. We'd wolf down our meals so we could run up front to choose a flavor of ice cream out of the cooler. For me, it was Superman, which was a mix of Blue Moon, red pop, and lemon.

Cam, Dan, and I hauled the gear to the porch behind my parents' garage. It was perfect for a band that wasn't ready to be in the public eye. I plugged my bass guitar into my amp, handed it to Cam, and said, "Let's see what you can do."

"I haven't heard your songs, so you gotta give me some time," he said.

"No problem," I replied.

We started with our shortest song, which was "You Got Stiff, You Passed Out." At only 56 seconds long, I figured it shouldn't be too hard for him to pick it up. We lit into the tune, and he followed along with Dan. By our third time with it, he added a little more flair.

We kept at it for an hour, and things went well. Between songs, there was a lot of talking, joking, and camaraderie between us. It felt like Cam had always been a part of the band all along. I looked at Dan, and he gave me a knowing glance.

When it came time to ask Cam if he wanted to join our band, there wasn't a lot of fanfare. I just asked him, and he said "yes." From that day forward, practices at my house were a regular thing.

The three of us sounded great together, but we still needed a drummer. I thought I might have a solution to that problem. I knew a drummer from Hamady named Rick Rokowski.

When we were younger, Rick was just another pimple-faced kid who played drums in the school marching band. His life did a 180 when he heard Mötley Crüe's *Shout at the Devil* album. He was so inspired by Tommy Lee's drumming that he sold his soul to rock 'n roll, figuratively speaking. He started going by the name "Rikki Roxx," which was a nod to Mötley Crüe's bassist, Nikki Sixx.

I first heard Rikki play at a Hamady High talent show. He and a couple of dudes did a cover of Crüe's "She's Got the Looks That Kill." The other guys were okay, but Rikki stole the show because he was such a powerhouse on the drums. I never forgot that performance.

I wanted to ask Rikki to sit in with us and hoped for the best. With his love of '80s hair metal, I wasn't sure he'd want to do that. I gave it a shot anyway, and to my surprise, he said he'd jam with us. If he was half as good as I remembered him to be, I'd offer him the gig on the spot.

On the day of his audition, Rikki blasted our songs into the stratosphere. His intense, hard-hitting style was the perfect complement to our hardcore punk sound. With him on board, we could do shows at the Capitol in as little as a month or two. From there, there was no telling where we could take it.

After we ran through the songs a couple of times, I asked Rikki to join our group. He told me he wanted to talk one-on-one, so we stepped into the garage. Once we were out of earshot from Dan and Cam, he thanked me for the opportunity to jam with us. I suddenly got a sinking feeling in my stomach.

He said, "I can't be in your band."

"Why not?"

He said, "I don't know about your style…"

"What do you mean?"

"The whole punk thing."

Rikki's words triggered a flashback in my mind. It felt like I was in a time machine. It took me back to the day Frank Puller said something similar in that same garage. I asked Rikki what he meant and he told me that he'd rather play in a metal band.

He was so bold and straightforward that he sounded like an adult, even though he's almost a year younger than me. It shook me a bit, but I quickly recovered. I suggested that he play in a metal band and jam with us, too.

"Nope," he said, shaking his head.

45

"Why not?"

"Not gonna work."

He probably thought that playing punk meant doing shows in my parents' basement or something. I told him about the thriving scenes in Flint and Detroit, but I couldn't get him to change his mind. At that point, all I could do was shake his hand and thank him for stopping by.

Once Rikki left, Dan and Cam asked me what happened. I told them we just lost our chance to jam with the best drummer in Flint. I said we could've really gone somewhere with him and they agreed.

Cam said, "What if I played drums?"

"Do you know how?" I asked.

"I could learn."

"I think it's a good idea," Dan said.

"Oh yeah?" I asked.

"Yeah," he replied. "If you play bass and sing and he plays drums, we won't have to rely on anyone else."

"That's what I was thinking," Cam added.

"Maybe you're right," I said.

And just like that, Cam became our drummer. It didn't matter that he'd never played the drums before. He also didn't own a drum set, but we weren't going to hold that against him, either.

Dan and I pooled our money and bought the cheapest drum kit we could find. We got it from none other than Rikki Roxx, and he sold it to us for next to nothing. I wondered if he felt guilty for blowing us off. Whatever the case, we happily bought the drums for Cam to use. That's how committed we were to the future of our band with no name.

We were all looking forward to Cam's audition as our drummer. Just like when he auditioned as our bassist, we started with "You Got Stiff, You Passed Out." I shouted, "1, 2, 3, 4!" and Dan and I ripped into the song. Rather than going all out, Cam laid back and did his best to throw down a basic beat.

When we finished, he asked to go through it again. The more we played, the better his drumming sounded. It was still going to take a while to get him up to speed, though. He literally never played the drums before, yet he was willing to step up to the challenge for the sake of the band.

We kept practicing throughout the early weeks of summer, and we were slowly developing. The goal was to get Cam caught up so we could play a 30-minute set at the Capitol. We'd need a name for our band whenever that day came, but we couldn't think of anything.

In the end, it was my dad, of all people, who solved the problem for us.

It all happened one Saturday afternoon while we were practicing. Dad led Nana, my maternal grandmother, behind the house to where we were jamming. She grasped onto my dad's arm for dear life as she took each jittery step. When I saw her, I hollered for the guys to stop playing.

I said, "Hi, Nana!"

"Hello," she replied, her voice wavering.

Dad told us we had to stop playing because the noise hurt Nana's ears. Dan and I turned off our amps, and Cam laid his sticks down atop the snare drum. It wasn't a huge disappointment because Cam had to work that night, and Dan and I were going skateboarding. Just for shits and giggles, I said, "Hey Nana! What do you think of our band?"

Dad replied, "I can't believe you have the audacity to ask that question."

"Audacity?" I asked. "What's that mean?"

"Look it up," he replied.

My father was a junior high English teacher and a voracious reader. Whenever I came across a word I didn't know, he'd tell me to "look it up." It meant I'd have to grab a dictionary and learn what the word meant myself. I developed a decent vocabulary because of this discipline that the old man instilled in me.

I led the guys to the living room, where I grabbed one of Dad's dictionaries. I thumbed through the "a" section until I found it. According to Webster, "audacity" means "a bold or arrogant disregard of normal restraints." I looked at the guys and said, "I think we have our band name."

Cam and Dan were in total agreement. We all knew that no other name would do. To me, it was a badge of honor that I planned to live up to it. My goal was to become the boldest, most arrogant punk singer that Flint had ever known. That wouldn't be too hard because that's pretty much what I was already.

I wanted to make Audacity a household name in Flint. It didn't matter that we weren't ready to play a show, the world needed to know who we were. I came up with a plan to do this, and it was more than guerrilla marketing. It would be in-your-face, seek-and-destroy marketing that was lacking in social graces. In other words, an extension of my personality.

I said, "We should make some flyers and hand 'em out to skaters and punks we meet."

The guys liked the idea, so I drew up a flyer with our logo on it. The three of us pooled our change and ran off a bunch of copies at the local Jiffy Print. With a stack of flyers in hand, we hopped into Cam's Chevette and headed to the Genesee Valley Mall. It was Flint's biggest monument to consumerism and conformity, so I had no doubt we'd run into a lot of people.

When we got there, I knew who we we needed to find. They stood out among all the squares who shuffled around the place like zombies. As invasive as our marketing approach was, it worked. We handed out flyers to about 20 punk fans. One of them was Ross Barkey, the bassist for Hammer 13. They regularly played the Capitol Theatre.

Marketing our band was added to our list of summer activities that included practicing and skateboarding. It was a lot more exciting than what most kids I knew were doing. For them, the summer was all about getting jobs and preparing for college. I didn't care about any of that because Audacity was my job, my passion, and my life.

I did feel guilty for luring Cam and Dan into my punk rock life. I had a feeling that their parents didn't like me because of that. They probably saw me as a "Pied Piper" who was leading their sons astray. The way I saw it, they were old enough to make up their minds.

With those two with me, the summer of '88 was like the biggest orange on the tree. It was big, bright, and bursting with flavor, and I planned to squeeze every drop of juice out of it. It was only natural that I wanted to share the sweetness of that fruit with my two best friends.

I was thinking about all that one day when we were hanging out on the back-porch after practice. We were just talking and drinking pops as the sunset in front of us. It gave us a gorgeous display of vibrant shades of orange, pink, and blue. The moment was so special that I took a mental snapshot of it and filed it away.

Something told me that I'd remember the summer of '88 for the rest of my life.

7.
Punk Rock Girls

A car horn blared outside my bedroom window one lazy Saturday morning. It was too early for me to get up, but I couldn't ignore the sound. I rolled out of bed and stumbled out the door, and found Cam parked in my driveway. This better be good, I thought.

He said, "I have to go to the mall to pick up some AC/DC tickets for a friend."

"Okay…"

"Well?"

"Well, what?" I asked.

"Do you wanna come along?"

"Sure."

I popped back into the house and threw on a T-shirt. I also grabbed The Undead's *Never Say Die* cassette for the road. The moment after my butt hit the passenger seat, I popped the tape into his cassette deck. We pulled into the mall's parking lot as the band ripped into "When the Evening Comes."

The mall was dead, so it didn't take us long to get the tickets. We decided to wander around, and we eventually ended up at Record Town. The darkly mystical sounds of Peter Murphy's "All Night Long" drew us inside. The music video was playing on a TV behind the counter, and I was digging Peter's post-Bauhaus sound.

As Cam and I browsed through the store's "college rock" LPs, a couple of punk rock girls sauntered into the store. One was a blond and the other a brunette, and they seemed to be about our age. I nudged Cam with my elbow, and he nudged me back. Good! He saw them, too.

I stole a couple of glances at the girls and felt drawn to the brunette. There was something about her short jet-black hair and even shorter jean shorts that did it. The U2 T-shirt tied off to expose her midriff also had its appeal.

49

The blonde was the exact opposite of her friend. She had that all-American girl look with a sexy punk rock edge. Her black mini skirt and "Boys Don't Cry" T-shirt accentuated an hourglass figure. I thought she was hot too, but she reminded me of a girl I struck out with during my senior year.

I sneaked another look at the brunette. It wasn't easy to do without getting caught because they were looking at us too. When our eyes met, she quickly turned away and giggled. It felt like I was in a John Hughes movie where the quirky, socially awkward guy meets the pretty punk rock girl.

I leaned my head toward Cam and whispered, "Back me up."

I made a beeline toward girls without a second thought. While I told Cam to follow me, it wouldn't have mattered if he did or not. I was bound and determined to talk to that brunette, and nothing was going to stop me.

Since they were looking at us and we were looking at them, I didn't feel the need to use some corny pick-up line. I just introduced us to the girls, and they responded in kind. The brunette was Belladonna Smith, and the blonde was Lily Brockhaus. The vibe felt good, so I went with it.

As we talked, I could tell that Cam was off his game. That meant I would have to rise to the occasion. Like the showman I knew I was born to be, I thrived in the spotlight. It wasn't long before I had the girls practically eating out of the palm of my hand. I instinctively sensed that it was time to set the hook.

"I see you have good taste in music," I said.

"Thanks," Belladonna replied.

"What bands do you like... besides U2 and The Cure?"

She rattled off a litany of new romantic groups like INXS, The Smiths, and The Cure. Lily added a few bands to the list, including Echo and the Bunnymen and Depeche Mode.

"What about Audacity?" I asked.

"I've never heard of them," Belladonna said.

"That's because we're not famous yet."

"You guys are in a band?" she asked.

"We are the band!" I proclaimed. "Well, there's a guitarist too, but he's at home."

"What do you sound like?"

I said, "Would you like to sample our sonic splendor?"

"Yeah!" Belladonna replied.

"Then come with uncles and hear all proper. Hear angels' trumpets and devils' trombones."

Cam, Dan, and I must have watched *A Clockwork Orange* about 15 times that summer. That's how I was able to memorize most of the dialogue. When I used that line from the movie, the girls didn't let on if they recognized it or not. It got them to come to the car with us, though, and that's all that mattered.

We blasted out a couple of songs from the tape we recorded at our last practice. I was pleasantly surprised that they showed interest in our scratchy, low-fi recording. We hung out and talked some more until Belladonna said her mom's boyfriend would be looking for them. I instinctively knew that was my cue.

I said, "Would you ladies be kind enough to give me your phone numbers?"

"Sure!" Belladonna replied.

Both of them scribbled their digits down on a matchbook that Cam supplied. I noticed that their phone numbers had a 517 area code, so I asked them where they lived. They said Owosso. I'd heard of that town before, but I'd never been there. Cam told me that it was about 30 minutes west of Flint.

I said, "On behalf of Audacity, I would like to invite you ladies to our first show."

"When is it?" Belladonna asked.

"When we book it, you'll be the first to know."

"Cool," she said.

We escorted the girls back to the mall. When we reached the sidewalk, a raggedy-looking car pulled up beside them. By the sour look on the driver's face, I figured he was Belladonna's mother's boyfriend. They said their goodbyes then piled into the backseat of that old rust bucket.

On our ride home, Cam was going crazy. My command performance surprised and impressed him. Up until that point, he was the ladies' man while I was the insecure loser who admired girls from afar. He said he'd never seen that side of me before. Frankly, neither had I.

As I sat in his car, I couldn't believe what had just happened. It was like some strange, otherworldly force took possession of me and made me talk to those girls. And now, I had their phone numbers. What the hell did I just get myself into?

Before I graduated from high school, I'd only had two romantic experiences with women. Both of them ended in disaster, and I was haunted by the humiliation of it all.

My first experience was with a chubby blond girl named Sally. She and I had mutual friends who thought we'd make a "cute couple." (Why do people use that tired old phrase?) Sally and I started talking on the phone and we clicked well enough to want to hang out one weekend.

When I met her, I was pleasantly surprised. She had a very thick hourglass shape with curves in all the right places. Her facial features were what I would call unique. She had a strong chin and angular cheekbones that gave her head a block-like appearance. While her beauty was non-traditional, it all came together well.

Sally and I started making out that night we met. It was the first time I'd ever kissed a woman, and it was exciting and awkward. As inexperienced as I was, I felt self-conscious. When things started to get hot and heavy, I pumped the brakes a bit out of fear of doing something foolish.

I apologized to Sally and told her I wanted to see her again. The next day, our mutual friend called me with some bad news. She said Sally wasn't interested in me anymore but wouldn't tell me why. I pressed her for details, and she asked me if I really wanted to know. I ignored her not-so-subtle hint and pressed her for the details.

She said, "Are you sure?"

"Yes," I replied.

"I don't know…"

"C'mon! I can handle it."

"Okay," she said. "Sally said you're a 'desperate loser who's grasping for a relationship.'"

A backdraft of negative emotion smothered me. It seared a path through my brain, and burned inside my head, face, and ears. I felt like an idiot for not listening to my friend. I was too stupid to take the hint, and that ignorance cost me.

I couldn't understand why Sally would say such horrible things about me. Did I do something wrong while we were making out? I was so nervous that night that it wouldn't surprise me. I figured that's what happens when you wait until your senior year to kiss a girl.

52

After that disastrous dating experience, I should have quit while I was behind. Too bad I was the kind of person who hit rock bottom then broke out a shovel. I blundered into another relationship while I was still reeling from the Sally Squarehead disaster. This time around, it was with a girl named Trudie from my neighborhood.

In a matter of days, Trudie and I went from hanging out to making out. A few days later, I got suspended from Powers for three days for breaking a preppy's nose. Since I had the time, I thought I'd surprise Trudie by walking her home from school. It was one of those silly romantic gestures that I hoped would impress her.

I got to Hamady just before the final bell rang. After a few minutes, I saw Trudie walking down the hall with one of her friends. As she got closer, she wouldn't look me in the eye. That didn't stop her little friend from shooting me a nasty look.

I said, "What's your problem?"

"You!" she replied.

"You got something you wanna say?"

"Yeah," she said. "She doesn't like you, so you can just leave."

"I wanna hear that from her," I replied.

Trudie burst into tears then ran into the girls' bathroom. Her friend shouted "loser," then followed after Trudie. All the kids in the hall saw that exchange, and I suddenly was surrounded by a sea of laughing faces. I wanted to smash them to a pulp, but I couldn't fight everyone. I got the hell out of there.

After that, I couldn't deny that I was years behind my friends when it came to dating. I didn't develop the mental and emotional toughness I needed to deal with rejection. The only thing I learned from those experiences was that liking someone led to pain.

Because of my bad experiences, I tore up Belladonna and Lily's numbers and flushed the pieces down the toilet.

That would have seemed crazy to any other 17-year-old guy, but I knew I did the right thing. I liked Sally and Trudie, and I got hurt. I was really attracted to Belladonna, so her rejection would have destroyed me. Getting rid of her phone number meant that I'd never take that risk.

I called Dan in the morning and asked him what he was doing. He said he had to help his dad with something, but he wanted to go skateboarding later. I told him I'd join him.

If I was going skating, I'd have to put a new set of wheels on my deck. When I went to the garage to do that, I saw Cam's Chevette roar into the driveway. The car came to a screeching halt, and he practically leaped out of it. As he walked up to me, I saw a wild-eyed look in his eyes.

"What's up with you?" I asked.

"Get ready!"

"For what?"

"We're taking a road trip."

"Where?" I asked.

"Owosso!"

"Owosso?"

I didn't know what he meant at first, and then it clicked. He wanted to go see Belladonna and Lily, and he wanted me to come with him. Oh shit! He probably thought I still had their phone numbers. I couldn't tell him that I flushed the matchbook because I'd have to explain why I did that.

I needed a way to get out of going with Cam. My mind frantically searched for some reason to give him for not being able to go. Then it hit me; I made plans to go skating with Dan. That's why I was putting a new set of wheels on my deck.

He said, "You can do that any time."

"But I promised him…"

"He'll understand."

"I don't know, man," I said.

Cam looked at me funny, then he said, "Something's up with you."

"No there isn't!"

"You bastard!" he said.

"What?"

"You called them!"

"No I didn't!" I said.

"Yes, you did!"

"I swear I didn't call them."

"Prove it!" he said.

I said, "I couldn't have because I lost their numbers."

"What?"

"My mom washed my jeans, and I forget to take the matchbook outta my pocket," I said.

"Damnit!"

"Relax," I said. "I remember Lily's last name."

"So?"

"There's probably not a lot of people in Owosso named Brockhaus," I replied.

"Okay…"

"If I find her parents in the phone book, we'll have her number…"

"So, you're coming, then?"

Damnit! I did say "we." That slip betrayed the fact that deep down, I wanted to go as much as he did. The girls were hot, and they showed interest in us. That was a lot more than anything I had going on in Flint.

I told Cam to hold on. I ran into the house and threw on my Schmitt Stix John Lucero T-shirt. It went well with the black jeans I was wearing, which were the same pair I had on at the mall the day before. (I knew that Cam wouldn't notice.) I also grabbed my The Vandals' *Peace Through Vandalism* cassette for the road.

We tore out of my parents' driveway like we were in the Daytona 500. I wasn't doing a good job of protecting my heart, but I didn't care. The wonder and excitement of the adventure numbed my fear of rejection. It wasn't until Cam stopped at a red light that I remembered my vow to avoid Belladonna.

A silence fell over the car as we lingered at the corner of Corunna and Elms roads. Serpents of heat slithered up from the asphalt before us. The mirage was a shimmering reminder of the drought that gripped the state that summer. Beyond that illusion was the reality that I was on my way to see a girl I swore to avoid at all costs.

Even at such a young age, I knew we teetered on the edge of a threshold. Sure, we could turn the car around and go back to our little world. That wasn't going to happen though. Our savage hearts pounded to the punk rock soundtrack of our lives. We couldn't resist something so powerful.

When the light turned green, Cam drove through the intersection and headed west down M-21 toward Owosso. I knew there was no turning back, not that either of us would have done that.

After about 30 minutes of witty banter and great tunes, the Audacity-mobile rolled into Owosso.

We stopped at a payphone outside a gas station. I grabbed the

55

phone book and flipped to the "B" section. Just like I suspected, Larry Brockhaus was the only person with that last name in Owosso. It had to be her dad. I dropped a couple of quarters into the phone and gave her a call, but no one answered.

Cam said, "What do we do now?"

"We're not gonna turn around and go home," I replied.

"Agreed."

"This town is small," I said. "We shouldn't have a hard time finding her house."

We asked a few people for general directions to her street, which wasn't hard to find. Within a matter of minutes, we pulled up in front of her place. I felt bold and totally sure of myself, just like I did the day before when we met the girls. I strode up to her front door and knocked. Lily opened the door and seemed shocked to see me.

She said, "Did you call here about 10 minutes ago?"

"Yeah," I replied.

"Sorry. I was sleeping."

"That's okay," I replied.

"Why did you guys come all the way out here?"

"We want to see you lovely ladies!" I replied.

Lily blushed but recovered quickly enough to invite us inside without it being awkward. After a brief meet-and-greet with her parents, the three of us piled into the car and picked up Belladonna. With both girls in tow, we drove around town until we eventually ended up at a small park.

As we talked, I put on a show with all the plumage and pageantry of a male peacock. Somewhere during my performance, I realized that I didn't need to do all that. The real me was good enough for both of the girls, so I toned it down a bit. As we continued to talk, the four of us bonded over our shared roles as outcasts in our communities.

I was having so much fun that I barely noticed the sun burning its well-worn path across the sky. Shafts of its light filtered through the trees to bathe Belladonna in a warm, amber glow. I wished that day would last forever, but I knew it couldn't. After about an hour, she said she had to go home. So did Lily.

The regret I heard in her voice echoed my feelings. Cam told them not to worry because we'd come see them again. We drove them home, and Cam and I got hugs from both the girls. It was a fleeting intimacy that promised bigger things to come. With nothing left to do, Cam and

I headed east, back toward the misery of our lives.

Out of nowhere, he said, "Do you like her?"

"Who? Belladonna?"

"Who else?" he said.

"I don't know."

"What do you mean?"

"I'm trying to figure it out."

"I wouldn't take too long if I were you," he said.

I didn't know what he meant because I was distracted by my thoughts. Being away from Belladonna, I remembered my gut feeling that she would be trouble. I was so into her, which meant that I'd get hurt if things didn't work out. Given my luck with girls, I had every reason to believe something bad would happen.

When I got home, I called Dan and apologized for standing him up. He asked me where I was all day, and I told him everything. He didn't sound surprised, and why should he? He'd had his fair share of girlfriends, so he knew how guys are when they meet somebody.

Dan said, "Just do me a favor."

"What's that?"

"Don't let this girl get in the way of the band."

"You don't have to worry about that!"

"It happens…"

"…Not with me," I said.

"You sure?"

"She's hot, but I'm not going after her," I said.

"You serious?"

"As a heart attack!"

"Good," he replied. "Because we finally have a band together."

"Exactly!"

"And we can start playing shows soon if we stick with it."

"That's what I want, too!" I replied.

I stayed true to my word about not pursuing Belladonna. That didn't stop me from going to Owosso every chance I had, though. What can I say? The girls made me feel like a rock star without me having to put in the work of being one. I became addicted to the attention.

No matter how much we went out there, I never made a move on

Belladonna. I was glad I didn't, because my gut feeling about her ended up being right. She was pretty; but, in my opinion, she was also very emotional and unpredictable. It was a struggle just to be friends with her, given how different our personalities were.

The more we went out there, the more I started gravitating toward Lily. I got so caught up in Belladonna's dark hair that I didn't see the gorgeous blonde who was with her. As the summer came to a close, I noticed, and I liked what I saw. Despite my growing attraction to her, I still didn't make a move out of fear that she could hurt me too.

It didn't take long to see that Cam was hot for Belladonna. He didn't do anything about it because I made the first move on her. After a month of me keeping her in the friend zone, he finally ran out of patience. It all came to a head one night while we were skateboarding at her apartment complex.

He and I rode down the hill to the end of the parking lot and came to a stop with a powerslide. Before hiking back up the road, we told me he wanted to talk. I stood there beneath the orange glow of a streetlight, waiting to hear what he had to say.

"What's the deal with you and Belladonna?" he asked.

"What do you mean?"

"Are you into her or what?"

"Only as a friend."

"You're not interested in her at all?"

"No," I said. "But I can tell you are."

Cam looked down at his shoes and I knew what that meant. He and I had an uncanny way of knowing when the other one was struggling with something. That unique aspect of our friendship made it easier for us to discuss uncomfortable things. At that moment, I knew that I would have to say what he couldn't.

"Look," I said. "I can tell that there's something between you two."

"You can?"

"Yeah. And I think you should go for it."

"Really?"

"Yes," I said.

He gave me a strange look, so I reassured him that it would be cool. I told him that for personal reasons, I just wasn't ready for a girlfriend yet. I had a feeling that he wouldn't press me for more details because of the the way I said it. Besides, Belladonna was on his mind, not me.

I said, "Go for it, dude!"

"I will," he replied.

"You'd be crazy not to."

"For what it's worth, I think Lily likes you…"

"…Like I said, I'm not ready."

Cam looked at me and said, "I think I understand."

"Good," I replied. "Now let's go. It's not good to keep ladies waiting."

By the end of that night, Cam made his big move outside Belladonna's apartment. Lily and I sat in the car watching them kiss until Belladonna's little sister came down and told Belladonna she had to come home. I wasn't the least bit jealous, but I did feel guilty. I couldn't shake the feeling that Cam jumped on a grenade for me, even if he didn't realize it.

8.
The Elephant in the Room

The summer of 1988 was one of the best times of my life, but it ended in the worst way possible.

August rolled into September, and school started up for Dan and Cam. It also meant that my mom and dad went back to their teaching jobs. Their friends' kids were going to college or entering the workforce too. I refused to have anything to do with the nine-to-five world, and my parents were furious with me.

I didn't care how many times they hounded me about getting a job and going to school. The only thing I cared about was my band. Too bad Audacity was on hold, thanks to Cam. Ever since he and Belladonna became an item, Dan and I never saw him. Without a drummer, we couldn't practice.

Dan and I went around and around on the pros and cons of firing him. The pro was the hope that we'd replace him with a drummer who'd have time for the band. The con was that he was our friend, and it would hurt his feelings if we booted him. In the end, Dan and I agreed to talk to him about his commitment to Audacity. The hard part would be pinning him down to do that.

We planned to talk to him about it one weekend. Too bad Cam went to Owosso, and Dan had to go up north with his parents. That left me stuck at home with parents who wanted to nag me about doing something with my life. Not wanting to hear that, I threw on my leather jacket and boots and walked to Tracie and Julie Godin's house.

The Godin girls were two of my closest friends, and I hung out with them a lot that summer. Both raven-haired and fair-skinned, they couldn't be more different from each other. Julie was the short, spunky spitfire, while Tracie was the dreamy, creative type. I never had to choose a favorite because I liked them both.

It didn't take long to get to their house on the corner of Orgould

Street and Ridgeway Avenue. The three of us hung out in the basement, goofing around and listening to music. At midnight, the girls' mom, aka "Mama Sue," came downstairs and offered to give me a ride home. I said I was fine to walk.

She said, "Are you sure?"

"I'm a big boy," I replied. "I can take care of myself."

What can I say? I was filled with the false bravado of a 17-year-old know-it-all. That made me feel like I was 10 feet tall and bulletproof, even though I was far from it.

When I headed out into that cool September night, I forgot that my neighborhood wasn't the same. By the summer of 1988, it had degenerated into a Mulligan stew of violence, drugs, and poverty. Many factors helped create those conditions.

In April 1988, *Colors* hit the movie theaters. That hard-hitting film glamorized California's gang sub-culture and its violence. Way too many Flintstones saw that movie as a call to arms. By May, gang symbols were spray-painted all over, and gunshots rang out almost every night.

Four months later, N.W.A.'s *Straight Outta Compton* became a mega-hit. The group's gangsta rap fueled every teenage boy's macho fantasies. Many Mayfair hood rats hopped on the bandwagon. They traded in their mullets and Mötley Crüe T-shirts for rat-tail haircuts and N.W.A. cassettes.

Some of the kids I grew up with started acting out the violence they heard in those songs. In their quest to earn street cred, they started hanging out with real gangbangers. I'm talking about the dudes who lived across Clio Road. That was the line of demarcation between Mayfair and the City of Flint. Almost overnight, I started seeing strange cars cruising like sharks through my working-class neighborhood.

I was well aware of these changes to my neighborhood, but I thought they wouldn't affect me. I felt reassured by this foolish notion for the first five blocks of my trip home. Things took a turn for the worse just three blocks from home. That's when a tan Chevy Celebrity Eurosport with tinted windows crept past me on Parkway Drive.

My stomach dropped when it pulled a U-turn and came back toward me.

I picked up my pace, but the car sped up until it was parallel to me. The window on the passenger's side rolled down, and someone shouted,

"Hey white boy!" I didn't get a good look at his face. All I could tell was that he was a black guy wearing a do-rag. It looked like there were about four or five people in the car.

Do-Rag shouted, "I'm talkin' to you, white boy."

"What's up?"

"Where the party at, dawg?"

"I don't know."

"Where you comin' from, then?"

It was none of his fucking business where I'd been, but I didn't say that. I knew better than to mouth off when I'm outnumbered. I started to walk even faster, but the car kept pace with me.

Do-Rag said, "You got any money?"

Okay. Now I knew this was getting serious. Do-Rag was playing something I called "punk the white boy." Since I grew up near Flint's north side, this was a "game" I knew all too well. Even though I'd only "played" it a few times, I always ended up losing.

Here's how it usually worked for me. A black guy saw me on the street and approached me in a certain way. On the surface, he seemed friendly, but there was a threatening undertone in his voice. I didn't know it at the time, but he was probing me for signs of fear.

I must have been nervous because the black dude started asking pointed questions. My fear increased, and he picked up on it. In an instant, he went from being nice to demanding my money or my possessions. Anyone who's ever been through this knows that it gets worse from there.

The last time I played "punk the white boy" was the summer of 1987. I got caught skateboarding in the "wrong neighborhood." At least that's what a group of black dudes told me. That was right after they came out of nowhere and surrounded me.

They demanded I give them my skateboard, which I did. As I timidly handed it over to the group's leader, he grabbed it from my hands and smashed me in the mouth with it. I saw stars dancing in front of me. Instead of finishing me off, my assailants ran away laughing.

One of them shouted, "That's what you get, white boy!"

My face was throbbing with pain, and I instinctively put my hand to my mouth. A torrent of blood and saliva filled my palm. The blow knocked out one of my teeth, and my lower lip dangled from my face by a thread of skin. I scanned the pavement for my missing tooth, but it

62

was probably embedded in what became my attacker's skateboard.

Two hours after the assault and battery, my dentist stitched my mangled lower lip back onto my face. He also attached a fake tooth to the rest of my teeth with something called a "Maryland bridge." My teeth were as good as new and my lip healed, but I remained traumatized.

Walking home from the Godin's house that night, I once again found myself caught up in that sick and twisted game. I wanted out of it as quickly as possible, so I told Do-Rag I didn't have any money. I knew that wasn't what he wanted to hear, but it was the truth.

"You best give it up, white boy!" he growled.

"I said I don't have any!"

Do-Rag wouldn't let up about the money, so I just kept walking. I needed a way out of that situation, but it never occurred to me to just run. I could have easily cut through the backyards of the nearby houses and lost them in the darkness. Another plan came to me in the heat of the moment.

There was a house to my right, and its owner had the front door open and the TV on. To me, this was a lighthouse in the storm. My brilliant plan was to walk up to the front door to give Do-Rag the impression that I lived there. I thought that would be enough to get them to leave.

I turned my back on Do-Rag, and he shouted something to me. As I made a beeline for the door, I felt overcome with a strange thought. Somehow, I just knew I was going to get shot. It was like a voice inside my mind told me it was going to happen.

With each step I took, I expected to hear a thundering blast behind me. Instead of a booming roar, I heard a loud crack that sounded like a firecracker. But firecrackers don't slam into your back like a sledgehammer and knock you to the ground. I went down to my knees atop the gravel and broken concrete in the driveway. My worst fear came true.

I couldn't just sit there and let Do-Rag fire off another round. I scrambled to my feet as the familiar sound of car tires tearing down a dirt road. I snapped my head to the left and saw the Celebrity's taillights disappear down Parkway Avenue. My chest suddenly felt like it was burning from the inside.

With that trigger-happy mother fucker gone, it was safe to check the damage. I unzipped my jacket and found a strange substance sticking to my shirt. It looked like maple syrup beneath the orange glow of the streetlights.

One part of my brain screamed, "You've been shot!" The other part of my mind insisted that he shot me in the chest. But how could he do that when I had my back turned to him? For some reason, I refused to believe that the bullet went through me. It was like a curtain of denial had been drawn through the middle of my brain.

Instead of going into a panic, the rational part of my brain kicked in. It was the same voice that told me I was going to get shot. This time, it urged me to stay calm and get help. I walked to the house that I'd tried to reach before and knocked on the door. I was lucky that the homeowner answered at that time of night.

I said, "Call 911! I've been shot."

"Bullshit!" he replied.

"Dude! I'm serious."

"Get off my porch!" he replied.

"Look!"

I opened my jacket and showed him the bleeding hole in my chest. He stared at me with his eyes open wide like he was the one who was in shock. I shouted, "Call 911, man!" That snapped him out of it.

"Fine," he replied. "But stay out there."

"Don't worry! I won't get any blood on your precious carpet."

I sat down on the crumbling concrete porch and waited… and waited… and waited for the ambulance. I worried that I might bleed to death before it got there. After what felt like an hour, some Genesee County sheriff's deputies finally arrived on scene. They didn't have an ambulance with them.

I know I shouldn't criticize people who are there to help. I also knew those paramedics couldn't find their asses with two hands and a flashlight. One of them desperately tried to jab an IV into my arm. No matter how hard she tried, she couldn't hit my vein. She just kept mangling me.

I said, "You're doing more damage than the bullet did!"

"Sorry," she mumbled.

I felt relieved when the ambulance finally showed up. The EMTs saved me from a slow and torturous death at the hands of that bumbling deputy. They put me on a gurney then plunged the IV in my vein on the first try. With that out of the way, they wheeled me into the meat wagon and sped off to the hospital.

The ambulance's lights bounced off the houses we passed on the way. This phantasmagorical display put me in a trance. We came to a stop beneath the emergency room awning of Flint Osteopathic Hospital. I remember thinking that the ride ended too soon, which was weird.

When they pulled me out, the gurney suddenly dropped to the curb. My head smashed hard against the metal stretcher after it hit the concrete. I growled "What the fuck?" and one of the EMTs mumbled a half-hearted "sorry." I wasn't convinced that was an accident. Being punk in Flint meant getting used to that type of crap from close-minded bigots.

They rolled me into the hospital and my family was waiting for me in the lobby. I didn't know how they beat me there. I didn't have time to ask them because they swarmed around me and put on a grand performance. It was like both of them had been practicing for the role of grieving parent and someone hollered, "Lights, camera, action!"

Dad proudly told the doctors to spare no expense when it came to his boy. Mom stood there and bawled like a helpless baby like she always did when things got too real. Some members of the hospital staff hugged her and told her everything would be all right. I had to give it to her. I took a bullet and she still managed to make it about her.

I was glad the attendants wheeled me away from that theater of the grotesque. When I got back to the room, a doctor gave me some bad news. As much as I denied that the bullet went right through me, that's exactly what it did. It punched through my flesh beneath my left scapula and bounced upward, tearing through my body, and exiting through my pectoral muscle.

What he said next really shocked me. The bullet missed my heart and lung by less than half an inch. If the shot was more to the center of my body, I could have been paralyzed. Any lower, and I would be shitting into a bag. I would've rather died than live the rest of my life like that.

As I sat there in my room, my mind went over everything that happened that night. This caused my heart to start racing, which made the monitor beep and whine. A nurse came into the room and jammed a needle into my IV. Within moments, a pair of velvet wings carried me off into an abyss that silenced the demons that started to torment me.

When morning broke, my inner demons attacked me with a vengeance. Why didn't I let Mama Sue drive me home? Should I have run away the minute the car turned around? I agonized over everything that I didn't do. What tortured me most was knowing that I let myself become a victim.

Long-repressed emotions burst out of the prison I'd kept them in for so long. I had to confront all those uncomfortable things that the shooting stirred up inside of me. Like most teenage boys, I thought I was tough. Do-Rag was playing at a much higher level than I could comprehend.

He tried to kill me, for real. It sounded unbelievable but there I was, sitting in a hospital room with a hole in my chest. The more I thought about Do-Rag, the more I considered him a vile and remorseless psychopath. Knowing that he was roaming the streets of Flint was a terrifying reality.

The more I thought about that monster, the more I became immersed in the dark emotions that roiled within me. It was all useless anger, though. Since I didn't know who Do-Rag was, there was no chance of getting revenge. Something fell from the corner of my eye and traced a path down my cheek. It was followed by others of its kind.

Punk as fuck, right?

It didn't take long to heal from the bullet wound. Getting over my emotional trauma was the real challenge. I needed time to decompress so I could sort out how my feelings. Too bad life had other plans for me when I got home.

My parents were worried about my mental state. Their biggest fear was me getting a gun and going out, looking for revenge. They became convinced that I was going to run around Flint, indiscriminately shooting people. They insisted that therapy was the only way to prevent that from happening.

When they asked me if I wanted to see a therapist, I said no. I didn't trust those people. My parents were teachers and they had fucked with my head for years. There was no telling what some professional therapist could do. Besides, those people didn't go through what I went through, so how they could help me?

When I told my parents to take their therapy idea and shove it, they came up with another plan. They had some of their teacher friends come over to talk to me. These visits followed the same pattern. Mom and Dad's friends started out with a pretense of concern before they launched into a full-on lecture. I heard more than I cared to know about the history of racism in America from slavery to the Civil Rights movement.

To make a long story short, they all believed that I had no right to be angry with Do-Rag. They insisted that he wasn't responsible for his actions. One of them even said that shooting me was an "important social and political expression from an oppressed minority." She had the nerve to say that to me days after I came home from the hospital!

If I thought the way they saw the shooting was bad, their advice on what I should do was worse.

My parents' know-it-all friends told me that I should reach out to Flint's African-American community. Some suggested I volunteer with a local organization, while others recommended books by prominent black authors. I didn't have any desire to do charity work or read the collected works of bell hooks.

The only good thing about those visits was that they finally ended.

Word of my unfortunate perforation reached my dad's family in New York City. My aunt and uncle felt inspired to come to see me on a mission of mercy. Their whole purpose was to share their religious perspectives with me, from a Catholic and a Buddhist perspective. After the visits from my parents' friends, I had no interest in putting up with my relatives.

When I tried to avoid their sermons, the two virtue vultures followed me from room to room. I got tired of them hounding me, so I begged my parents to make them back off. Mom said she couldn't believe I was being so disrespectful to people who were "just trying to help." Dad said he'd "knock my fucking head off" if I didn't show my aunt and uncle the respect they deserved.

Wow! What kind of father threatens to beat up his son who had just been shot? Only my dear old Dad, Flint Schools' Educator of the Year, and an inspiration to all his students. If they only knew how he really was!

It was up to me to deal with my aunt and uncle. Since I couldn't reason with them, I did the only thing I could do. That was to make a show of listening to them, but I let their words go in one ear and out the other. After two weeks of philosophical torture, they finally packed up and headed home.

My parents thought my aunt and uncle were "helping" me. This false belief blinded Mom and Dad to the dark side of what my relatives did. My parents lived for what other people thought of them. That's why they shouted me down when I wanted some space. They were scared to death of offending anyone, so I had to put up with those "life coaches."

I hated that they let those idiots have free access to me. Their so-called "help" was nothing more than intellectual masturbation. They jerked themselves off with their words until they came in my ear, then left me to clean up the mess. They thought they were heroes while I fell through the cracks, just like most victims of violent crime.

Not a damn one of them really meant it when they asked me, "Are you okay?" I think they were afraid of their own feelings and emotions that would be stirred up by that discussion. That didn't change the truth about it, though. I was almost murdered because of the color of my skin. And, because of the color of the shooter's skin, I wasn't allowed to talk about it.

I was willing to bet that in another 30+ years, people would still be tiptoeing around that elephant in the room.

9.
Hurt People Hurt People

September 1988 was a month that was colored red with anger. While I struggled to overcome the trauma of getting shot, the kids in my neighborhood had a lot to say about it.

I left Hamady to escape the stifling confines of their narrow minds. Now here they were, dragging me down into the cesspool of their ignorance once more. One kid told Dan that I got shot because I "must've been mouthing off." Another one said, "That's what he gets for walking around with a mohawk." When I heard that, it felt like I was being victimized all over again.

Out of all these armchair sociologists, one name kept coming up. It was Randy Willis, a little shit from the neighborhood. He used to be a heavy metal kid, but he traded in his mullet for a cheesy little rat tail haircut and a gold chain around his neck.

"Li'l Rand" was running his mouth because he thought I wouldn't do anything about it. That was a huge mistake on his part. Once the hole in my chest healed, it was time to teach him what happens when he talks shit about someone who knows where to find him.

The little loudmouth hung out at Playland, a video game arcade on Pasadena Avenue. When Hank Werner opened his arcade in 1967, he didn't expect his business would host street justice. Neither did the new owners who bought it sometime during the 1980s. I didn't care what they wanted because all I could think of was getting revenge.

I told Cam and Dan to pick me up after they got out of school. When they showed up, I hopped in the car and said, "Go to Playland." From the backseat, I heard Dan say, "Oh shit!" He knew what was up, and Cam would find out soon enough.

I barged into the building and walked around the circular island of video games in the front room. All I saw were three strangers playing Bubbles, Major Havoc, and Ring King. I checked the back room, but

Randy wasn't there either.

When I walked back to the front, Dan said that he found Randy in the side room. He was playing Donkey Kong Jr., so he didn't notice me walk up on him. When he finally saw me standing next to him, he had a nervous look on his face. That told me everything I needed to know.

Since I'd probably only have a few seconds to get my licks in, I didn't bother talking to him. I just snatched that disgusting little rat tail and yanked on it. It was an old dirty wrestling move known as "the turkey peeks over the log." It causes pain in all those tender nerve endings where the hair meets the back of the neck.

The little punk shrieked out in pain. I slammed his head into the video game to shut him up. Seeing his head bounce of the game's wooden cabinet was so satisfying that I did it again.

I said, "How's that feel?"

He shouted, "What did I do?"

"Talkin' shit about me!" I growled.

"I didn't say nothing!"

I pressed my forearm into his throat and said, "You callin' me a liar?"

"No!"

I blasted his head with a quick elbow shot then said, "What?"

"I swear!"

The commotion attracted the manager of the arcade. He shouted for me to let Randy go, but I jerked that greasy rat tail even harder. That lifted Randy's head, and I smacked him with a hard, open-handed slap. It hit his ear with a crack and made him stagger around like a drunk.

"That's enough!" the manager shouted.

When I spun around to face the guy, I saw him flinch. That told me everything I needed to know. That shrimp with spaghetti stick arms wasn't going to do anything. As far as Randy was concerned, I knew he got the message. The little rat wouldn't be running his mouth about me anymore.

We tore out of the parking lot so fast that Cam's tires were spitting gravel like bullets.

I got into another fight that summer, and this one happened closer to home.

One Sunday afternoon, Dan asked me to come over. Since it was during the day, I decided to ride my skateboard to his house. I absentmindedly rode through the parking lot behind the big box retail store on Pierson Road. I didn't get far before a white van screeched to a stop in front of me.

A voice shouted, "No skateboardin' on the premuhseez."

It was that hillbilly security guard who'd been hassling me ever since I started skating. When he used to confront me, I would take off through the trails in the woods behind my house. That day, I decided I wasn't running from that slack-jawed yokel.

"I'm skateboardin' through the premuhseez," I replied, mocking his southern accent.

"What'd you say, boy?"

There was a daring tone in his voice. It was one I'd heard many times from the bullies at school and on the streets. If you said something that pissed them off, they gave you one chance to take it back. They did this by asking you to repeat your offensive words.

When I was younger, I would lower my head and say, "I didn't say nothing." The bully would say, "That's what I thought you said!" and I would slink away in shame. That security guard didn't know that I wasn't the scared little kid that I used to be. That day, I looked him in the eye and said, "You heard me, motherfucker!"

His face became contorted in a look of pure rage. My eyes were drawn to his teeth, which furiously bit down on his lower lip. Out of pure instinct, I shot an overhand right through the van's open window. My fist smashed him in the face, and his head snapped back and bounced off the seat.

In half a second, he was scrambling to get out of his van. With an inhuman burst of speed, I lunged forward and slammed my shoulder into the van's door. It smashed into his body, then slammed his back into the metal door frame. With him pinned there, I pushed on that door with all my might, crushing him against the door frame once more.

I felt something hit the side of my head. By the time I realized that he punched me through the van's open window, he hit me again. I felt rage fill my veins, adding strength to my body. I roared like an injured bull and leaped forward, smashing his body with the door a third time.

In my fury, I wanted to crush the life out of him. Something stopped me from attacking, though. It was the sickening noise that slithered from his chest. It was like the last, desperate gasp from a dying pterodactyl. I jumped back and he crumpled to the asphalt.

71

As he laid there, struggling to breathe, his confidence drained from him and he looked pitiful. That's when the panic flooded my mind. What if someone saw us fighting and called the cops? I hopped on my skateboard and got the hell out of there.

When I got to Dan's, I had him bust out his dad's clippers and shave off my mohawk. I hoped that would make it harder for the security guard to identify me. I knew I couldn't walk home either because if the cops were looking for me, they could pick me up. I called Cam and was lucky enough to catch him before he left for Owosso.

I told him what happened, and he agreed to pick me up before he left. I expected the cops to be waiting for me when I got home, but they weren't there. My parents didn't say anything to me either, but I was on pins and needles the whole night.

Over the next few days, I thought the police would come over at any minute. After hearing nothing for a week, I figured I was in the clear. I developed a sense of respect for that hillbilly security guard. He might have been a close-minded bigot, but he took his ass whipping like a man.

Cam came over one day and said we should check out a show at The Capitol Theatre. I agreed. If our band was going to be successful, it was time to get serious about it. That meant finally being part of our local music scene. It also meant that Cam still cared about our band.

Dan couldn't go out with us, so it was just the two of us. It felt good to hang out with Cam, though. I hadn't seen him in almost a month, so we spent most of the ride catching up with each other. We also briefly discussed his commitment to the band, which he said remained strong despite his relationship with Belladonna.

In about 20 minutes, he steered his Chevette through the mix of shadow and neon that was downtown Flint. When he turned onto Second Street, The Capitol rose before us like a monument to my punk rock ambitions. Cam parked the car, and we walked to the building as quickly as we could without breaking out into a run.

I'd heard about the shows at the Capitol Theatre for more than two years but never went to one. That night, I was finally there, and it was everything I expected and more. It felt good to be with kids who dressed like me and liked the same kind of music. I didn't feel like an outcast, which was the opposite of being in the square world.

Since we showed up between bands, Cam and I hung out in the lobby. As we did, I noticed this kid staring at us from the other side of the room. He was a tall, skinny dude with a Dead Kennedys T-shirt and parrot's beak bangs. His mean-mugging had me on edge, and it felt like lightning was shooting through my arms and legs.

I pulled Cam aside and told him what was going on. I also warned him not to look at the guy. So, what did he do? He craned his neck to see the kid, then had the nerve to say I was "paranoid." I couldn't believe it! I'd been around long enough to know when someone was mean mugging me, and that kid was.

The band started playing, so we went into the theater. The group on stage was Hammer 13, and their bassist was Ross Barkey. He was one of the punks we met at the mall. The band was good, but after five or six songs, I had to take a leak. I kept an eye out for Mean Mug as I walked to the bathroom but didn't see him.

On my way back to the pit, I found Mean Mug. He was shouting at Cam and jabbing a finger in his face. I charged forward like a raging bull and knocked some poor girl to the floor. I didn't have time to see if she was okay, though. I kept plowing forward until my shoulder slammed into that kid.

The blow knocked him back, and his arms flailed in a desperate attempt to regain his balance. As he got his feet under him, I grabbed his T-shirt and yanked him toward me. As he stumbled forward, I swung a hard right at his temple. In the chaos of battle, I only grazed his head.

Mean Mug's arms turned into a windmill of punches. I went into a defensive crouch, and his fists crashed into my back. He managed to pound the scar that marked the point where Do-Rag's bullet entered my body. I felt an intense pain sear through me. It probably was more psychological than physical, but it made me roar like an injured lion.

The sudden burst of adrenaline powered my looping right hook. My fist cracked against Mean Mug's face, and it felt like a hammer hitting a raw steak. I quickly followed up with a left hook, a right hook, and another left hook. This rapid succession of blows rocked him, but my focus on speed robbed my punches of their power. This left my opponent on his feet and angry.

Before he could launch another attack, I put everything I had into a leaping right hook. Instead of hitting Mean Mug in the face, my fist slammed into the side of his neck. I watched as the dude's knees buckled, and he fell to the floor in slow motion. On his way down, his head almost hit the base of a theater seat.

The piercing sound of a girl's shrieks yanked me back to reality. My eyes focused on the two security guards rushing toward me in real-time. I shouted to Cam, and we bolted toward the lobby. As I got to the door, a gigantic hand clamped down on my shoulder and shoved me down to the sidewalk outside.

I jumped to my feet and whirled around to face my attacker. I suddenly found myself staring at two security guards. Both of them were built like professional wrestlers, and one of them even looked like Big Bossman from the World Wrestling Federation.

Big Bossman shouted, "Why were you fighting?"

"Why'd you push me?"

"Answer my question!" he bellowed.

"I didn't attack no one."

"Bullshit!"

"It was self-defense, man!"

Just then, I heard someone shout, "Can you prove that?"

The crowd parted and this funny looking dude walked up to me. He was about 5' 4" and had long hair, a tie-dyed shirt, and bell-bottom jeans. He also wore a big peace symbol on a leather strap around his neck.

The hippie said, "To prove self-defense, you have to establish a reasonable basis to fear for your safety."

"He jumped my friend!" I said.

"He didn't attack you?"

"No..."

"And did you have a chance to retreat or escape?"

I knew he had me at that moment. Technically speaking, we could have run away from Mean Mug, I just didn't want to. The little hippie picked up on my hesitation and started yapping about how violence didn't solve anything, blah, blah, blah. I didn't like the way he was talking down to me.

I said, "Hold on!"

"What?" he replied.

"Who the hell are you?"

The kids in the crowd laughed, which gave me a bad feeling. I soon found out who that annoying little hippie was. He was none other than Scott Repperton, aka "Big Daddy." Great! I had to piss off the guy

74

who booked the bands at the Capitol.

I felt like an idiot, so I just stood there as Big Daddy kept talking. In the middle of his lecture, Mean Mug staggered outside. He took one look at me and shouted, "That's him!" That sent him into a coughing fit, and he had to sit down on the sidewalk to catch his breath.

Once Mean Mug came around, Big Daddy said he wanted to have a "dialogue" with us. After we had some back and forth, Mean Mug said some metalheads jumped one of his friends downtown. He saw Cam's stupid mullet and thought he was one of them. I told Big Daddy that this was our first time at The Capitol.

Big Daddy said, "So, this is a case of mistaken identity…"

"Sounds like it," I replied.

"Then let this be a lesson to you," Big Daddy continued. "The answer to words is more words, not violence; never violence."

We all mumbled in half-hearted agreement. Big Daddy looked at the three of us, then asked if this was over. We all said that it was. With that settled, he then told everyone to go back inside and enjoy the show.

We slowly filed back into the Capitol. As I walked past Mean Mug, he refused to look at me. Whatever. He got what was coming to him. As I went to walk through the open door, Big Daddy pulled me aside and said he wanted to talk to me.

"What?" I asked.

"I'll cut you a break this time," he said. "But if this happens again, we'll make you sorry you ever came here."

There was no small irony in getting threatened by the hippie who just lectured me about violence. It wasn't a cute or funny kind of irony, either. It pissed me off, but I couldn't do anything about it. Like it or not, I had to put up with Big Daddy.

When Cam dropped me off at home, he said we needed to talk. I always got defensive when someone said that to me, and this was no exception. We sat down at the picnic table in my front yard like we'd done many times before. I asked him what's up, and he said, "What's gotten into you?"

"What do you mean?" I asked.

"All this fighting."

"What about it?"

"It's not like you," he said.

75

"Hurt people hurt people I guess."

Cam laughed because I quoted a guidance counselor at Hamady. He always said "hurt people hurt people" whenever kids got into a fight. I never knew what he meant by that, so I asked him to explain it to me one day at school. He said I'd eventually figure it out, and he was right.

I'd been hurting for a long time because I always was the one who got pushed around and disrespected. The drive-by shooting was the last straw. After I got home from the hospital, I couldn't take it anymore. Rat-Tail Randy pulled the trigger on my rage, and I went looking for any excuse to go off on someone. I tried my best to explain all that to Cam.

He said, "You need to get laid."

"That's your answer?" I asked.

"It'll change your attitude on a lot of things," he replied. "Trust me."

"It ain't gonna happen."

"Why not?" he asked.

"'Cause no woman wants me."

"Come off it, man!"

"What the hell does that mean?" I asked.

Cam said Lily liked me and I was an idiot if I didn't see that. I did see it, but I didn't want to act on it. My paralyzing fear of rejection always held me back. I also couldn't tell Cam about that because I had no interest in relieving my humiliations from the recent past.

"Well?" he said.

"I don't have a chance with her now," I replied.

"You could if you tried."

"I don't know how to talk to girls," I said. "Not like that, I mean."

Cam told me to relax and just be myself. That was good advice, but I told him I didn't know when I'd ever see Lily again. He said he was bringing Belladonna to Flint the next day, and he was sure he could talk Lily into coming along. I believed him because he could sell a ketchup Popsicle to a woman wearing white gloves.

The sun was going down as we drove the girls due east on M-21. We had a case of beer and a pint of rum courtesy of Cam's stoner connections. That was everything we needed to have a good time except a place to take them. Then an idea hit me.

I said, "Let's go to the asylum."

76

"Yeah!" Cam replied.

The "asylum" was an abandoned group home complex. It was in a secluded spot where Mt. Morris, Flint, and Flushing townships came together. It wasn't far from Dan's house, and he and I skated its empty parking lot a few times that summer. I knew that no one would bother us there.

The car's headlights cut a swath through the darkness of that barren place. Cam parked and he and Belladonna got out, while I stayed in the backseat with Lily. If it was ever possible to get cozy in a Chevette, we did it. It felt like we were safe from the world in our womb of glass and steel.

She handed me a cassette so I put it into the tape deck and pushed play. The Cure began to serenade us with "Friday I'm in Love." Echo and the Bunnymen continued to set the mood with "Bring on the Dancing Horses." Her mixtape also had songs by The Smiths, Depeche Mode, and other New Romantic bands.

The lights from the dashboard illuminated her crystalline blue eyes. I felt drawn to them and her beautiful face. I barely noticed that she was drawing closer to me until the tips of our noses nearly touched. As if on cue, our lips met in the soft and perfect union. As first kisses go, it was graceful and passionate.

We kissed through The Church's "Under the Milky Way." It felt like the band was performing just for us as we held each other beneath the glittering canopy of stars. If there was such a thing as magic, the air was practically crackling with it. All the anger that consumed me just drifted away, and the moment left me spellbound.

It seemed all too soon when Cam finally knocked on the fogged-up windows. It was time to take the girls home. I released Lily from my embrace, but we held hands all the way back to Owosso. Our kiss beneath the streetlight outside her house was a continuation of the magic I felt earlier.

My head was in the clouds all the way back to Flint. I could barely hear Cam as he congratulated me for making it happen with Lily. All I knew was that I would never forget that night because it was the night that all the love songs made sense.

10.
One and Done Again

I finally got to play the Capitol Theatre on November 18, 1988.
Too bad I had to crawl through a mile of broken glass to do it. That's
what I get for listening to Cam "The Scam" Leon.

In late September, he came up with a brilliant idea to quit his job
and move to Owosso. He planned on finding work there and eventually
getting a place with Belladonna. He asked me to come with him
because he knew I wanted out of my parents' house as much as he
wanted out of his. It sounded good, but a tiny voice in my head told me
not to go.

I said the whole thing seemed rushed. How long would it take for
us to find jobs? Before we got a place, where would we sleep? And
how would we eat? Cam said we'd sleep in the car, and we had enough
money between us to live until we got settled. I didn't want to sound
like a wet blanket, but I said it didn't sound like a good idea.

He said, "You'll get to see Lily every day."

"Let me pack a bag," I replied.

I quickly threw some clothes, deodorant, and all my cassette tapes
into a gym bag and hopped into his car. We stopped by Dan's to say
goodbye, and he begged us not to go. He told me that moving away
would put the band on hold. I knew he was right, but I'd found
someone more important to me than the band.

Once again, the cracked asphalt of M-21 beckoned us forward. It
was like a long and winding river that led to its own heart of darkness.
The Colonel Walter E. Kurtz that awaited us was the deep-seated
xenophobia that was the dark undertow of that town. Even though
we'd been there a bunch of times, we had no idea what we were driving
into.

Cam and I placed job applications all over town. After two weeks
of constant dead ends, we started to get desperate. I knew what I had

to do, and it went against all the middle-class values my parents instilled in me. That was to go on welfare, and I swallowed my pride to do it.

In 1988, Michigan still offered General Assistance, aka GA, to everyone who qualified. Being homeless with no job meant that I qualified. All I got was food stamps, but it kept us fed. We could have gotten more if Cam would have gone on GA, but he refused. I figured it had to do with that blue-collar pride he got from his dad.

With makeshift meals in our belly, we did another round of job hunting. We expanded our search to the nearby towns of Corunna and St. Johns but still came up empty-handed. Feeling dejected, we spent our days at the local library until the girls got out of school. I managed to finish Anthony Burgess's *A Clockwork Orange*, which was the most productive thing I did.

Our desperate shot at autonomy came to its inevitable end in November. Belladonna dealt the first blow when she broke up with Cam. The second shoe dropped when the cops impounded his car, which doubled as our home. Since he didn't have any money, he couldn't afford insurance. Without insurance, it was illegal for him to be on the road. Now we were truly homeless.

It was decision time, and I thought going back home was my best bet. I wasn't sure if my parents would have me, but it was my only shot. I was sure Cam would go home too, but he was dead set against it. He said he'd get a ride to Detroit and crash with some punks he knew. Whether I agreed with his decision or not, that's where we left things.

Lily cut class to drive me home. She offered to stay with me when my parents got home, but I told her I had to face them on my own. Our lips met in a long kiss that seemed like much more than teenage puppy love. As she pulled away from me, I saw the tears form in her eyes.

I said, "Give me a chance to get my shit together so I can take care of you."

Her eyes welled up again as she nodded her head. I didn't know how the hell I was going to make good on my promise, but I desperately wanted to do that for her. At that point, there was nothing left to do but let her go home to her parents so I could face mine.

Mom and Dad blasted me with Operation Dragon Fire as soon as they got home. Before I moved out, Dad said I wouldn't last six months out there. Coming back home with my hat in my hand gave him the perfect chance to say, "I told you so." That night, he said it over and over. It was his moment to shine, and he milked it for all it was worth.

Mom took the guilt-trip route. She told me that she worried herself sick while I was gone. That made me a "selfish, rotten piece of shit" for putting her through all that. That hardly phased me because she put me down like that since I was a kid.

All I had to do was let Mom and Dad get their pound of flesh without going off on them. I bit my tongue and took it until they finally ran out of gas. At that point, they laid down the law. I could only stay there if I got a job and went to school. I immediately agreed because I was willing to do anything to get on my feet.

Despite Flint's decline in the late 1980s, I got a job in less than a week. It was at a small grocery products warehouse in Swartz Creek. Enrolling in night classes at Mott Community College was easy, too. With these two things locked down, there was something I needed to do for myself.

I called Handsome Dan and said, "Are you ready to get the band going?"

"You're the one who put it on hold," he replied.

I apologized and told him that he was right. I should have never listened to Cam. I quickly pivoted back to my original question about getting Audacity back together. Dan reminded me that Cam was missing in action, so I promised him that I'd find us a drummer. He seemed skeptical.

I said, "I don't know how I'm gonna do it, but I will."

I might have bitten off more than I could chew with that one. My history with drummers was horrible, yet I promised Dan I'd find one. It was going to be hard but not impossible. It was a good thing I had a plan.

I whipped up a "drummer wanted" flier and took it straight to Bill Schaffer's Drum Shop. William Schaffer was a legendary drummer inside and outside the Flint music scene. He played in symphony orchestras, TV and studio sets, and as a backup for big-name performers. His store was huge with practically everyone who played drums, so it was the perfect place to hang our flyer.

A few days later, I got a call from Rikki Roxx of all people. He said he saw my flier at Schaffer's, and I got excited. Did he change his mind and decide to drum for us after all? No, he didn't, but his friend, David

Bierman, was looking for a project.

I said, "Give me his number!"

I called David Bierman after I hung up with Rikki. I introduced myself and told him about the bands that influenced me. The list included The Misfits, The Sex Pistols, and The Vandals. His influences were KISS, Alice Cooper, and Queen, which had me wondering if this was going to work between us.

I asked him why he'd want to drum for a punk band. He said he was looking for some live playing experience. I told him he'd get plenty if he jammed with us. He seemed okay with that, so I invited him to practice with us that weekend.

That Saturday, Dan and I set up in my parents' garage. It wasn't long before a van pulled into the driveway. The passenger door opened, and I got my first look at David Bierman. I knew he was into the whole hair metal thing, but I was still shocked by what I saw.

His voluminous dark brown hair was quite a spectacle. He must have teased it with vast amounts of heavy metal hair care products. He was only five feet, four inches tall, but that hair nearly put him over six feet.

David walked over and shook my hand and Dan's. He then introduced us to his dad, David Bierman, Sr. The two of them unloaded Junior's drum set, which was almost as massive as Luis Cardenas' 360-degree kit. Despite its size, they got it together rather quickly. Then David Sr. hopped in the van and left so we could see if his son was Audacity material.

When David sat behind his kit, all I could see was the top of his gigantic hair. If nothing else, I figured the experience of jamming with him would be interesting. He asked us if we could run through a few covers to get warmed up, but we didn't know any hair metal hits. We wouldn't play them even if we did because Audacity was a punk band.

Dan and I jumped right into one of our originals. The little guy with the big drum kit and even bigger hair rocked out like a beast. Despite our musical differences, his hard-hitting style fit our sound. To be honest, he took our songs to the next level.

After three or four songs, I needed to talk to Dan. We stepped away from the mics and went around the corner of my parents' garage. It was about as much privacy as the situation could provide, and we still had to whisper.

"Well?" I said.

"He's good!" Dan replied.

"Yeah, but what about the whole hair metal thing?"

"The punk drummer we had moved to Detroit."

"Good point," I said.

We came back to the garage and asked David if he wanted to join the band. He said "sure," and Audacity became a power-trio. I was glad he said "yes," but part of me wondered if the punk kids downtown would accept him. We'd find out soon enough.

The family van pulled into the driveway not long after David Jr. joined Audacity. When David Sr. got out, something seemed off about him. He had that look in his eye of someone who had a couple of drinks. He confirmed my suspicions when he swaggered over to me and stood a few inches from my face.

David Sr. said, "What d'ya think of my boy?"

"He's good," I replied.

He snorted then said, "He's the best."

"And now he's in our band."

David Sr. looked at his son and said, "Is this what you want?"

"Yeah," Junior replied.

The old man turned back to me and said, "My boy's gonna show you what you need to know about the music business."

There was an awkward moment of silence between us. I looked him in the eye, and he glared back at me. It felt like a standoff from an old spaghetti western. Junior broke the tension when he asked his dad to help him load his drums.

With a new drummer on board, Dan and I drove the band full speed ahead.

We put together a setlist of punk cover songs and our originals, and we practiced once a week. David rose to the occasion by coming up with a drum part for each song, then committing the tunes to memory. Within a few months, we knew that we were ready to play the Capitol.

While I wanted to book the show myself, it was better to have Dan do it. Big Daddy never forgave me for knocking out Mean Mug. It was the way he looked at me every time I was downtown. Dan could get us a gig without all that drama being part of the process. Two days after I asked him to, Dan told me he got us on a bill.

I said, "Did Big Daddy give you any shit?"

"Who's that?" he asked.

"The dude who books the shows."

"I talked to Joel," he said.

"Who's Joel?"

"Joel Rash."

That was the first time I'd heard the name Joel Rash, but it wouldn't be the last. He's the guy who usually booked the shows downtown. He's also the guy who liked taking adventure vacations in America and Europe. Whenever he did that, he put Big Daddy in charge.

Joel was back in Flint, which was a good thing for Audacity. The only downside to our gig was the fact that Lily couldn't be there. She had to go out of town with her family that weekend, and her parents wouldn't let her out of it. I told her not to worry because there would be a lot more gigs with David in the band.

When Saturday rolled around, Dan and I loaded our gear into my car and drove to David's house. We then loaded everything into Old Man Bierman's van. With father and son in the two-seat cab, Dan and I rode in the back from Montrose to downtown Flint.

We were the headliner that night, which had its pros and cons. The pros were that we were the headliner. The biggest drawback was that we had to sit through all the other bands' sets. At least Hammer 13, with Ross Barkey on bass, was one of them.

I was all wound up by the time we took the stage. It was the moment I'd been waiting for since 1986. With my bass guitar strapped across my chest and a microphone in front of me, I felt like a god on that stage.

We unleashed our sonic fury, and it whipped the crowd into a frenzy. The pit became a swirling mass of punks. I saw Dale Brownfield and Corey Robinson among the whirlpool of leather jackets, torn jeans, and T-shirts. It looked like they were really getting into it.

As we launched into our second song, I spotted another friend in the pit. It was Tony Serr, and he burst through the churning mass of bodies and ran toward us. When he reached the edge of the stage, he pounded his fists on it and shouted my band's name over and over. Many of the kids joined him in his chant.

The crowd's reactions got me higher than any drug ever could. As I basked in that glory, I felt something smack against my right hand. I looked down and saw a big glob of spit glistening beneath the stage lights' glare. It left a trail as it oozed down my hand like a slug.

Seeing that drained my excitement and replaced it with a white-hot rage. I shouted for the guys to stop playing. A tense silence filled the room, and Dan looked at me like, "What the fuck?" I answered his questioning gaze by yelling, "Someone spit on me!" into the mic.

I said only a coward would do something like that. Then I dared the mystery spitter to own up to his dirty deed in front of everyone. From somewhere out in the darkness, I heard someone shout, "I did it!"

"Come up here and say it to my face!" I bellowed.

A form emerged from the darkness and came into view. I recognized the dude's face, spiked black hair, and glasses with thick, Coke bottle lenses. It was the guy who worked at Record Town in the mall. I talked to him many times over the summer of '88, and he was always cool with me. I wasn't always cool with him, though.

One day, Cam and I stopped into the store with Lily and Belladonna. I must have felt the need to be the center of attention that day because I started making fun of Coke Bottles. The laughter from Cam and the girls was like a drug, and I maintained that high by going in on Coke Bottles some more. I didn't care that I'd upset him.

I wasn't surprised that he spit on me that night. He had every right to be pissed. The thing was, I couldn't let it go. Everyone at The Capitol was watching to see what I would do.

As Coke Bottles got closer to the stage, I took off my bass and ran toward him. When he came within range, I swung that heavy guitar like a battle-ax. I aimed straight for that idiot's pitted face, but my bass sailed through the air with a harmless swish. I had no choice but to follow through with the heavy swing.

As the bulk of my bass flew past my foe's head, the leather strap attached swung around and hit him across his cheek. A loud smack echoed in the dead air. A second later, Coke Bottles ripped out an agonizing scream and fell to a knee. He clutched his face and wailed in pain.

The crowd exploded in a mix of reactions. Some laughed, others shouted, and one girl let out a shriek of terror. I dropped my guitar and lunged at Coke Bottles, but a security guard grabbed me. Two more security staff yanked Coke Bottles to his feet and dragged him out of the theater. Once he was gone, the security guard let go of me.

I ran to the mic and launched into a tirade about what happens to anyone who disrespects me. Dan nudged me in the back and said, "You made your point." The intense look on his face shocked me out of my rage. I strapped my bass across my chest and we ripped through The Misfits' "Last Caress" to close the show. The crowd went nuts.

A bunch of kids came up to me and said we put on a great show. Some of them laughed about me blasting Coke Bottles in the face. All that attention made me feel like a legend after just one performance. I wanted to stay there and bask in my glory all night, but I had to get Dan home.

We jumped into Bierman's van and made the long trip back to his house. On the way there, I kept raving to Dan about our show. I swore that we would take over the Flint scene, and he mustered up a weak "yeah." I couldn't understand why he wasn't as excited about our show as I was.

We got back to David's house sometime after 1 AM. I was cold, tired, and ready to call it a night. Dan and I put our gear into my car then said goodbye to David Jr. As we were leaving, David Sr. said he wanted to talk to me.

I handed Dan my keys and told him to warm up the car. Then I walked over to where David Sr. was and said, "What's up?"

"I'm gonna tell you somethin' and you're not gonna like it," he said.

"Oh yeah?" I replied.

"You need to work on your stage presence if you want to make it in this business," he said.

"What do you mean?" I snarled.

"My boy's been doin' this a long time..."

"So?"

"He's more than just a drummer ..."

His words and the stench of alcohol hung in the air. It was clear that David's dad had something to say, and he wanted me to ask him to say it. I wasn't going to play that game with him. I stared into his bloodshot eyes until he finally worked up the nerve to give me his pitch.

"My boy should be the singer of this band," he said.

I shouldn't have been shocked that he was so bold. Hadn't I learned my lesson with Frank Puller? I thought that I did, but I must have forgotten it somewhere along the line.

So, David Sr. thought his boy was the be-all, end-all to music. As we stood outside in the cold, he went on and on about how little Davey was a better singer than me. He also told me that I should consider

85

myself lucky to have him in my band. As he shared all that, his breath assaulted my nose with the unmistakable smell of alcohol.

I said, "I think I get your point."

"I'll bet you think I'm just a stupid old man…"

"I didn't say that," I replied.

"It's what you're thinking."

"I didn't know you could read minds."

Dan honked the horn before Old Man Bierman could respond. I excused myself from the lecture and walked away. When I got to the car, Dan asked me what that was all about. I told him about my conversation with the wise and venerable David Sr. I also called the old man every name in the book.

Dan said, "You should've said that to him."

"We'd lose our drummer if I did."

"I think we already did," he replied.

I pulled the car over and started pounding my fist into the center of the steering wheel. I also screamed "fuck" with each punch. Dan gave me a look of worry and revulsion. It was the same look he had on his face during my outburst on stage that night.

I put the car back into drive and got the hell out of there. It was a long ride from Montrose to Mayfair, and Dan and I didn't talk the entire way. The most he said to me was "bye" after I dropped him off. That bothered me.

David Jr. called me a week after our show. He got right to the point and told me he was quitting Audacity, effective immediately. I sensed what sounded like regret in his voice. During his brief time in the band, he and I had become friends. I wondered if he'd miss our back and forth as much as I would.

He never really gave me a reason why he was quitting, even though I asked him. I got the sneaking suspicion that his dad was behind it. He tried to get me to step down from my position as lead singer after the show. Since I didn't back down, the old man probably told David Jr. to start a band of his own. As close as he was to his dad, there was no way Davey would say no.

David Jr. destroyed Audacity as far as I was concerned. I was mad at him but even more pissed at his dad. I was disgusted with how David Sr. was so damn supportive of his son's music. My old man did everything he could to crush my musical dreams. I was stupid to think that David Jr. was ever my friend. I hated him.

I gave Dan a call. When he answered, the story of David quitting poured out of my mouth like a tidal wave. All I wanted was Dan's reassurance that we could make it through this setback, but I didn't get it.

Dan said, "I'm in the middle of something right now."

The way he said it was so cold and off-putting. All I could say was "goodbye." When I hung up the phone, I knew that was the last time I'd talk to Dan as a bandmate. He didn't say anything about quitting, but the frigidity of his tone told me everything I needed to know.

I knew what drove the wedge between Dan and me. It was me. More to the point, it was all of my angry outbursts. He was a very calm guy who didn't like all that yelling and drama. Too bad that's all I could do back then.

My temper was the byproduct of me getting shot. I needed to deal with my problems, but I just kept burying them instead. It would explode to the surface any time I faced adversity. I should have never burdened Dan with all of that negativity. That was too much to ask of anyone, even my best friend.

We drifted apart in the weeks after that phone call. I didn't call him because I got a strong feeling that he didn't want me to. Sure, I could have misjudged the situation, but he didn't reach out to me either. Months later, my worst fear came true when I found out that Dan formed a new band.

Dan bought a bass and learned to slap and pop like Flea from the Red Hot Chili Peppers. His new group had that punk/funk/soul fusion sound that was all the rage in the early 1990s. He named it "Kung Fu Joe" after a character in *I'm Gonna Get You Sucka*. He loved that crazy movie.

While Audacity was a one-and-done band, Kung Fu Joe quickly became a living legend in the Flint scene. Every time I turned around, they were playing at The Capitol. I avoided their shows by convincing Lily to do other things like dinner and a movie. I just wasn't ready to see my former best friend and bandmate playing without me.

The only silver lining to it all was Lily. I still had a loyal girlfriend who loved me. That made her more valuable than any band ever could be.

11.
The Last Ride of a
One-Trick Pony

It was a normal weekend for Lily and me. I got out of work on Friday and picked her up, then drove to The Capitol. Joel Rash took another one of his adventure vacations and left Big Daddy in charge of booking the bands.

We paid our cover at the door like we always did, then we walked into the lobby. That's where we ran into David Bierman Jr. The first thing I thought was what the hell was that two-faced, heavy metal poser doing down here?

David said, "Hey, J.P.!"

"Hey, bro!" I replied. "What brings you down here?"

"We're playing tonight," he said.

"Oh yeah?" I said. "What's your band's name?"

"King David," he replied.

Wow! I thought. Only an egomaniac like David Bierman would call his band "King David." As I tried to wrap my mind around that, David started jacking his jaw about becoming "Flint's best solo rock performer." Just hearing him say that pissed me off, but I managed to shake his hand and wish him luck.

Lily said, "So that's David?"

"Yeah," I replied. "And I can't believe he's playing here."

"Is he any good?"

I said, "We'll see."

Lily and I sat in the front row when King David took the stage. I quickly realized that Davey was a better drummer than a singer. He sounded like a constipated screech owl caught inside a blender. He had absolutely no business being a frontman yet there he was, stinking up the joint.

88

The crowd didn't appreciate him shrieking through Black Sabbath's "Changes." That's when a plan formed in my mind. If I could pull it off, I'd get some much-deserved payback on David and his old man.

I went to the center of the pit and plopped down on the floor, right in front of the band. I saw a couple of punk girls I knew so I asked them to join me. They asked me what I was doing, and I said, "These metalheads think they can invade our club!"

"No kidding!" one of the girls replied.

"I think they suck," I said.

"Definitely," she replied.

That was all I needed to hear. I thrust my fist in the air and shouted, "You suck!" I did it a few more times before the girls joined in. As we kept this up, about 30 other punks joined us. The power of our collective shouts rose above the clamor of the band.

Flint is famous for the General Motors Sit-Down Strike of 1936-1937. That single act of defiance led to the formation of the United Automobile Workers union. I knew my sit-down strike was equally successful the moment David's eyes locked with mine.

I was glad he knew that I was the ringleader of that chorus of boos. Now he knew what it felt like to be betrayed by someone he thought was a friend. It was far better to slam the ice-cold dagger of betrayal into his heart instead of his back. I got to see the look on his face when I did.

When I walked back to Lily, she had a look on her face. It robbed me of the joy I got from booing David off the stage. What was her problem?

She said, "That was mean!"

It felt like she was taking David's side, and I said that to her. We went back and forth about it. I couldn't understand why she was so mad at me for doing what I did, so I called her out on it.

"People have the right to leave you without being punished for it," she replied.

I shot back with, "You're acting like a back-stabbing bitch."

She dropped it and didn't say much for the rest of the night.

Some people thought I was a hero for booing King David off the stage. One of them was Phil Bateman, a guy I knew from Powers. He was a skater kid who played guitar. He told me that I was "too intense" when I asked him to jam with me back in high school. He was singing a different tune at The Capitol.

Phil said, "Are you still doing music?"

"Not since Dan started Kung Fu Joe," I replied.

"They're really good!"

"If you like that sort of thing," I grumbled.

"Well, I'm looking to put something together."

"Oh yeah?"

He asked me if I wanted to play bass and sing for his band. I asked him who'd play drums, and he said, "Jim Connor." I knew that kid from Powers, too. So, Phil and Jim formed a band and wanted me to be in it. That sounded good, but I just had one question.

I said, "What do you wanna call this band?

"How about Audacity?" Phil said.

"Nobody knows who we were," I replied.

Phil told me that a lot of kids remembered my old band. He said they liked the I-don't-give-a-fuck attitude that came through in my songs. He also said everyone was talking about how I hit Coke Bottles with my bass. I only smacked him with my guitar strap, but Phil's version made me look like more of a badass.

I said, "If you wanna be Audacity, we'll be Audacity."

"Righteous!" he replied.

Between work, school, and Lily, it was hard to squeeze in practices. I found the time to do it, though. Good thing it didn't take us long to come together as a band. We sounded nearly as good as the original Audacity, and I started to feel like my old self again.

When it got to the point where we could play those tunes in our sleep, I told Phil to book a show. He got along with Big Daddy much better than I did, so I thought it best to let him run point on that. Phil called me one Friday and said we had a gig in a month.

Lily and I planned our weekends around who was playing downtown. Every Friday after work, I'd stop by Wyatt Earp's and grab a flyer for the shows that weekend. On the nights that Kung Fu Joe played, we always did dinner and movie instead.

One weekend, I forgot to stop by Wyatt Earp's. When Lily and I got to the Capitol, the place was packed. We walked into the lobby, and there was Dan O'Hallahan, my old pal and former bandmate. At that moment, I knew exactly who was headlining that night.

When Dan saw me, he walked over and thanked me for coming out. We caught up for a bit before he went back to his new friends. I told Lily I wanted to leave, and she asked me why a little too loudly. I told her to calm down, which was as successful as any time a man says that to a woman.

It was obvious that Lily wasn't going anywhere. That pissed me off, but I crumbled like a cookie. Back in November, I'd lost my band and my best friend; I didn't want to push my luck and lose my girlfriend, too. But even though I was stuck at The Capitol, I didn't have to watch Kung Fu Joe play.

When Dan's band took the stage, I milled around the lobby. Even from there, I could hear Kung Fu Joe warming up. Just as Dan was going through some funky bars on his bass, Lily came marching into the lobby. She demanded I watch the band with her.

Before I could object, she grabbed my hand and practically dragged me into the theater. She plopped down into a front-row seat, of course. Great! I'd be watching Dan's band up close and personal. That wasn't my idea of an awesome Friday night.

I suffered through all of Dan's bass guitar gymnastics. I would have never admitted it to anyone, but Kung Fu Joe brought the house down. As the band blasted out that funky music, the pit exploded with kids jumping and moshing.

Lily leaned over and said, "They're really good!"

"If you like Red Hot Chili Peppers clones," I replied.

"Grow up!"

After 30 minutes of entertaining torture, the band ended in a funk-filled fury. When the lights came up, I couldn't wait to get out of there. I didn't want to come face to face with Dan because I'd have to tell him that his band sounded great. That would have killed me.

I grabbed Lily by the hand and guided her to the lobby. As I tried to make my way through the crowd, she yanked hard on my hand. That brought me to a stop.

"What the fuck?" I said.

"Why are you in such a hurry?"

"I wanna go…"

"…Well I wanna hang out," she said.

I leaned toward her ear and whispered, "Let's park and hang out in the car."

"That's the last thing I want to do!" she snapped.

I never was good at handling rejection. I'd had too much of it in my life and the emotions it triggered always overwhelmed me. When Lily said that, her words burned my pride to a crisp. Without thinking, I called her something that a man is never supposed to call a woman.

That single-syllable word came out much louder than I intended. The entire lobby got quiet, and all eyes focused on me. The silence was shattered by the shouts of someone. It was Moonbeam Flaxseed, a hardcore man-hating feminist with a nasty habit of going off on dudes. In less than a second, she was nose-to-nose with me.

"Don't ever say that to a woman!" Moonbeam shrieked.

"I just did," I replied.

A wild look lit up her eyes, which blazed with the intensity of a forest fire. She insulted everything from my IQ to the size of my penis in her attempt to shame and humiliate me. I'd survived a drive-by shooting, so the lunatic ravings of a wannabe neo-hippie feminist didn't faze me.

"Go fuck yourself!" I said.

Moonbeam leaped toward me, and the bony point of her shoulder crashed into my collarbone. Her attack also made our heads knock together like a couple of coconuts. She crashed to the floor in a heap of tangled hair, tie-dye, and paisley. I thought I knocked her out until she rolled her head to the side and eked out a painful moan.

Angry voices suddenly exploded all around me. Many people in the crowd thought I hit Moonbeam. All I saw in front of me was a mob of angry faces and gnashing teeth. My ears started to pound, and everything seemed to move in slow motion.

The security guards barged into the lobby and were swayed by the crowd's hysterics. One of those giants bellowed at me about how it's wrong to hit a woman. I said I didn't hit her, and the head bouncer grabbed me by the arm. I jerked free from his grasp and told him not to touch me.

"Get outta here!" he snarled.

"Gladly," I replied.

I stormed toward the door and didn't care if Lily followed me or not. She did, but only because I was her ride home. From the sidewalk, I heard Moonbeam leading a chant of, "Hey hey! Ho ho! Misogyny has got to go!" I was furious.

Lily and I didn't say a word to each other on the ride back to

Owosso. It was the most uncomfortable 30 minutes of my life. I let her off in her parents' driveway then sped off into the night. I was tempted to drive back downtown and beat the shit out of that asshole security guard, but I wasn't going to do anything to jeopardize our upcoming show.

I rolled out of bed in the morning and headed to Phil's house. Our Saturday morning jam session would be the last one we'd have before our show. Phil met me at the door when I got there, and he had a strange look on his face. I asked him what was wrong.

"You can't play the show," he said.

"What do you mean?"

"You can't play The Capitol anymore."

"What the fuck?"

He told me it was because I punched Moonbeam in the face. I told him I didn't do that, and he said I needed to explain that to Big Daddy. He was the one who banned me, after all. That hardly came as a surprise to me. Moonbeam was one of his friends.

I used the phone in Phil's room to make the call. The little shit ripped into me for allegedly punching Moonbeam in the face. I told him I didn't do it, and he said that slapping a woman was just as bad. I said I didn't slap her either, but he wasn't having it.

"I'm serious!" I said.

He said, "Every minute, 20 women are assaulted by a man."

"But Moonbeam wasn't one of them," I replied.

Phil shook his head from side to side. He didn't think my attitude was helping, but he wasn't the one being called a woman-beater. Even though I had every right to be pissed, Phil was right. I'd have to reign it in if I wanted to fix things.

Big Daddy said a lot of people saw me hit Moonbeam. Once again, I tried to tell him I didn't hit her, but he talked right over me. He said he couldn't give a platform to someone who could do such a thing. His conscience wouldn't allow it.

"What are you saying, then?"

"You can no longer play at The Capitol," he said.

"Dude! We have a show next weekend…"

"You should've thought about that before you hit my friend."

"I already told you, I didn't hit her."

"I'm sorry but my mind is made up," he added.

"That's bullshit!"

He said, "My decision might seem arbitrary, but I have to do what's in everyone's best interests."

"So, what are you saying? I'm banned for life?"

"Yes," he replied. "But you can still attend shows if you want to."

At that point, I only had one card to play. I told Big Daddy that Lily saw the whole thing, so he should ask her what happened. That was a huge risk because I didn't really know what she'd say if he did. It was worth the risk at that point.

He said, "I can't trust that you won't threaten or coerce her into saying something that's favorable to you."

"What do you mean?"

"You have all the signs of an abuser," he said.

"That's bullshit!" I said.

"My friends wouldn't lie."

"Are you fucking kid…"

Big Daddy slammed the phone down and the line went dead. I turned to Phil and told him what he already knew. He said we could probably get that lifted when Joel got back but no one knew when that would happen.

I said, "I won't hold it against you if you want to get another singer and go in a different direction."

"You sure?" Phil asked.

"Yeah," I replied.

I wasn't going to ask him to keep the band going with me. My reputation in my hometown scene was shot, and I couldn't play there anymore. It was easier if I cut myself loose than put Phil in the awkward position of telling me he was quitting. That's what would have happened under the circumstances.

As I headed home, the reality of everything that happened hit me like a baseball bat. I tore down the highway like a bat out of hell and didn't let up until my car screeched to a halt in my driveway. When I called Lily, I exploded on her the moment she answered.

It was all her fault, and I wasn't shy about saying it. She was the one who insisted we stay for Kung Fu Joe. She demanded that we hang out in the lobby afterward. None of that shit with Moonbeam would've happened if we would've left like I wanted to.

She said, "Nobody made you call me a cunt in public."

94

She was still pissed about that, but I didn't care. She wasn't the one who got banned from playing The Capitol. It was utterly humiliating when Big Daddy told me that. It was even worse when he told me that I could still come to see the other bands play on the stage he wouldn't let me play on.

I shouted, "We're done going down there anymore!"

"Speak for yourself," she replied.

"What?"

"I'm not gonna stop going there just 'cause you fucked up."

"You're saying downtown is more important than me?"

"I'm saying I'm going down there," she said. "You can come with me or not."

"That's the same thing."

"If you say so," she said.

When Lily gave me her ultimatum, I should have stood by my convictions. Too bad I didn't have the self-confidence to do that. I'd already lost so much by that point that I was afraid of losing her, too. If she hung out downtown by herself, she could meet someone else, and I'd go back to being the loveless loser I was in high school.

Lily wasn't the only reason I didn't take a stand. As angry as I was, I didn't really want to sever my connection with The Capitol. Punk rock was the foundation of my precious identity, and going downtown was my only connection to that. It was like my very existence depended on the local music scene. If I cut that out of my life, I'd disappear.

On the weekend, I slunk back to The Capitol with my tail between my legs. What made it worse was Lily dragging me by the hand like I was a little kid in trouble with his mommy. When we got there, Big Daddy looked surprised to see me. After what he did, any sane person would have said, "Fuck this shit!"

He took our money and stamped our hands like he always did. As we walked inside, I heard hushed whispers ripple through the crowd. They still thought I hit Moonbeam, and they hated me for it. That embarrassing experience inspired me to write a song.

"Like a Beaten Dog"

Like a beaten dog, I come crawling right back

Seeking love when I'm under attack
Flay my flesh, I got plenty of slack to flog
Like a beaten dog

Wound me, gore me
You kill me when you ignore me
Ain't got not pride; whip my hide
Kick my ribs, rip out my hair,
We both know I ain't going nowhere

Like a beaten dog, I come crawling right back
Seeking love when I'm under attack
Flay my flesh, I got plenty of slack to flog
Like a beaten dog

Bash me, thrash me
Take a whip and lash me
It's not assault; it's all my fault
You can smash my face, break my nose
I got nowhere else to go

Like a beaten dog, I come crawling right back
Seeking love when I'm under attack
Flay my flesh, I got plenty of slack to flog
Like a beaten dog

Now look what I made you do
You wouldn't beat me if it wasn't true
I shouldn't get on your nerves
I only get what I deserve

Wound me, gore me
You kill me when you ignore me

12.
Broken, Severed, and Disconnected

My relationship with Lily was the foundation that supported me through tough times. By the summer of 1990, that foundation was crumbling beneath my feet.

The Moonbeam incident was a wound that never healed for either of us. Yes, I said that to Lily, and it was mean. I still thought she should have backed me up, though. When she didn't, I felt betrayed, and I wished I had the guts to break up with her. I didn't, so I lashed out at her instead.

Every time we were together, I'd blow my top. Even the smallest things set me off. One nasty incident happened while we were on our way to see The Jesus and Mary Chain at the Latin Quarter in Detroit. Lily said something, and I ranted and raved at her the whole way down there. That was an hour's worth of misery for her.

Things between us finally snapped one night after we watched *Fresh Horses*, of all movies. I thought that Molly Ringwald's character was a cold-hearted, manipulative whore. The way she played Andrew McCarthy's character reminded me of what Belladonna did to Cam. My tirade went on for a while until Lily finally spoke up.

She said, "It sounds like you got a thing for her."

"Who?" I said.

"Belladonna."

"No way!" I bellowed.

"I don't know," she said. "You seem to talk about her a lot…"

"That's bullshit!" I replied.

I was initially attracted to Belladonna when we met, but I thought I buried those feelings a long time ago. Lily uncovered that very uncomfortable truth and rubbed my nose in it. I was embarrassed by how she saw right through me. I did the only thing I could do, which was huff, puff, and deny everything. She wasn't buying it, though.

She said, "We need to talk."

"About what?"

"I think we should take a break," she replied.

"What are you talking about?"

"We need to take a break from seeing each other," she said. "Just for a little while."

"Why?"

"We need it."

"Bullshit!" I said.

"Okay. I need it," she added.

I demanded to know why she needed this so-called "break." She said she went straight from high school to being my girlfriend, so she needed to "find herself." When she suggested that I do the same, I balled up my fist and pounded my chest.

"What are you doing?" she asked.

"I just found myself," I replied.

"I knew you wouldn't understand."

"What's to understand?"

"I'm doing this whether you like it or not."

"For how long?"

"I don't know," she replied.

"If you're so sure you need this break, you should know how long it will be," I said.

"I'm not sure."

"Wow!" I said. "Some plan."

"Two weeks!" she snapped.

"What?"

"I need two weeks," she said.

I was pissed but not surprised. My popularity at The Capitol was on the decline, while Lily was a rising star down there. She was the darling of a group of friends she started hanging around. I thought they were a bunch of snobs, and that created some tension in our relationship.

Every time I saw her with them, I'd launch into a tirade. I was like a spitting cobra flinging venom into her eyes. She didn't really fight back, which I thought was strange. Little did I know she was saving up all those petty hatreds so she could drop one big bomb on me.

98

I knew that I was losing her, and I should have manned up and faced it. I collapsed into her lap instead and begged her not to go through with this break. I knew it made me look desperate and weak, but fear of loss is a powerful thing. It was strong enough to make me trade my dignity for a small amount of comfort.

"No," she said. "I have to do this."

"Are you not attracted to me anymore?"

"I didn't say that..."

"But you didn't not say it," I replied.

She said, "It's not that I'm not attracted to you..."

"...Then what is it?"

"Things have changed."

"Like what?"

"You're not in a band anymore..."

"What's that got to do with anything?" I asked.

She said, "That was a big part of what I liked about you."

That devastated me. How could I want to stay with her after she said that? It was so superficial, but I didn't say anything about it. I felt emotionally gutted, and it took everything I had to walk out the door.

The sadness I felt soon turned to anger. The more I dwelled on it, the more I suspected Lily of cheating on me. Two weeks was long enough for her to test drive a new guy. If she didn't like the ride, there was always me waiting in the wings like a sucker.

I shared my suspicions with my friends and family, but they gave Lily the benefit of the doubt. That pissed me off because I was sure she was messing around. The mental anguish I put myself through left me exhausted. That made me realize that Lily had all the power in this situation.

I desperately needed something to tip the balance in my favor.

My devious mind soon came up with a plan. I left some things at her house, so I planned to pick them up when she was at work. She might think that I met someone else while she was figuring out what she wanted. That would put her through the same Hell that I was going through.

I took a day off work and drove out to Owosso. When I knocked on the door, her little sister answered. She was the only one home, and she was happy to let me in. I ran up to Lily's room, grabbed my stuff, and made a point of saying goodbye to her sister. I knew she would tell Lily that I was there.

Lily called me a couple of times, but I had my family tell her I wasn't home. I was lucky they agreed to play along. My elusiveness must have driven her crazy because she came over just six days into her "two-week break." I was leaving for Wyatt Earp Records to pick up The Pixies' *Bossanova* album at the time.

Lily asked me to get into her car. I asked her why, and she said we needed to talk. I told her we'd talk in two weeks, just the way she wanted it. She asked me to get in the car again, so I did. I stayed cold and detached so I could pick up any signs that she might be messing around with someone.

Lily asked me why I got my stuff from her house, and her voice had a regretful tone. I resisted the temptation to hold her face in my hands and melt into a kiss. I couldn't get over how much she hurt me with everything she said that night. If I just forgave her, I'd be giving her permission to treat me like that again.

She said, "Why won't you talk to me?"

"Because you said two weeks," I replied. "I'm respecting your wishes."

"I wanna talk now."

"There's nothing to talk about," I said.

"So, all this was for nothing?" she asked.

"My life isn't gonna stop just 'cause you showed up."

"I know, but..."

"...Talk to me in a week."

"My friends were right," she said.

"What friends?"

"This was a mistake," she added.

I got out of her car and slammed the door so hard that the window shattered. Hundreds of pieces of glass shined like diamonds on the passenger seat of her car. Lily's eyes opened wide and she started yelling at me.

"Get the fuck outta here!" I bellowed.

She peeled out of the driveway and tore off down Jennings Road.

At Wyatt Earp Records, I proudly told Doug how I stood up to Lily. I was practically out of breath by the time I finished. He looked at me through those narrow eyes of his and asked me if I was sure that's what I wanted.

"Hell yeah!" I said.

"I hope it's not somethin' you'll regret," he replied.

"No way, man!"

While I was all bluster and bravado inside the store, Doug's words wormed into my head. As I drove home, I started to second guess my decision. Did I really do the right thing? What if she wasn't cheating on me after all? By the time I got home, those doubts became nagging demons that tortured me.

The next day, I broke down and called Lily. I told her I was sorry about her window and offered to pay for it. She said I couldn't afford it, which stung my pride because she was right. I hardly made any money as a part-time grill cook at a Ponderosa steakhouse.

Instead of exploding, I humbly asked her to take me back. She was dead set against it. I went into a panic and started begging. I was making a complete fool of myself, but I was too desperate and scared to stop. Lily said I had my chance then she slammed the phone down in my ear.

That time, it was for real. We were broken up, and I knew I couldn't talk her into coming back.

I fell to the floor and started crying. It was an ugly and retching thing that twisted my face into a grotesque mask of suffering. My two biggest fears were losing my band and my girlfriend. Now both came true. I crashed headlong into a deep depression as a result.

I took to hanging out in my room with the shades drawn, listening to Depeche Mode. I also started to pass through my day-life like a robot on autopilot. I couldn't find the joy in anything, not even hanging out at The Capitol. Too bad I kept going down there.

Lily was having the time of her life since I stopped being a part of it. I hated seeing her hanging on the arm of a new guy practically every weekend. She took sadistic glee in parading her new lovers past me.

As a result of our breakup, some of my friends quit talking to me. The most I could get out of them was icy stares. A few asked me for my side of the story. Great! Now I have the chance to do what I love most, which is to put on a show.

I'd pull out my flask and take a long draw of bourbon. Then I'd deliver painful orations about how "my woman done me wrong." I went from punk rock singer to alcohol-and-misery-infused spoken word artist. I was like Henry Rollins and Charles Bukowski… minus the talent and fame, of course.

My sidewalk performances were quite the novelty act at first. People would crowd around me and laugh at the outlandish shit that poured out of my mouth. They quickly lost interest after I lamented the same sad tale over and over. It got so I couldn't give away tickets to that shameful spectacle.

When the crowds started to avoid me, I knew I'd become a bad joke. I kept going downtown, though. I foolishly thought that I would lose my spot in the scene as if I even had one at that point.

One night, I finally learned where I really stood with some people downtown.

It started as just another weekend downtown. I put on my pathetic one-man show like I always did. I stood at the corner of East Second and Harrison streets and brayed like a wounded beast. My ridiculous behavior attracted just enough attention to encourage me to keep making a fool out of myself. I was too stupid to remember that the cries of injured animals attract predators.

After I ran out of steam, I went into The Capitol. The lobby was buzzing with people buying soft drinks and snacks at the refreshment stand. I got a fountain Coke in a caution-yellow plastic cup then plopped down in a seat to watch a band.

I heard someone shout my name. I looked up and saw Pete Mendelsohn, and he was making a beeline toward me. I thought that was strange because I barely knew the guy. I might have talked to him a grand total of two times, and it wasn't more than saying, "What's up?"

Pete sat down in the row of seats behind me and asked me how I was doing. As we talked, the spicy odor of his clove cigarette rolled off its burning tip in pungent, powder-white wisps. A bunch of kids in the scene smoked cloves back then.

He said, "Are you doing any music these days?"

"Not really," I replied.

"That's too bad. You're a good songwriter."

That comment was just a scrap of validation, but that was all it took. I opened the floodgates of my big mouth and blabbed about my band breaking up, being banned from playing the Capitol, and how Lily did me wrong. Pete lent a sympathetic ear to all my pitiful victim talk.

102

In the middle of our conversation, Pete sprang up from his seat and said a quick goodbye. I watched him speed-walk up the aisle until his form was swallowed by the lights in the lobby. I thought that was odd but maybe that's just how he was. I returned my attention to the band that had the privilege of playing on that stage.

I suddenly felt like I slammed headfirst into a wall. It was like a wet blanket fell from the balcony and smothered me. That was followed by the feeling that I had to puke. I knew I had to get out of there, so I forced myself to slog to my car.

My nausea got worse as I drove down Saginaw Street. I hopped onto westbound I-69 and drove as fast as I could. It was hard to control the car as a wave of dizziness swept over me. By the time I got onto northbound I-75, I started to shiver. I didn't know what the hell was happening to me.

About five miles from home, the brake lights of the cars in front of me became fuzzy. The road started to wiggle like a snake, making it harder to stay in my lane. My biggest concern was crashing into another car. I don't know how I did it, but I managed to make it home.

Did Pete's clove cigarette make me sick? Its acrid smoke wafted past my nose the whole time while we talked. Then again, I'd hung out with people while they smoked cloves before, and that never happened to me.

I figured the best thing I could do was sleep it off. When I crawled into bed, my room start to spin like a witch's wheel. I looked up and saw a vortex of dark clouds swirl around the ceiling. I knew it wasn't real, but it still freaked me out.

The urge to vomit started clawing up my throat like a beast sprung from its cage. I ran to the bathroom and grasped the edges of the toilet's gaping maw. With a heave, chunks of half-digested food and a river of Coke and bile exploded from my mouth. My senses were assaulted with the unmistakable smell and taste of vomit.

I puked into the bowl over and over. The noises of my sickness attracted the attention of my mom. She stood in the doorway and shrieked at me about being drunk. When I turned to answer her, I saw a bunch of bats fly out of her hair and flap around the bathroom. I turned back to the toilet and vomited.

I crawled back to bed, and the hallucinations eventually stopped. I was mentally and physically exhausted from everything I went through and needed some rest. Instead of falling asleep right away, my mind tried to explain what happened to me.

There was no damn way that smoke from a clove cigarette did all that to me. Like that old Ramones song said, "Somebody put something in my drink." It could have been the person who served me the Coke, but I didn't think so. "Sneaky Pete" was my No. 1 suspect.

Why was he was so interested in talking to me that night? He wanted to catch me with my guard down and drop something in my drink. With me yapping away like an idiot, I would have never noticed if he dropped acid in my Coke.

The next morning, my mind screamed for revenge, but my body cried out in pain. It felt like my muscles had been stretched to their limits, and my mouth felt like a desert. It was an effort just to get up and grab a drink of water. I decided to spend the rest of the day in bed.

I was ready to avenge myself the next day, and I had a plan to do it. I'd park up the street from his house and wait. He'd eventually have to leave, and when he did, I'd get him. I wasn't going to give him a chance to get in the fight. I was just going to run up behind him and hit him in the back of the head with my brass knuckles.

It was a good plan, but the only problem was that Pete was no longer in Flint. A friend told me that Pete shipped out for the Peace Corps. The Peace Corps? That rotten bastard was really passing himself off as someone who wanted to help people? What a joke!

I knew I should have walked away from The Capitol after Big Daddy banned me. I kept going down there for Lily and I kept doing it after we broke up. That's when I started showing my ass by always putting Lily down. If Sneaky Pete spiked my drink, was that the reason why?

It sure felt that way to me.

I took what happened as a message. I was spending way too much time at The Capitol. The people who hung out there didn't like me, and they didn't want me down there. I didn't really like any of them, either. So why was I hanging around?

After I lost everything I cared about, I let my life spin wildly out of control. All of the stupid and embarrassing actions played on an endless loop inside my mind. There was only one way to make those shameful images disappear.

I was 20 years old, and my life was going nowhere. I had no one and nothing, and I was tired of being that way. I was yearning to make something of myself, but I knew that wasn't going to be easy.

I had a terrible relationship with success, thanks to my parents. All my life, they told me that their friend's kids were world-beaters while I was a failure. I called this "success shaming" because they shamed me with other people's successes. It made trying to be something an uphill battle for me.

After three years of hanging out downtown, I walked away from it so I could move on with my life.

13.
A Wedding Proposal with Fries and Gravy

My decision to improve my life seemed like a new concept to me because it was.

One of the improvements I noticed was my experience at Mott Community College. When I started going there, my mom insisted that I should be a physical therapist. I had no idea why she chose that career for me. She just made up her mind about my future, and that was that.

I went with it because I didn't know what I wanted to do. I quickly learned that it wasn't the career path for me. I struggled with higher-level math and science courses, which were a huge part of that program. There was no way I could keep going down that road.

On a fluke, I got involved with the college newspaper. As I dug into the writing, I discovered that I really liked it. After I saw my first piece in print, I knew that was what I wanted to do.

Mom wasn't crazy about me becoming a journalist. I told her that was what I was going to do, and I wasn't going to argue about it. She didn't like it but what was she going to do? It was my life.

My immediate plan was to get my associate degree from Mott. From there, I planned to transfer to a university with a good journalism program. The long-term plan I devised was as simple as it was modest. I'd write for a newspaper until my books took off. Life would be good when I got on the *New York Times* Best Sellers List.

When I started focusing on myself, I found it easier to make new friends. One of them was Nick Sauermaische, who I met through a mutual friend. I liked him right away because he was into punk, and we had the same twisted sense of humor.

I started hanging out at Nick's house, and it didn't take long for him to become like a little brother to me. One day, I asked him if his last name was German. He told me his family line was from Rottweil, and he wanted to get the village's crest tattooed on his arm.

I said he needed a German nickname. After doing some research, I found out that "Klaus" is the German nickname for Nicholas. I started calling him Klaus, and he was cool with it. One day, he asked me what kind of name is Ribner, and I told him it's Slovak.

"So, what does your last name mean in Slovakian?"

"You mean Slovak?" I asked.

"Yeah."

"All I know is that it used to be Ribnicky…"

"Ribnicky?"

"That's what my aunt told me."

He said, "Okay, you're P.J. Ribnicky."

"Sounds good, Klaus," I replied.

"P.J. Ribnicky" started hanging out at Klaus's house every night. We'd usually lift weights, listen to music, and play Dr. Mario. He always beat me because he'd jam me up with extra pills on my screen.

We also watched The Comedy Channel, which became Comedy Central. My favorite show was *Supercar*. It was one of those British marionette shows from the 1960s. Klaus teased me mercilessly every time I sang the theme song.

Somewhere along the line, my new friend told me that he wanted to start a band. Since I used to be in one, he asked me what I thought about him playing guitar. I told him it might be better if he played bass. Singers and guitarists were a dime a dozen, but it's harder to find a good bass guitar player.

Klaus took my advice to heart and bought a bass guitar and an amp. He was dead set on us starting a band together, but I told him I got banned from playing The Capitol. He said we could find other places to play, but I thought he'd get sick of me holding him back. He disagreed, which I thought was touching but tragically unrealistic.

The more he pushed for us to start a band, the more I wanted out of our friendship. That seemed crazy on my part because the loyalty he showed me was what I wanted in a friend and bandmate. It didn't matter, because I wanted to cut and run… and I knew why.

If I started jamming with Klaus, I'd end up hanging out downtown. Even though I didn't let on to anyone, I was still in love with Lily at that time. Going to The Capitol would mean seeing her with her boyfriend-of-the-week. That would dredge up the emotions that I was trying so hard to keep buried deep inside of me.

I needed to get away from the Capitol, while Klaus was headed straight for it. I wrestled with what I should do for months before I finally made my decision. One day, I just ghosted on him. It was a terrible thing to do, and he didn't deserve it, but I did it anyway.

Klaus wasn't the only casualty I created when I cut ties with downtown. I foolishly stuck to my no-downtown edict even when Glenn Danzig played The Capitol. The very man whose music inspired me to pick up a microphone played my hometown on October 19, 1990. It was a stop on his *Danzig II: Lucifuge* tour.

Everyone I knew went to that legendary show. They told me that Glenn, Eerie Von, John Christ, and Chuck Biscuits really tore it up. One of my friends even got to meet Glenn on his tour bus after the gig. That could have been me, but I blew it by keeping a promise I made to myself.

I made a new friend during my last semester at Mott.

His name is Aaron Harrington, but everyone called him "Frenchy" because he French-inhaled once during a smoke break. He and I bonded over our love for Social Distortion. We even caught their *Somewhere Between Heaven and Hell* show on May 5, 1992, at St. Andrew's Hall in Detroit.

Our friendship picked up again during the fall semester of 1992. It consisted of us hanging out in the student lounge between classes. One day when we were there, a voluptuous blonde sat down at our table. As soon as her butt hit the seat, she went in on Frenchy for skipping class.

I told her she couldn't just roll up to our table and start dogging on my boy. The blonde said that Frenchy was her friend too, and he told me it was cool. I felt stupid for a moment, but I thought I could turn the situation to my advantage.

"What's your name?" I asked.

"Alanna," she replied.

"Alanna, what?"

"Kovács."

"That sounds Eastern European."

"Hungarian…"

108

"Really!"

"Yeah."

I'm Slovak," I said.

"I guess that makes us neighbors," she replied.

I liked her response. It was witty, and it showed some awareness of where her people came from. We started talking, and the two of us got so caught up in our conversation that we barely noticed Frenchy leave. By the time I had to leave for class, I got Alanna's phone number.

I didn't bother waiting for the "mandatory" two days to call her. We'd see each other at school anyway, so there was no need to play coy. I called her that night, and we picked up again the next day at school.

Shortly after meeting, we spent a lot of time together. We quickly became intimate as well. Our relationship was a storybook romance set in the post-industrial wasteland of Flint. She was all the things Lily wasn't, so it was easy for me to tell her those three little words three weeks after we met.

I practically spent all my free time with Alanna. It was fun, but there were things I was ignoring, like my schoolwork. Even her mom got sick of me being over the house all the time. I saw where things were heading, so I told her that I needed some me-time.

She looked at me and said, "I knew it."

"Knew what?"

"You don't love me."

"Yes I do."

"No," she replied. "You're in love with the idea of being in love."

That sounded so ridiculous. I'm in love with the idea of being in love? What the hell did that even mean?

I had a vague suspicion that Alanna was running a game on me, but I took the bait. She challenged my honor, and I responded by trying to prove her wrong. I started shouting and bellowing about my word being true. She played it cool by saying things like "okay," "yeah," and "sure" like she didn't believe me.

By the time I dropped her off that night, I agreed that we should keep seeing each other. When I got home, I was convinced that Alanna played me. I let her words trigger my emotions and make me feel that I had to defend myself. I developed that nasty habit after years of my parents' verbal abuse.

I'd be lying if I said I wasn't concerned with how Alanna manipulated me. I talked myself out of those concerns when I thought about how much she wanted to be with me. It felt like shooting a mega-dose of "feelgood" into my veins. A woman hadn't felt that way about me in a long time, and I didn't want to give that up.

The next day, I met up with her in the student lounge. I asked her to take a walk with me, and she did. When we found a secluded spot beneath the trees, I declared the depths of my love for her. She accepted my proclamation, and we continued to spend all our free time together.

My relationship with Alanna was magical, but something threatened to shatter the glass castle we built for ourselves.

My time at Mott was coming to a close while hers was just starting. That meant I'd be applying to colleges with journalism programs. Michigan State University was the only choice for me. It had a good journalism program, but that wasn't the reason I wanted to go there.

Years before, I got hooked on the East Lansing/Okemos area. Since it wasn't far from Owosso, Lily and I used to hang out there. We shopped at Flat Black and Circular and other stores in and around the Campus Town Mall. It was a fun and relaxing escape from Flint.

As far as I was concerned, MSU was the only school for me. I still applied to the University of Michigan and Central Michigan University to cover my butt. I didn't mention any of this to Alanna. I had a feeling that she wouldn't like me moving away in the fall.

One day, I got a response in the mail. Its maize and blue letterhead betrayed its source as U of M. That lofty institution of learning located in Ann Arbor denied my application. It was the only time I wasn't devastated by rejection.

I got another letter a few weeks later. This one had MSU's telltale green Spartan helmet on its letterhead. My heart pounded as I tore the letter open, then it sunk like a stone when I read its contents. Those short-sighted idiots in the school's admissions department rejected my application. That crushed me.

The third letter to arrive was thicker than the other two. It was from CMU, the only college that accepted me. While I should have been happy, I wasn't. My parents went there. After growing up in their shadows, I wanted to blaze a new trail.

Getting shot down by the other two schools meant one thing. I had to accept CMU's offer. The only thing left to do was break the news to

Alanna. She responded pretty much the way I expected she would.

"So, you're just gonna leave me behind?" she said. "Is that it?"

"It's not like that," I replied.

"That's how it feels!"

"I've done all I can do at Mott…"

"Then go to U of M-Flint."

"They don't have a journalism program."

"Get an English degree."

"I don't want that degree," I said.

She didn't want me to leave because she saw it as me abandoning her. I told her we could still be together, but she said that long-distance relationships didn't work. I couldn't argue with her because she broke up with her out-of-state boyfriend to date me.

I told her I couldn't turn down the opportunity, but that didn't reassure her. I said she should transfer to CMU, but she said, "That will take too long." That was hardly an argument, so it didn't change my mind. By the time I left her house, we were both angry.

The fallout from that argument hung over us like a dark cloud that whole week. On Friday, I took her out to eat. We went to Angelo's on Franklin Avenue, which was Flint's iconic coney island restaurant.

We ordered Flint-style coney islands. This hot dog features a made-in-Flint Koegel's wiener and a sauce made from seasoned ground beef heart. It's topped with chopped onions and mustard. I risked losing my Flint card by adding a stripe of ketchup. (That much savory deserves a touch of sweet to balance it out.) We also got fries with a side of gravy, which is another Flinttown favorite.

The food was great, but Alanna's mood sucked the joy out of it. Halfway through dinner, she started up about going away to school. Once again, I said she should apply to CMU and join me there. She refused, and it became a rehash of the argument we had before.

I said, "Well, I'm going to CMU, and there's nothing else to do about it."

"Yes, there is," she replied.

"What's that?"

"We should get married and go there together."

The hustle and bustle of the restaurant faded away, and I sat there in stunned silence. Did Alanna just propose to me? Yes, she did. I could tell by the look on her face that she wanted an answer.

The choice of who to spend the rest of your life with is one of the most important decisions anyone can make. If you choose wisely, you'll have a good shot at a life filled with prosperity and happiness. If you marry the wrong person, you could end up poor and miserable. Instead of taking that into consideration, I could only focus on one thing, and that was sex.

Alanna was the second woman I'd ever slept with. Marrying her would make her the last. Sure, our relationship was fiery and intense at that time, but getting married could become something that I'd regret later. Was I really ready to settle down so soon? Was she?

Sure, I had my concerns, but I also had a reason to say "yes." It was my fear that if I broke up with her, I'd never find someone else. I was 21 years old, and I'd only been with two women. When I did the math, it didn't inspire confidence in my ability to attract women.

I looked at her from across my plate of Coney dogs and said, "I do."

PART TWO

1998-2003

14.
Southbound to Murder Town

There's nothing more embarrassing than living with your parents at the age of 30. In the winter of 1998, I packed up the teetering contraption that was my life and moved in with Mommy and Daddy.

The move was kicked into motion by my divorce. After six long years of struggling to make it work, I filed for divorce. That kicked up a shit-storm between both of our families. Our families never got along with each other. The dissolution of our marriage turned us into the Hatfields and the McCoys.

Members of my family had their theories as to why my marriage ended. They weren't shy about sharing those opinions, either. In the end, the one thing everyone agreed on was that we were too young to have gotten married. Maybe so, but it taught me that those who don't pay attention to statistics are doomed to become one.

After we got divorced, Alanna and I were in a rush to prove that it was the other person's fault. Each of us wanted people to know that we did all we could while the other person didn't try. In the grand scheme of things, it didn't matter. There was my truth and her truth, and people believe what they want to believe.

So, like it or not, I was moving back to Flint. It was the city that almost killed me back in 1988. Thinking that out loud could get me in trouble with many people I knew. There's a deep sense of pride that many Flintstones have for their city. I get it... to a point.

While I'm a proud Flintstone, I'm also realistic about my hometown.

Flint has ranked as one of the most dangerous cities in the US for decades. After I got shot in 1988, I wanted to get as far away from there as I could. How would I heal from my trauma if I was constantly reminded of it? After being away for a while, I was returning to the scene of the crime. Flint hadn't gotten better in the time I was gone.

I had other negative associations with Flint. To me, coming home meant that I had failed. I'd failed at my job, my marriage, and my life. The thought of that upset me. Instead of focusing on what made me happy, I let my mind become contaminated by dark thoughts.

I hated my former employers.

I hated my ex-wife.

I hated the Friend of the Court and the power it had over me.

I felt the same way about the judge in my divorce.

I also hated my student loans and declaring bankruptcy.

Most of all, I hated myself, but I didn't realize it. I was convinced that Mom and Dad were to blame for my situation, but I didn't know exactly how. All I knew was that I was returning to that environment. That embarrassing fact encouraged me to indulge my resentments.

My mental state was a far cry from how hopeful I once was. I graduated from Central Michigan University in December 1996 with a Bachelor's degree in journalism. I leveraged that to land a job at a small newspaper. It was an opportunity for me to hone my craft and work my way up through the ranks to become an editor.

As a cub reporter, I worked for an editor from the old school of journalism. He wasn't afraid to tell me when my reporting fell short. His constructive criticism would have helped me master my craft, but I wasn't mature enough to handle it. I didn't realize it at the time, but it all had to do with my unresolved childhood issues.

When my boss criticized me, it triggered flashbacks of Operation Dragon Fire. I felt like I was under attack, and that made me defensive and angry. Things finally came to a head over a disagreement with how I handled a particular story. I decided to take a job at another newspaper in the next town.

My new job was a replay of my old one. As I struggled with more criticism from my new editors, my marriage to Alanna reached its inevitable conclusion. After about 10 months of struggling to deal with my life, I lost my second newspaper job. The bosses showed me the door, but not before I was able to line up a job at a small newspaper in Flint. It was my only option.

I brought three things from up north back to Flint with me. There was my bachelor's degree in journalism, student loan debt, and my on-again/off-again relationship with my new girlfriend, Annie Haggblom. I called her "Nellie Oleson" because she was Swedish and spoiled rotten, just like the character from *Little House on the Prairie*.

115

It was hard to please Nellie on my post-divorce paycheck, but I did my best. I got up at five o'clock in the morning to work the breakfast shift at McDonald's, then shuffled off to my job at the paper. What little I had left after taxes and child support, I spent on Nellie.

That wasn't good enough for her, and she rubbed my nose in my failures just like my parents did. I let her put me down because I was the king of low self-esteem and bad decisions. It added to my misery of being back in Flint.

Being back in my old stomping grounds gave me another chance to play music.

I started listening to a lot of GG Allin back then. He was the most decadent, depraved, and deranged punk rocker ever. He performed naked, took craps on stage, and threw it at the audience. He'd also get into fistfights with the crowd.

I admired GG because he brought danger back to rock and roll at a time when punk evolved into alternative rock. I identified with that rage because I failed my first time around and left Flint with my tail between my legs. After GG died of an overdose on June 28, 1993, I swore to keep his spirit alive.

The new songs I was writing summoned the fury inside me. That would be the tip of the spear in my revenge against everyone in the scene who did me wrong. If I wanted to succeed in that, I'd have to record my songs. Since I didn't have a band and a fat bank account, I needed a plan. I came up with one, and it meant I would have to take advantage of an old friend.

I picked up the phone and called Dan O'Hallahan, aka "Handsome Dan." In the time I was gone, he'd given up playing in Kung Fu Joe for a wife, two kids, and his dream job. He was happy to hear from me, and I was excited to talk to him, too.

I knew that Dan always felt bad about me getting shot. I was going to take advantage of that sympathy. No, I wasn't going to ask him to join a band with me. I wanted Dan to hook something up between me and his friend, Andy Harris.

I'd met Andy through Dan, and we hung out a couple of times at Dan's house. From what I could tell, Andy seemed like a cool guy with a quick wit. He also was a musician, and a walking encyclopedia of funk, R&B, and soul music. Most importantly, he had a recording studio

116

in his house.

I knew taking advantage of Dan's sympathies was wrong, but my selfishness had a way of trumping my morality. I justified the whole thing by convincing myself that he owed it to me for quitting Audacity. The more I thought it, the more I believed it was true.

While I caught up with Dan on the phone, he invited me over for dinner. Great! That would give me the perfect opportunity to set my plan into motion. I figured I'd casually mention that I'd like to get back into music. I hoped that would be enough for him to put in a good word for me with Andy.

When I got to Dan's, I felt like a total loser. He and his wife had a beautiful home in Flint's East Village. I was dead broke, working two jobs, and living in a mother-in-law apartment attached to my parents' house. My envy got so bad that I went to the bathroom and threw some cold water on my face to get myself together. I looked in the mirror and told myself to keep it together so I could make it through dinner.

After we ate, Dan and I sat on his back porch and had some beers. As we talked, I wondered how to bring up the subject of recording music. I couldn't come right out and tell him I wanted to record with Andy. As luck would have it, Dan asked me if I planned on doing anything in music.

I said, "I'd like to do some recording."

"Do you remember Andy Harris?"

"The name sounds familiar…"

"…You met him."

"…When?"

"Over here," he said.

"Is he the guy who's into Prince?" I asked.

"Yeah."

Dan told me that Andy had a home studio. He said he'd talk to Andy about me. I told Dan that I didn't have a lot of money, but he said, "Don't worry about it." He'd call Andy and take care of everything, then he'd call me. I was barely able to conceal my evil grin as I thanked him.

I ran into Andy Harris one day at Border's Books & Music on Miller Road. The café was a hangout for many of Flint's musicians, and I liked to go there and soak up that vibe. I would usually sip Chai tea and sing Irish folk songs with my friend, Kevin Tyler (RIP).

On the day that I met him, Andy was on the other side of the magazine rack. I said hello, and he walked over and shook my hand. As we talked, I wanted to ask him if he had spoken with Dan. That would have been awkward if Dan didn't have a chance to call him.

I was relieved when he brought up the subject. We grabbed a table in the café. I told him I wanted to record a few songs, but my divorce left me in a bad financial situation. He said not to worry about it, then asked me what I had in mind. I said I'd been writing short, fast punk songs with controversial lyrics.

He said, "Do you wanna put a band together?"

"If I can find the right people," I replied.

"Just to be upfront, I'm happy to record your project, but I won't have time for a band."

"No problem," I replied.

"And as your producer, I'll make sure that your vision isn't compromised."

"I appreciate that," I said.

"Yeah, I hate it when producers trample all over an artist's vision."

"Does that happen a lot?" I asked.

"It's pretty common with some producers, but not with me."

"That's cool," I said.

Andy told me what he had in mind for my recordings. I'd come over and lay down a basic guitar and bass tracks to a drum track he programmed. Then I'd do my vocal tracks. That would give us the basis of each song. "From there, we'll bring in other musicians to lay their parts over what we've done," he added.

"That sounds good," I replied.

"If you have any musicians in mind for this project, you should reach out to them," he said.

"I have someone in mind," I replied.

I didn't know any guitarists or bassists for my project, but I did have a drummer in mind. Reaching out to him would be a gamble because he shot me down the first time that I asked him to be in my band. That person was none other than Richard Rokowski, aka Rikki Roxx.

He wasn't big on punk in 1988. Since then, the musical landscape changed, and hair metal was no longer king. The explosion of grunge was a gamechanger for anyone who fancied themselves a rock musician. But would that be enough to change Rikki's mind about jamming with me?

I didn't know where Rikki lived, but it wouldn't be too hard to find him. His parents still lived down the road from mine, so I could call them and leave a message. As it turned out, I didn't even have to do that because I ran into him at Border's Books & Music.

I walked inside the store like I'd done many times before. I heard someone bellow my name from the register aisle. I turned and saw a dude in a long, black leather jacket walking toward me. When he got closer, I saw that it was Rikki. I didn't recognize him at first because his haircut bore no traces of the feathered mullet that once adorned his shoulders.

I reached toward his oncoming palm, and we met in a firm handshake. After a minute of small talk, I told him I'd been meaning to get a hold of him. He asked me why, and I told him I was back in town and getting a project going. He sounded interested, so we grabbed a table in the café.

Rikki said, "So, what's your project all about?"

"It's hard, fast songs with controversial lyrics," I replied.

"I see nothing's changed."

"You got me there," I said.

I thought it was time for the moment of truth. I asked Rikki if he wanted to work on my punk rock project, and he said he did. He told me he hadn't done anything for a couple of years, so he was eager to get back into the studio. A couple of years? I didn't do anything in over a decade, not that anyone was counting.

Rikki assured me that he'd do everything he could to help bring my vision to life. He understood that this was my project. At the most, he said he'd make suggestions if he thought it would help; but, at the end of the day, he'd respect my direction. It was pretty much the same thing Andy told me.

"I really appreciate that," I said.

"No problem."

I wanted to work with Andy and Rikki for years, and now I would be. What impressed me most was how much respect they had for my vision. I've always had definite ideas for my projects, but that changed when I brought on new band members. With Andy and Rikki, I felt confident that I'd stay in control.

119

There was something else that didn't escape me. In both cases, I was looking to call Andy and Rikki, but I ran into them at Border's first. To some people, those incidents might have seemed like coincidences. To me, it was a sign that my project was meant to be.

So, I had a producer, a drummer, and a studio, but I didn't have a name for my project. As fate would have it, my then-girlfriend "Nellie Oleson" came up with that. She didn't mean to, though. It was just something that happened as a result of an unfortunate back rub incident.

Nellie asked me for a massage one night, and I was all too happy to oblige her. To set the mood, I lit a couple of candles and put on some soft, Celtic instrumental music. She wiggled out of her clothes and laid down on my bed.

I brought out the lotion and rubbed her back, shoulders, and arms until my hands were in knots. I laid down next to her, her naked body pressed against mine. I naturally began kissing the back of her neck. That's when she jumped up and shrieked, "What are you doing?"

"What do you think?"

"Why can't a back rub just be a back rub?"

"Huh?"

"Why does it always have to be about sex with you?" she said.

"You're buck naked in my bed…"

"…So, I owe it to you?"

"I didn't say that."

"It's what you're thinking!"

Nellie didn't have me fooled. She was making up a reason to be angry so she could leave. I think she wanted to get back to her estranged husband, or maybe one of the other guys she was seeing. She proved my point by struggling with her clothes. Once she was dressed, she glared at me and said, "Don't even think about calling me!"

"Don't worry. I don't like being put on hold."

"What's that supposed to mean?"

"You know what I mean," I replied.

Nellie didn't appreciate my observation in the least. Her piercing shrieks drowned out the lilting pipes and thumping bodhrans that softly emanated from my stereo. Amidst her tirade, she unleashed a torrent of names upon me, and "pure spun evil" was one of them.

"What did you call me?" I asked.

"Pure spun evil!" she said. "Did that hurt your precious feelings?"

"No," I replied. "You just gave me the name for my band!"

"Fuck you!" she screamed.

She barged out the door in a rather dramatic fashion, and I knew that was the last time I'd see her. I didn't care. Things between us were strained from the start, and she had other options on the table. I was more interested in my music, especially since I now had a name for my band. And oh, what a name it was!

I wanted my new songs to summon the fury that had been brewing inside me since 1990. I also wanted to bring danger back to Flint's underground music scene and get revenge on everyone who put me down. For all that, there was no better name than Pure Spun Evil.

I couldn't wait to tell Andy and Rikki.

15.
Adventures in the "Blue Room"

For years, I dreamed of recording music with Andy. Now that it was finally about to come true, I was a total mess. I was all passion and fire when we talked at Border's. Now that it was time to walk the walk, I remembered that I hadn't done anything in music for 10 years.

Since I'd already pulled into Andy's driveway, it was too late to turn back. Besides, I didn't have it in me to run. I'd already come that far. If I quit now, I'd regret it for the rest of my life.

I rang Andy's doorbell and, a moment later, he opened the door and welcomed me inside. Once I got settled, he handed me a guitar. It was a metallic silver Gibson Les Paul. That gave me something familiar to anchor to and help relieve my anxiety.

I strummed the chords to one of my songs to warm up. As I did, I heard Andy chuckle behind me. Was he laughing at my meager guitar skills? I snapped my head around and looked Andy in the face.

He told me that he was laughing at an email he got. It was from a guy he used to record. According to Andy, the guy started recording his industrial music project, then dropped off the face of the earth. Last week, he sent Andy an email, which he printed up and handed to me.

"when we started this you was cool but now your acting different. I listend to all yur problems cuz I have no problem bein there for a friend. But then when I call what I thought was a friend to tell him bout what's goin on with me you said "what's up" like you didn't even care man. I don't deserve to be treated like that. I know you think all my music is lame and angry but what do you expect when I got people like you always dicing me. now I'm just gonna worrie bout my ownself cuz people don't give a fuck bout nothing or nobody but ther damn self."

The newspaper reporter in me focused on the guy's atrocious spelling, grammar, and punctuation. The human part of me picked up on how he thought Andy dismissed him. Andy told me that all the dude brought to the studio were a few unfinished drum tracks.

"You need more than that to build a song," I said.

"Exactly!" Andy replied.

The funniest part of the email was when the guy accused Andy of "dicing" him. It reminded me of a line in that old K-Tel Veg-O-Matic commercial. "It slices, it dices, it makes julienne fries!" I was sure that the dude meant "dissing," and Andy and I had a good laugh over that. Then he got quiet, and an intense look came over his face.

I said, "You okay?"

"I know I have some avoidant tendencies, but I don't remember saying that to him," Andy replied.

"You mean that whole 'what's up' thing?"

"Yeah."

I could tell that bothered Andy, which surprised me. The dude who wrote the email seemed like someone who shouldn't be taken seriously. It still touched a nerve with Andy, though. The moment between us was so awkward.

"Don't worry about it, man," I said. "That dude's an idiot."

"I don't wanna talk about it anymore."

I recoiled from the abruptness of Andy's response. I mean, he was the one who showed me the email in the first place. It made me wonder if he could go cold on me the way the dude in the email said he did to him. No, I thought. Andy is a friend of Dan's, and he offered to record my songs for free. That meant I could trust him.

Andy said we should jump into recording, starting with my guitar parts.

I took a deep breath then exhaled as his LinnDrum machine counted off the song's intro. I came in on time and hammered away on some power chords. It was a decent imitation of Johnny Ramone's iconic style, and I knocked out the first song in a few takes. My performance was the result of some solid coaching from Andy.

What little confidence I'd built up suddenly evaporated when it was time to record the vocals. My fears and insecurities came rushing back to me. I worried about singing out of key. I couldn't show any fear to Andy, though. I stepped inside the booth, aka "the box," where the microphone loomed before me like an inescapable fate.

From the booth, Andy told me to do a mic check. I felt my throat tighten to the size of a raisin as I sang a few bars. As I did, he kept saying, "Louder." I pushed through it as best as I could until he told me he had what he needed.

He cued up the song and asked me if I was ready. I nodded, and he pushed a button on the console. The count off rang inside the headphones then the song suddenly began to blaze away. Even though I knew it was coming, it still caught me off guard. I came in about a half step behind.

Andy stopped the song then told me to try it again. I repeated this sad routine at least 15 more times. No matter how hard I tried to nail the vocals, I couldn't make it happen. I either came in too soon, too late, or slightly out of tune. After nearly an hour of miserable failures, I felt mortified.

He said, "You sound a little tight."

"Yeah."

"Hold on..."

He left the booth and went into the kitchen. While he was gone, I wondered if he would tell me to come back when I could sing. Or would he tell me not to come back at all? It would have served me right if he did.

During the '90s, I whined about how Big Daddy robbed me of my chance to play. That gave me a lot of downtime. I could have used that to my advantage by practicing and refining my craft until I was a master musician. I descended into a paralyzing depression instead.

Andy came back with a steaming mug of tea. It's an old trick that many singers use to relax their throats. I drank it like it was some magical potion that would fix all my flaws. I didn't know if it would, but it gave me some confidence to get back into the box.

Andy said, "Let's give it another try."

He turned off the lights then flipped a switch. Shimmering shades of soft blue light filled the booth. It looked like I was underwater, and Andy said that ambient lighting has a relaxing effect. It was something he read in *Mix* magazine.

Once again, I put on the headphones and stepped up to the mic. Andy cued the song and told me to come in on the four. I can't remember if it took one take or 20, but I finally got it done. Andy gave me a thumbs up from the booth.

I listened to it with him, and it felt weird to hear my voice on tape. It sounded higher than the way it sounds in my ear. Andy said it's like that for everyone, and it would take a while to get used to it. The whole thing was an unsettling experience for me, and I wasn't sure I'd ever get used to hearing the sound of my voice.

We listened to the different takes a few times then picked the best one. He then matched my vocals and guitar with an electronic drum track, and it started to come together. There was still a lot to do before it became a song, but it was the most I'd ever recorded. That was reason enough to be proud.

Andy told me it was a tradition to go to The Torch Bar & Grill after a late-night recording session. When we got there, he suggested I try the Torchburger. When I took my first bite, I could see why it always gets named the best burger in Flint. Since he was a vegetarian, Andy got the grilled cheese sandwich and fries.

He asked me why I moved back to Flint. That was all it took for me to open the floodgates of my big mouth. I swamped the poor guy with all the uncomfortable details of my divorce. I also inundated him with all my anti-government talk and ridiculous conspiracy theories. If he gave me any subtle hints that I was going on too long, I was too busy making an ass out of myself to tell.

Andy ended my pathetic spectacle by bringing the conversation back to my project. He said we needed a couple more sessions before we had Rikki lay down the drum tracks. I couldn't have been more excited about the momentum we had going.

Over the next few weeks, Andy and I plowed forward with the project.

I improved on the time it took me to lay down my vocals. I'd like to say it was due to my talents, but it was all due to Andy's patient and helpful guidance. In less than two months, we had five songs recorded, and we were ready to bring in Rikki.

Rikki showed up on a Saturday night, and I introduced him to Andy. They made some small talk as Rikki set up his drums, and the

125

two of them clicked right away. That hardly surprised me since they were both musicians.

I got out of their way so Rikki could do his thing. I heard him playing from the other side of the door and was thoroughly impressed. He'd only gotten better over the past 10 years. More importantly, his drumming raised the bar on my simple, three-chord punk songs.

Since Rikki knocked the first song out in two takes, we had him do the other four. Just as I suspected, he smashed out more punk rock percussion gold down to the last cymbal crash. As the three of us listened to the tracks, Rikki asked if I wanted any backing vocals on the songs.

I said I wanted some Misfits-styled "whoah ohs" on the choruses. Rikki went into the box and knocked them out in just a few takes. Andy and I thought he nailed them, but Rikki asked to do it again, and again, and again. After more than an hour, Andy and I thought that was the end of it.

Rikki insisted on doing something else with the backing vocals. It was a take with him shouting the choruses. He said his old band did this at a recording studio in Lansing, and it "added some punch to the hooks." I asked Andy what he thought, and he said, "It's your project."

I thought it was a bit much, but I couldn't say no. I wanted Rikki in this project so badly that I would have let him yodel while hanging upside down if that's what he wanted. Just like his previous backing vocals, he took a while to knock out the new ones. It was hard to tell which of the 30+ takes had his best shouts.

In the end, Rikki was happy with his backing vocals, and that was all that mattered.

Andy and I introduced Rikki to the tradition of going to The Torch after a session.

The three of us talked, and I noticed that we all had a similar sense of humor. A cool vibe started to form among us. It stayed that way until Rikki and Andy started talking to each other. It was some high-level musician stuff and I couldn't keep up, so I sat back and listened.

I felt a familiar and uncomfortable feeling return to haunt me. It was the same one I used to get during my years as a socially awkward schoolboy. I called it "The Curse of the Friend Connector." Every time I introduced two of my friends to each other, they would hit it off.

Before long, they would start hanging out with each other, and I'd get left out in the cold.

As I sat there listening to them, I felt like that lonely little schoolboy all over again. No matter how upset I was about being ignored, I controlled my emotions. I forced myself to keep my mouth shut so I wouldn't look like an ass. After a while, Andy apologized for leaving me out of the conversation.

"It's cool," I replied. "I liked listening to you guys talk music."

That was the first thing I thought to say, and I hoped they bought it. The last thing I wanted to do was betray how I really felt. I took advantage of the lull to take control of the conversation. I steered the topic back to my CD project because that put me back in control of the conversation.

As I continued to blab away, I knew I was pushing things a bit. There was no reason for me to believe that Andy and Rikki would end up icing me out. That was high school stuff, and I was foolish to think it would happen in my 30s. The three of us were too mature for all that.

So, why didn't I shut up and let things play out naturally?

16.
Two for the Price of One

For someone who wanted to have the best punk band in Flint, I was a piss-poor scenester. I'd been back home for almost a year but hadn't set foot downtown. I'd have to do that again if I wanted people in the scene to know me. And that meant going to Metropolis.

When my life crashed and burned in 1991, I tucked tail and fled Flint like a scalded dog. While I was gone, The Capitol Theatre ceased being a thing. The scene moved to a club called Metropolis, a two-level bar at 510 South Saginaw Street. That building used to house the Hot Rock Café back in the day.

I'd been to The Hot Rock a grand total of one time on May 24, 1989. Lily and I went there to see Detroit psychobilly legend, Elvis Hitler. The band was promoting its *Disgraceland* album, and everybody who was anybody in the scene was at that show.

Elvis Hitler played all 13 tracks off that classic psychobilly record. My favorite was "Battle Cry of 1,000 Men." I went nuts when they tore through it near the end of their show.

The Hot Rock cooled for good after I pulled my disappearing act. Sometime during that gilded decade known as the '90s, the place was reborn as Metropolis. From what I'd heard, Metropolis was unlike any other bar in Flint. It was a two-level nightclub with a full bar on each floor. Live bands played upstairs, while DJs spun tunes on the first-level dance floor.

If the Capitol was high school for my generation, Metropolis was our college. In 1999, it was time for me to go back to school.

As I drove down the bricks of Saginaw Street, memories of my downtown days came back to me. It was the first time I'd been there since I moved back home. The closer I got to my destination, the more

I wished I had someone with me to give me courage.

I went inside Metropolis, and it took a moment for my eyes to adjust to the shadow and neon. When they did, the décor was the first thing I noticed. Someone painted the walls to look like Fritz Lang's 1927 silent film, *Metropolis*. Nice touch. There also was a Volkswagen van parked just off the dance floor for people to sit inside.

As I walked through the bar, I recognized a lot of scenesters from back in the day. They didn't see me because I stuck to the shadows. I wasn't there to reminisce about the good old days, no matter how much I missed them. I was there to see the bands.

I headed upstairs and slammed face-first into a painful realization. The scene I once knew was gone. Punk wasn't dead, but it had mutated into a strange and monstrous hybrid called "nu-metal." The genre infected Flint, and symptoms of the disease were all around me.

I saw a horde of kids covered in neck tattoos, oversized hoodies, and facial piercings the size of car parts. The kids in the band were almost young enough to be my kids. I couldn't relate to what they were playing.

They trudged through a song on guitars tuned so low that the strings practically rattled. The singer, if you could call him that, growled like an angry hellhound. It was a far cry from the fun, three-chord simplicity of my youth.

As I watched the bizarre rituals of that strange and savage tribe, a memory came back to me. It was at a time when I was about their age, and an Earth Day event was going on at the Capitol. There were a bunch of bands on the bill, including Flint legends Dark Reality, Guilty Bystanders, and The Will. This attracted "The Old Timers," a group of punks who helped establish the scene in the early '80s.

That day, The Old times stood huddled together on the sidewalk, shivering in the midday sun. They watched the strange and savage tribe that was my friends me. The look in their eyes was a sad and silent acknowledgment that it was a new era. When I noticed the resignation in The Old Timers' eyes that day, I never thought I'd be replaced by another strange and savage tribe.

That night at Metropolis, I felt like a dinosaur. What was I thinking, starting a band in my 30s? These nu-metal kids didn't want to listen to some old, washed up dude trying to relive his youth. They'd probably laugh me off the stage.

I wanted to get out of Metropolis as fast as I could. Instead of bolting, I slunk through the darkness toward the exit. As I headed downstairs, I almost ran into a guy who was walking up the steps. I mumbled a quick "excuse me" and shuffled down the stairs.

The guy said, "P.J. Ribnicky?"

I froze mid-step. There was only one person in the world who called me that. I snapped my head around and met a pair of brown eyes that looked all too familiar. It was my old friend, Nicholas "Klaus" Sauermaische.

"Klaus!"

"I thought that was you," he replied.

Klaus scooped me up in a bear hug and lifted me off my feet. He almost put my head through the low ceiling of the stairwell. He set me back down, and we were both started talking at the same time. That was getting us nowhere, so I said, "Let's go downstairs and grab a beer."

"You're buying," he replied.

"Fair enough."

I caught Klaus up on my life since I left Flint. He heard about my marriage, my daughter, and going to college. He also learned about my divorce, bankruptcy, and shitty job prospects.

As we talked, I expected him to ask me why I ghosted him back in the day. I'd always felt bad about that, and I never gave him an explanation for why I did it. I was glad he didn't say anything about it. He just caught me up on what was going on in his life, which included a job, house, and his band.

I said, "Let me guess. You're playing bass?"

"That's right," he replied. "And I owe it all to you."

"C'mon, man…"

"…It's true," he said.

"I just showed you a few things."

"If it wasn't for you, I might not have tried."

"You could've picked it up along the way," I said.

"Just take the compliment."

"Okay," I replied. "Thanks."

"You're welcome."

"I'll bet you've come a long way since then," I said.

"Let's put it this way," he replied. "Les Claypool is my biggest influence."

"Gotcha," I said.

Klaus named his band Polk High and I got the reference right away. It was the name of Al Bundy's fictional high school in *Married With Children*. He loved that show, so it didn't surprise me that he named his band after it.

A tall, thin guy with black hair and a pencil-thin mustache grabbed a barstool next to Klaus. Klaus introduced me to him. The guy's name is Matt Falconi, aka "Falcon," and he played guitar for Polk High. The dude shook my hand and said, "So, you're the infamous J.P. Ribner."

"Infamous?" I replied.

"Yeah," Falcon replied.

"What did I do this time?"

"You taught my friend how to play bass," he said.

I said I only showed Klaus a few scales. He became the player he is through his hard work and dedication. That wasn't humble-bragging, either. I only played bass because I couldn't find anyone else to do it.

Falcon still thanked me for inspiring Klaus to play bass. Klaus then told me that he and Falcon had been in bands since 1991. They had played The Capitol more times than they could count, plus a bunch of other gigs. I couldn't help but think that could have been me if I didn't bail on Klaus.

I said, "When can I hear some Polk High?"

"Right now!" Klaus replied.

Klaus wasn't kidding when he said he was a Les Claypool fan. As I listened to the Polk High CD, his manic bass-thumping skills jumped out front and center. I could almost see his flipper-like hands slapping and popping the strings.

After the last song played, I had an impression of Polk High. It was a band filled with talented musicians who all competed for the lead in each song. Klaus's bass licks were impressive, but they were all over the place. So was the drummer, vocalist, and oddly placed saxophone player. Falcon's playing was tight because it was his role to lay back so the others could indulge in their virtuosity.

As the three of us sat in his car, an idea crept its way into my mind. It was every bit as wicked and self-serving as the trick I pulled on Dan to get Andy to record my songs. I knew what I was doing was wrong, but my conscience didn't try to stop me.

I said, "I forgot to tell you that I've got something going too."

"A band?" he asked.

"Recording project…"

"…That's cool," Klaus said.

"…But I'd like it to be a band…"

I described Pure Spun Evil to Klaus and Falcon. I told them what it sounded like and who was in it. I ended by saying that if I had a bassist and guitarist, my project could become a band. It fell silent inside his car, and I could practically hear the wheels turning inside Klaus's head.

He laughed, and I asked him what was so funny. He said that he's a bassist and Falcon plays guitar. I said that didn't do me any good because they were already in a band. He said he could do both if I was willing to book Pure Spun Evil shows around Polk High's gigs.

I said, "Of course."

"Then count me in!"

"Great!" I said. "Pure Spun Evil has a bassist."

"What about Falcon?" he said.

"What do you mean?"

"Don't you think he might wanna be in the band too?"

"We just met, so I didn't want to assume anything," I said.

Klaus turned toward Falcon and said, "Do you wanna play guitar in Pure Spun Evil?"

Falcon said, "Sure."

His response didn't gush with the same excitement that Klaus displayed, but I was okay with it. From what I could tell, Falcon had that laid-back, too-cool-for-school personality type. I was so desperate that I would have let a stop sign join the band as long as it could play guitar.

"Thanks, man!" I said.

"No problem," Klaus replied.

"It shouldn't take long for you guys to pick up my three-chord punk tunes."

Klaus said, "And once we lock those down, I can start writing some songs, too."

When he said that, it was like someone ripped the needle across the record. Everything came to a screeching halt, and I sat there like a deer in the headlights. Did Klaus just say what I thought he said? Yes, he really did.

"Well?" he asked.

"Well, what?"

"What do you think about me writing some songs?"

"That would probably have to come in time..."

"I hope it doesn't take too long," he said. "Because I'm not that same kid you used to know..."

"...I know that," I said.

"I'm a damn good songwriter."

"I know," I said. "I just heard your stuff."

"That's right!" he replied.

And that presented a problem. I knew I wasn't the best musician in the world. I wasn't the best singer, either. My lyrics and songwriting were the only talents that I brought to the table.

My biggest fear was that another band member could write a better song than me. If that happened, I would have to live with the shame of being eclipsed in my band. I couldn't ignore the irony that I got into music to help me with my insecurities, yet there they were again.

Not wanting Klaus to write songs presented a problem. If he knew how I felt, he and Falcon would quit Pure Spun Evil as quickly as they joined. If that happened, it would go back to being a recording project. I wanted Pure Spun Evil to be more than that.

Damn! Why the hell did Klaus have to screw the pooch by saying that?

As much as I wanted to work with Klaus and Falcon, I was tempted to take a pass. That's because I always wanted to be the songwriter in my bands. I always had a definite vision for Pure Spun Evil and my lyrics were a big part of that vision.

After agonizing over all that, I wondered if I was making a big deal out of nothing. For all I knew, Klaus was just blowing smoke. Why would he want to waste his songs on my band when he could use them in Polk High? That would make more sense.

The more I thought about it, the more I believed I was being crazy. He'd probably be so busy with Polk High that he'd forget about his crazy idea to write songs for my band. I asked Klaus to write his number down, then I told him and Falcon that I had to get going.

"I call ya when we're ready to practice," I added.

17.
The Big Drama Show

"Here's what a real song sounds like!" Klaus said.

He and Falcon ripped into the tune, and Rikki fell in with the groove. It was a decent song, but there were a couple of problems. The first was that I could have written two songs with all the chord changes Klaus had in that one tune. Secondly, the song's style was great for Polk High, but not Pure Spun Evil.

When they finished, Klaus asked me what I thought. I said it sounded good, which wasn't a lie. It wasn't the whole truth, either. It was an awkward situation, and I didn't know what else to say.

"Damn right it does!" he replied.

"Do you have any lyrics?" I asked.

"We can get together and write some," he replied.

I said, "We should do that," but didn't commit to anything. The next thing I know, Klaus and Falcon were tearing into another song. Just like the first, it was good, but it was more Primus than Pure Spun Evil.

I called Rikki after practice to discuss this situation. He had a knack for reading people and situations. When I asked him what I should do, he said I needed something to distract Klaus from wanting to write songs for the band.

He said the best thing to do was come up with some mutual goal. It would have to be something that all of us could work on to achieve. I said I'd book a gig within a few weeks. That would only give us enough time to work on the songs I'd written.

"That might work, but it's a short-term solution," Rikki said.

"What do you mean?"

"It won't take him long to realize that you don't want to play his songs."

"Then what?"

"Then he'll probably quit and take Falcon with him," Rikki replied.

"I guess we'll cross that bridge when we come to it," I said.

Joel Rash was booking gigs at Metropolis at that time. He always came through for me in the past, and I was counting on him to do it again. I told him I needed something in a couple of weeks, but he was booked solid for the next two months. I almost went into full panic mode until he suggested I try Churchill's Food & Spirits.

Churchill's is a small bar down the street from Metropolis. They booked punk and nu-metal bands, but they didn't pull the crowds that Metropolis did. Still, if I could get a gig there right away, I'd take it. I didn't care if we played to five people as long as it put a hold on Klaus's songwriting ambitions.

Joel put in a good word for me at Churchill's, and they gave us a gig in three weeks. Since we only had 12 songs, we'd have to find another band to headline our gig. That band would also have to have a PA system we could use because Churchill's didn't have one.

I definitely had a challenge ahead of me. It was one that I'd have to overcome to keep creative control of my band.

I needed to find a special kind of band to share the bill with at Churchill's. They had to be good enough to draw a crowd, but not so good that they would upstage Pure Spun Evil. And they had to have a PA that they were willing to let us use.

I remembered a nu-metal group I saw at Metropolis. They were called Unknown Ceremony, and the lead singer's name was Kyle. I didn't know if they'd want to split a gig with us, but there was only one way to find out. I knew I could find him hanging out at Metropolis with all the other nu-metal kids.

The key to the con job is to appeal to the mark's ego. The first thing I told Kyle was that I really liked Unknown Ceremony's sound. I added that it reminded me of Tool while still sounding original. His face lit up like a Christmas tree. I knew it was time to sink the hook.

I told Kyle that we wanted to do a double bill with them at Churchill's. To seal the deal, I added that we'd be more than happy to open for them. (More flattery.) He asked me the name of my band, and I told him. He said he'd never heard of us, so I mentioned that Klaus and Falcon from Polk High were in my group.

Kyle said, "Polk High kicks ass!"

"So does Pure Spun Evil," I replied.

"Right on!"

Kyle agreed to the gig, and I knew how I wanted it to go. We'd go on first and kill it. Unknown Ceremony would have to follow our blistering performance, and they wouldn't be able to do it. At best, they'd chug away at their brand of down-tuned mediocrity.

Unknown Ceremony's relative inexperience was exactly why I picked them to do the show with us. Well, that and their PA system.

A crowd of familiar and unfamiliar faces filled Churchill's. The folks from Unknown Ceremony must have hyped our show as much as we did. The time had finally come to unleash my fury onto the Flint scene. My anticipation was like a dark tide poised to bust through a crumbling dam.

I shouted, "1, 2, 3, 4," and the guys erupted into a ferocious wall of sound. A wave of sonic mayhem swept past me and swallowed the crowd in its ferocity. Shoulders hunched and arms gnarled, I stalked back and forth before the crowd like a wild beast sprung from its cage.

Our furious energy carried us through our entire set. We ripped through 12 songs in less than 30 minutes, then ended with a crashing finale. Everyone was shouting and clapping, and I fed on that energy like a vampire.

Kyle and the guys from Unknown Ceremony had hopeless looks on their faces. They knew that they couldn't follow us. Even though they made that show possible for us, I savored each precious second of their despair.

After we packed away our gear, I slumped into a chair. Rikki sat down at my table. So did Andy, who came out to experience our first show. Klaus and Falcon sat at a table next to us with their Polk High entourage.

Klaus drank pitcher after pitcher of beer. As he did, his friends told him how great he was. It was like our entire performance was a one-man show. I could tell that my old friend reveled in the delusion that he and he alone was that man.

Klaus raised his glass and said, "I have free reign over nothing."

That might have sounded weird to Rikki and Andy, but I knew what Klaus was doing. He was hint-whining, which was his little way of letting me know he was pissed off. It all had to do with me not letting him write any songs for my band. It had to be.

I went to the bar to get another pitcher of beer for my table. While I waited in line, Klaus got behind me. I sensed him standing there, practically breathing down my neck. I turned around and asked him what the hell he meant by that "control over nothing" comment.

He said, "You can indulge in my downfall or continue to ignore it."

"What the fuck does that mean?" I asked.

"It doesn't matter," he replied.

The rest of the night was just as awkward. The more Klaus drank, the louder his crybaby routine got. Falcon, the strong silent type, just sat there with a scowl on his face. Their friends clustered around them and continued to heap compliments on them. In short, it was a sad circus.

I called Rikki the next day and told him that we needed to meet. He asked if Klaus and Falcon would be there and I said no. Rikki said not letting them be a part of it would be a bad idea. He pushed for a full band meeting, but I refused.

I said, "All they'll do is dominate the meeting with Klaus's songwriting grievances."

"That's the whole point," Rikki said. "You could finally address it with them."

"I'm not ready to be a target just yet," I replied.

"Fine," he said. "Where do you want to meet?"

"I got a six-pack in the fridge so why don't you just come over?"

When Rikki got there, we discussed the goods, the bads, and the uglies of the band. We also talked about the things we should do to increase our reach. Rikki took notes of everything in his leather-bound binder.

When it was his turn to talk, he got straight to the point. He said there was something personal behind Klaus's insistence on writing songs for the band. I asked him what it is, but he said he didn't know. The only thing Rikki was sure of was that I needed to address it in a band meeting.

I said, "You're back on that kick again?"

"Yes. And they will be too until you address it."

I knew exactly what would happen if I opened that door. Klaus and Falcon would attack me, which would have been bad enough. If Rikki had some issues with me, he'd probably join in with them. If that happened, things could get ugly for me.

Instead of hitting the problem head-on, I chose to go around it. I told Rikki we should do another Churchill's show. He asked me if I was sure I didn't want to confront Klaus and Falcon, and I said no. They wanted to write songs for Pure Spun Evil, and I don't want them to. There was no room for negotiation.

"Well," he grumbled. "You can book another show, but you'll need to find a new bassist and guitarist after that."

"You really think they'll quit?" I said.

"Yeah."

I called Kyle and got him to agree to another gig in a couple of weeks. Once again, I had to keep the window short to keep Klaus from wanting to write songs. After that, I knew I couldn't keep running and hiding forever. I'd have to address the issues with Klaus one way or the other.

Rikki called me a couple of days later with some bad news. He said he dropped off his drums at Falcon's house, aka "The Falcon's Roost." When Falcon came out to greet him, he spotted Rikki's binder on the armrest of the car. Rikki said it was open to the pages with the notes from our "top secret" band meeting.

When Falcon saw that, he asked Rikki what it was all about. Caught off guard, Rikki spilled the beans about our meeting. Falcon asked him why he and Klaus weren't invited, and Rikki told him it was my idea.

I said, "Why the hell would you leave your notes out like that?"

"I told you not to hold a meeting without them," he replied.

"It wouldn't have been a problem if you put your binder away!"

"Let's not point fingers here…"

"Fine," I said.

"The important thing is to find a way out of this mess you made," he said.

"Are you fucking serious?" I asked.

"If you can't handle the truth, then you shouldn't have me in your band," he replied.

"How about we focus on the real issue right now?"

"Fine," he said.

"Do you really think they'll quit the band after the show?"

"Yeah…"

"Good!" I said. "It'll save me the trouble of having to fire them."

"Why would you do that?"

"If I give in to them on this, it'll never stop."

"I don't think that's true," he said.

"I've seen this kind of thing before."

After I hung up with Rikki, I wondered if what happened with Falcon was really a mistake. I mean, what are the odds that Rikki's binder just happened to be open to the notes from our meeting? And what were the odds that Falcon just happened to see those notes?

Did Rikki leave the binder out as a way of letting them know without coming out and telling them? Or did he just tell Falcon about the meeting? Either way, I didn't have any proof, so I couldn't accuse Rikki of anything. I had enough problems on my hands with Klaus and Falcon.

Before our second Churchill's gig, Rikki borrowed a 200-watt PA head and some monitors. That was a huge help because it meant I didn't have to sing through a guitar amp anymore.

We used the PA a couple of times at practice. I loved the way it sounded, but Rikki said I needed to dial up some more mid-range tones on my vocals. I had no idea how to do that, but I said I'd take care of it before our next practice.

I got to The Falcon's Roost early and started messing with the PA head's settings. I had no experience working a PA head, but I figured it was like a stereo system. My plan was to fiddle with the settings until I got a better tone.

Falcon walked into the room as I desperately tweaked the knobs. Great! He was a gearhead, so he would know how to fix these things. I asked him what I needed to do to get more mid-range tones.

Falcon said, "You need to learn to work your equipment!"

The words exploded out of his mouth, and it caught me off guard. Falcon always was the "strong silent type," which meant he kept things bottled up inside of him. Once he had so much in there, it didn't take much to unleash his emotional explosion.

Falcon's feathers were ruffled, and it had nothing to do with my inability to run a PA. It was about the top-secret band meeting, and me not letting Klaus write songs for the band. I didn't know what to say, which was probably a good thing. With a week before our show, I didn't want to give him an excuse to quit.

The four of us jumped into practice after Klaus and Rikki showed up. As we played, the tension in the room was obvious. Klaus and Falcon phoned in their parts, and we only went through our setlist once. Rikki and I got the hell out of there. We knew that nothing good would come from hanging out with those two after practice.

By the time I got home, I'd made up my mind about those two. They didn't have a future with Pure Spun Evil beyond our next show. There was just no way I could go on with them after the way Falcon that jumped my shit like that, not to mention Klaus's songwriting desires.

To keep from dwelling on it, I focused on the show itself. It was going to be our last one for a while, so I wanted to go out with a bang. In the spirit of GG Allin, I knew exactly what to do. It would be a bold and daring move, especially for me, and it would terrify and entertain the audience in equal measure.

I was going to make sure people talked about Pure Spun Evil long after our show.

Setting up for our show was more than a bit tense. Klaus and Falcon were angry with me, and I was mad at them. I was also pissed at Rikki, who was upset with me. All those roiling emotions transformed the band into a simmering cauldron of resentment.

GG would've been proud if he saw us at Churchill's that night. The band's barely repressed anger roared out of us from the first note. It continued to build as we shredded through our songs. All through the set, I slammed the microphone into my forehead until I gushed blood like a fountain.

Our raging second performance made our first one tame by comparison. The crowd was in a near frenzy near the end of our set. That's when I knew it was time to unleash my big surprise. The guys jumped into a grinding blues instrumental as I slowly stripped out of my T-shirt and jeans. In a matter of moments, I was standing before the crowd wearing nothing but a jockstrap and a dog collar.

With a mixture of blood and sweat pouring down my face, I must have been quite a sight. The crowd exploded into laughter and cheers. Little did they know that they were about to become part of the show.

I shouted, "Protect yourself at all times!"

The guys ripped into our last song as I charged into the crowd like a jockstrap-clad rodeo bull. Those jaded punks scattered like a flock of startled pigeons as I barreled through empty tables and chairs in pursuit.

I herded the terrified audience into a back corner of the bar. The fearful, quivering group stood before me as I belted out the lyrics to our last song.

As our set came to its thundering conclusion, I abruptly turned and walked away as if nothing happened. The room erupted into cheers as I pulled my blue jeans over that dirty, blood-stained jockstrap. No one came near me until I was fully dressed, and I washed the blood off my face and hands. That's when many people told me they hadn't seen a show like that in a long time. I basked in all that attention.

When Unknown Ceremony took the stage, I sat down next to Rikki and Andy. The three of us looked at the pictures Andy took with his digital camera. He got some great shots, including a few with me in my jockstrap. His skills in so many mediums make him a master artist in every sense of the word.

Klaus and Falcon sat a few tables away from us. I went into the show feeling angry at them, but I let all of that out on stage. That caused me to have a change of heart. They put on a hell of a show, and it seemed a shame to throw it all away. As a last-ditch effort, I bought a pitcher of beer and took it over to them.

Klaus said, "What's this?"

"Looks like beer," I said.

"We didn't order it."

"I got it for you."

"That's not coming out of our end!"

"It's on me."

"Uh huh."

I put the pitcher down on the table then walked away. I hate it when people stomp on me after I've done something nice for them. My parents were notorious for pulling that shit. My brief exchange with Klaus triggered those memories, and that filled me with rage.

I had no doubt how it would end for those two. I also knew how serious the repercussions would be. My decision would end up costing me a friend. That sucked, but I'd waited too damn long to be back on stage. I couldn't let anyone take control of my creative vision.

Rikki saw the look on my face, and he said I should call them over to the table. I asked him why, and he said I should let them go right then and there. Even though they didn't work out, he said they deserved to hear it directly.

"It's what any band leader would do," he added.

He was right, but he was crazy if he thought I would do that. If I couldn't face those two in a band meeting, there was no way I could fire them right there at the bar. In the end, I decided to get rid of them in a more passive-aggressive way.

Two days after our show, I hung a "musicians wanted" flier all over town. Someone would see it, and they'd tell Klaus and Falcon. It probably didn't matter because I was pretty sure they quit Pure Spun Evil the minute we got done playing.

Since Andy was the quintessential "fifth member" of the group, I figured I'd tell him what happened. I called him and told him the story of how everything went down, and how I'd gotten rid of Klaus and Falcon. He listened patiently, then let out a chuckle when I said, "I don't know how the hell I'll replace them."

He said, "I've been wanting to talk to you about that."

"Oh yeah?"

"What would you say about me playing bass?"

"I'd say I love it!" I replied. "Why? Are you interested?"

"Yeah."

"That's great!" I said.

"Really?"

"Yeah," I said. "I would've asked a long time ago, but you said you didn't have time for it."

"I've seen what you've been going through with Klaus…"

"…Uh huh."

"And I wouldn't try to take over your band or change what you got going."

"Thanks, man!"

Just like that, Andy became a member of Pure Spun Evil. He only had one condition. With his job and upcoming marriage, the day would come when he'd have to step away. I said I understood, and I asked him to give me some notice when that day would come. That would buy me a little time to find someone to replace him.

I called Rikki and told him everything. He was just as happy about the news as I was. With the three of us being so close, I was sure there wouldn't be any major personality conflicts in the band. Now, I just had to find the ideal guitarist who could play plus fit in with our unique personalities.

18.
The New Kid in Town

I didn't want to hang a "guitarist-wanted" flyer on the corkboard of every guitar shop in town. That strategy attracts all the freaks and losers from the darkest fringes of the music scene. Then again, I was desperate to replace Falcon and keep Pure Spun Evil rolling. So, with flyers in hand, it was off to the music shops I went.

It didn't take long for the calls to start rolling in.

The first came from an exuberant guitarist who wanted to make an impression. He told me that listening to punk changed his life. I told him I could relate, then asked him if he'd played in any bands. He dropped a few names, but it wasn't anyone I knew. That didn't mean anything one way or the other.

When it was my turn to talk, I told him what Pure Spun Evil was all about. I said we liked to push the envelope with songs that were bold, fierce, and inflammatory. In other words, punk rock. I added that the guitarist I was looking for would be someone who could handle that.

He said, "I'm fine as long as you don't say anything about Christianity."

"What do you mean?"

"I won't play any blasphemous songs."

"Are you Christian?"

"Born again in the spirit of Christ," he replied.

"Well, I have one song that refers to the Bible as a 'filthy book of lies,'" I said.

"Are you serious?"

"Yeah," I said. "But other than that, religion doesn't really come up in my lyrics."

"Well, that's one song you won't be doing if I'm in the band!" he replied.

"Are you serious?"

143

"Yes!" he said.

Despite that one line in my song, I didn't really hate Christianity. I was going through some things at that time, and I detested any type of authority. The song really didn't mean that much to me, but I couldn't let some stranger tell me which songs I can play in my band.

Something else occurred to me as I talked to "Mr. Jesus Freak on a Leash." Why would a hardcore Christian want to audition for a punk band named Pure Spun Evil? Why would he want to play in any punk band for that matter? Most of them weren't as gentle about the subject of religion as I was.

I said, "This isn't gonna work out."

"Probably not," he replied.

I got a call from another guitarist who saw my flyer. The minute I got him on the phone, he gave me a complete rig rundown. I guess he thought that would impress me or something. I was more interested to know if he could play the gear that he bragged about owning.

I asked him if he was in any bands and that was a thing. He lit up like a Christmas tree when he told me about his group. He played bass for a band called Harvest of Flames, and just by listening to him, it was the greatest group ever.

I said, "Why do you want to join my band if you're already in one?"

"I like to play different styles."

"How much time will you have for us?"

"I can do it," he replied.

"I would hope so…"

"…Oh!" he said. "I also do backing vocals."

All of a sudden, he starts singing. I didn't recognize the song, but he did a decent job with it. He stressed all the highs and added a resonating tremolo to the lows. While his performance was impressive, it also was awkward. When he finally finished his serenade, there was silence on the line.

I knew right then that I didn't want this guy in my band. He was in another band, which meant that Pure Spun Evil would always be second place. Plus, the whole singing-over-the-phone thing was just weird.

I said, "You seem like a talented guy, but you're not a good fit for us."

"That's cool," he replied.

"But thanks for thinking of us…"

"…Oh!" he said. "If you're not doing anything on Saturday,

144

Harvest of Flames is playing Metropolis!"

When the "Flaming Fool" said that, I wondered if he called me just to plug his band. I told him I'd take a pass on seeing him play and he sounded disappointed. I had no interest in being part of the local band circle-jerk that went on every weekend. A bunch of dudes saying "Oh, you're so great!" to each other was just sickeningly fake.

A week later, I got a call from a third guitarist. He also wasted my time telling me about his gear. Yawn. When he finished, I dug deeper by asking him who his favorite punk bands were.

"Punk?" he said.

"Yeah. Punk rock."

"Oh..."

"...Did you read our flyer?"

"...Yeah."

"Then you know we're a punk band."

"I don't wanna play punk."

"What the hell do you wanna do?" I said.

"I wanna play something totally original, just like Tool!"

"But we play punk," I said.

"Trust me!" he said. "When you hear my sound, you'll forget all about that."

I was all out of diplomacy at that point, so I just hung up. Why should I even talk to that idiot? "Mr. Total Tool" was a jackass, but it wasn't just him. The experience of talking to all those guys was frustrating and depressing. If they were the best Flint had to offer, Pure Spun Evil was doomed.

The phone quit ringing and I was starting to give up hope. It looked like I'd never find that last piece of the puzzle I needed. Worst yet, I was sure Klaus and Falcon were laughing at me because Polk High was booking show after show.

I'm not saying there was a competition between Klaus and I, but there was a competition between us. I was determined to win it.

One day at work, I complained about not being able to find a guitarist. I said that I wished there was a way to get an answer to my situation. That's when my coworker said I should call Christopher Paris.

I said, "Does he play guitar?"

"No," she said. "He's a tarot card reader."

"A psychic?"

"Yeah," she replied.

"Is he any good?"

"Some things he told me happened exactly how he said they would."

To be honest, I didn't know how I felt about seeing a psychic. A lot of people think that stuff is fake, but some people say there's something to it. It all depends on finding the right reader. Since I didn't know what else to do, I took a chance and set up an appointment with Christopher.

The next night, I drove to his house off Court and Crescent streets. His place was one of a few apartments that were partitioned off an old home. To get to his door, I had to walk up this old, rickety set of wooden stairs that shook with each step. I thought the thing would crumble beneath me and send me crashing to the ground, but it managed to hold.

Christopher didn't look like what I thought a tarot card reader should look like. He was a husky, dark-haired guy with short hair, and warm, friendly eyes. There was nothing outlandish about him, and that made me feel comfortable.

I stepped inside his apartment and shamanic drumming emanated from his CD player. Candles gave the room a warm amber glow, and ornate tapestries covered the windows. There was pagan-themed art on the walls, which went the extra mile to give the place a mystical feel.

When I sat down at the table, I saw that he placed bunches of pennies piled around each leg of the table. I asked him what that was all about and he said it was an old, Italian folk belief he got from his grandmother.

I said, "What is it supposed to do?"

"Bring good luck and fortune."

"I need to put some pennies around my table legs, then," I replied.

He started my reading by laying out the cards in a Celtic cross pattern that nearly covered his table. Then he said his reading would tell me what to expect if I stayed on the course I was on. I nodded.

One of the cards he flipped was the "King of Wands" in the reversed position. He said it represented someone who was a big part of why I sought the reading. He described this person as "dominating and pushy," with a "strong desire to be in control." I immediately thought of Klaus, but I didn't say anything. If there was any truth to

Christopher's advice, he wouldn't need any prompting from me.

The next card he drew was "The Emperor." He described it as a "leader who represented structure and a solid foundation." This was the card that represented me. I felt flattered, but I was sure Klaus and Falcon didn't see me that way.

He said, "I sense there was a clash between you two."

"Can you tell me why?" I asked.

"It was a battle for control," he said.

"Yeah?"

"He challenged your authority, but you didn't cave in," he continued. "You made the right choice."

"Thanks."

"Was this a business? Or something like a business?"

"You could say that."

"It would have suffered under his control."

"That's what I thought."

"If you haven't parted ways with him, you probably should."

"I did, but it left a hole that has to be filled."

I'd just broken my promise not to give too much away, but I had to know. The answer, Christopher said, was in the last card in the spread. He flipped it over and it featured a staff that glowed in a vibrant shade of gold. Christopher told me that the card was the "Ace of Wands." It meant that the person I was seeking was coming my way.

"Oh yeah?"

"Yes," he said. "And he's looking for you, too."

"When will we find each other?"

"I can't answer that," he replied. "But when you do, it will be a very strong beginning for both of you."

"It sounds like he'll be the right fit," I said.

"That's the message I'm getting."

"Is there anything else you can tell me about him?"

"You'll know him when you see him," Christopher replied.

I wasn't sure if what he said was "real," but it gave me hope. It would be great if there was a guitarist out there looking for me as much as I was looking for him. Pure Spun Evil was something good, and the right person could help take it where I wanted it to go.

About a week after my reading, I got a call from a guy named Rocky

147

Keane. He said he played guitar, and was looking to play in a band. Whether this was a good thing or a bad thing depended on how he answered my questions.

I asked him who his influences are, and he said Metallica. I said they're big Glenn Danzig fans. He said he loved their covers of "Last Caress/Green Hell" and "Die, Die My Darling." That earned him some bonus points with me. He also liked The Dead Kennedys and Suicidal Tendencies, which was cool.

I got a good feeling off Rocky, but I didn't want to get ahead of myself. Ten minutes of phone conversation didn't tell me anything about his character. I had to put him to the test, so I told him to check out the three songs we loaded onto MP3.com.

"If you like what you hear, call me back in 20 minutes," I added.

"Okay," he said.

My phone rang about 20 minutes later, and I didn't bother to look at the caller ID. It was Rocky, and he raved about our songs. So, that meant he was interested, but I needed to know a few things first.

I barraged him with a series of questions. I was looking for anything that might show if he was the type who'd try to control my band. He passed with flying colors.

We had a practice scheduled for Saturday, so I asked him if he could swing by. He practically jumped through the phone when he said "Yes!" I gave him directions to my apartment then realized it might be awkward to audition a stranger. I said, "Are you doing anything tomorrow night?"

"No," he said.

"You wanna meet at Border's so we can get to know each other better before practice?"

"Sure!" he replied.

"I'll see you there at seven."

The next night, I picked a spot at one of magazine racks. It looked casual, but it was a good place to keep an eye on the door. As I waited for Rocky to show, I flipped through an interview with guitar god Tom Morello of Rage Against the Machine. I felt inadequate by comparison.

After a few minutes, a guy walked in wearing torn jeans, black boots, and a black leather jacket. That has to be him. I walked over to meet him, and the first thing I noticed was his complexion. He had golden blonde hair, blue eyes, and fair skin.

There was something about him that seemed familiar, then it hit me. He looked like the luminous Ace of Wands card from my tarot

148

reading. Just then, I remembered the last thing Christopher Paris said to me that night. He said, "You'll know him when you see him."

"Rocky?" I said.

"Hey J.P.!" he replied.

I wanted to learn more about who he was as a person, so we grabbed a table in the café. He told me he grew up in Grand Blanc and started playing guitar when he was about 10 or 11. I also found out that he led a busy life. When he wasn't taking classes at the University of Michigan-Flint, he was working a part-time job in Ann Arbor.

"Ann Arbor?" I asked.

"Yeah! The 48103."

"Are you gonna move there or something?" I asked.

"No. I wanna live in California."

"Cali?"

"The 90077, baby!"

He raved about the beauties and wonders of Los Angeles. The more he talked, the more I realized that I would never call him Rocky again. He was so obsessed with geography that I nicknamed him "The Zip Code Kid." Well, in my mind, anyway. I didn't know him well enough to actually give him a nickname.

I knew I liked him well enough to invite him to audition with us, but I had one more test. We had two more songs that we didn't put on MP3.com. I had them on our CD out in my car, so I asked The Kid if he wanted to go out and listen to them.

We hopped into my car and I fired up the CD. Rocky listened patiently, no doubt making note of the keys and chord changes. When the songs ended, I asked him if he'd like playing stuff like that and he said, "Hell yeah!" I handed him the disc.

"How many can you learn before practice?" I asked.

"As many as I can," he replied.

"Cool," I said. "I guess we'll see you on Saturday."

When I got home from my meeting, I called Andy. I told him we'd be auditioning our new guitarist that Saturday. He asked me why I felt so sure about it and I said, "Call it a hunch." That was as close as I was willing to get to admitting that a tarot card reader predicted it.

I felt excited about The Kid's audition. He must have, too, because he was the first to show up for practice. His punctuality made a good impression on me. I asked him if he had enough time to work on the other songs. He said he thought he had them down. I hoped so.

When Andy and Rikki showed up, I introduced them to The Kid, though I called him Rocky. He shook their hands, then complimented them on the work they did on our CD. Once everyone was ready, I turned the mic stand so that I faced the guys. That would let me see what everyone was doing in real-time.

"Ready?" I said.

Andy and Rikki nodded, and The Kid gave me a thumbs up. It was time to see what he could do. I called out the name of the song, and Rikki counted off the intro on his sticks. We went into it, and I kept a watchful eye on our prospective guitarist. He locked in with Rikki and Andy, and the three of them put down a solid groove.

We jumped into the next song and again, I watched The Kid. He stayed in the pocket with Rikki and Andy, and there was some real musical chemistry there. I also noticed his guitar style added a metal element to our punk sound. That didn't surprise me, considering his influences.

At the end of the third tune, The Kid asked me if I liked what he was doing. I told him it was good, but I'd never imagined my songs having such a metal edge to them. He apologized and said that he was used to playing along with Metallica. I told him there was no reason to apologize because I liked it.

He said, "You sure?"

"Yeah," I replied. "Everyone in the band adds something to our sound."

"Cool!"

"Let's do 'em again," I said.

At that point, I felt comfortable enough to turn my back on the band. The guys launched into the song, and I put everything I had into my vocals. We went through all our songs, and The Kid sounded good with us. It was the perfect blend of punk and metal. In other words, it was Pure Spun Evil.

When we finished, I told The Kid to grab a beer out of the fridge while I talked to Andy and Rikki. The three of us stepped outside, and the guys asked me what I thought. It was a big moment, and the importance of it wasn't lost on me. Whatever decision I made would affect the future of our band, good or bad.

I said, "He's our guy."

Rikki said, "I think so too."

"Me too," Andy added.

"Then it's settled," I said. "But let's fuck with him a little bit."

We walked back into my apartment, and the guys followed my lead. We surrounded The Kid, and I folded my arms across my chest. I then tipped my head back and looked down upon him through narrowed eyes. He looked up at me, and he seemed nervous.

"So, you think you're some kind of guitarist?" I said.

"Yeah... I guess."

"Well, which is it?"

"What?"

"Are you a guitarist? Or do you *guess* you're one?"

"I... I am one."

"Good," I said. "Because Pure Spun Evil doesn't need someone who guesses they can play."

"What are you saying?"

"You got the gig," I said, cracking a smile.

"Awesome!" he said.

I extended my hand, and we shook to seal the deal. It felt great to have a full band again. We needed a win after the failed experiment with Klaus and Falcon. The Kid also saved me from having to deal with the weirdos who answered my guitarist-wanted flyer. The irony that he found us through that same flyer wasn't lost on me.

19.
Evil Invades Metropolis

The Zip Code Kid was a workhorse. Andy, Rikki, and I loved this because we were all about putting in the practice time, too. We started jamming for three hours at a time at least twice a week. We did it to make sure we'd be our best when we played our first show together.

In addition to practices, I spent more time with The Kid. Every weekend, we'd hang out at Metropolis to get to know the people and the bands down there. In the past, I never put much stock in doing that. That hurt me when Big Daddy banned me, and I didn't want to make that mistake again.

The Kid and I formed a solid friendship. There was something familiar about it, and it was Andy who brought it to my attention. He said that seeing me and The Kid hanging out reminded him of the stories he'd heard from Dan. The comparison between the two guitarists was spot on.

One weekend, we jumped into the mosh pit at Metropolis. While smashing and slamming into strangers, we met a guy named Brett Steel. He was a short, stocky dude with tattooed forearms, a goatee, and a shaved head. We introduced ourselves and told him about Pure Spun Evil. Without even hearing us play, he bought a copy of our self-titled CD.

Brett said, "This better be good."

"You'll like it," I replied.

Brett asked us when we were going to play Metropolis, and I told him I didn't know. I needed to get us on the bill, though. For an original punk band in Flint, there was no better platform. One show could expose Pure Spun Evil to the largest number of local music fans.

The next day, I called Joel Rash and asked him if any slots opened up. He said he could squeeze us in on an upcoming gig, but we'd have to be the opening act. Ideally, it was better to play in the middle of the bill when most people were there. I still agreed to take Joel's offer because we needed to get our foot in the door.

"Great!" Joel said. "I've been wanting to see you guys play."

"I've been wanting you to see us play, too," I replied.

The Metropolis show was the break I'd been waiting for. I couldn't afford to screw up, so I pushed the guys to work harder than we ever did before. We practiced three times a week for at least three hours at a time. It was the only way we could be sure we did our best when the time came.

My boot camp band practices started to wear on the guys after a while. I could tell by the looks on their faces. I wanted to back off a bit, but I was possessed by a demon named "Making Up for Lost Time." That infernal beast tormented me with the fact my friends' bands had played hundreds of shows, and I needed to catch up.

While my obsession was stressful, it benefited us on the back end. We became a well-oiled musical machine. I could point my finger to get the guys to deliver the hits. It reminded me of the stories Andy told me about how tight James Brown's band was. That level of tightness told me that we were more than ready to play Metropolis.

On the night of the gig, I found out just how much of a crowd each member of Pure Spun Evil could draw. Some of Andy's family showed up, and it was the same for The Kid. Even some of Rikki's coworkers were there. I didn't bring as many people, which had to do with my falling out with Klaus and Falcon.

We took the stage all charged up and ready to go, but we didn't get our cue from the sound guy. It looked like he fell asleep behind the mixing board. I tapped my finger on the head of the mic. The thumping noise echoed through the PA monitors and filled the near-silent room.

I saw the sound dude's eyes snap open. It was like he suddenly realized where he was and what he needed to do. He leaned toward the microphone on the soundboard and said, "Making their Metropolis debut, here's Pure Spun Evil!"

I dropped my hand, and the guys ripped into our opening number. A thunderous sound filled the room, and the pit degenerated into a frenzied mass of mayhem. It was like some virus had infected everyone.

We launched into our second song, "predator.com." It was a

cautionary tale about the disappointments of online dating. When The Kid tore into his solo, someone threw a computer keyboard onto the stage. In true GG Allin fashion, I snatched it and started bashing it into my forehead. The crowd went insane as plastic cracked, keys flew, and blood trickled down my forehead.

I tossed the shattered keyboard into the crowd just in time to sing the song's last verse. I could see the dudes in the pit stomp on what was left of that bloody computer accessory. After a few minutes, someone threw it back on stage. Great! I grabbed it and started hammering my forehead with it again.

We maintained that shredding intensity level throughout our set. As we ripped through our last song, I saw a familiar face in the pit. It was Brett Steel, and he was singing along with the chorus of our closing song, "The American Way." He obviously liked our CD.

When we finished, I was reminded of the phrase "leave it all on the field." I used to think it was just some corny thing that high school football coaches said. That night, I realized there was something to it. We didn't hold anything back, which meant we left it all on the stage. That was exactly what we were supposed to do.

As I helped the guys pack the gear, someone tapped me on the shoulder. It was Justin MacNeill. He played lead guitar for Mooseknuckle, one of the hottest metal cover bands in Flint. Andy had him play the guitar solo on the CD version of "predator.com."

Justin said, "You put on a hell of a show!"

"Well, we tried, anyway," I said.

"I'm serious," he replied. "You're probably the best frontman in Flint right now."

"Thanks, man!" I said.

"You can thank me by buying me a new keyboard," he replied.

"That was you?"

"Yeah."

"Thanks for the prop!" I said.

Between playing Metropolis and Justin's compliments, I felt like I was on a powerful drug. The glow of our post-performance haze didn't last forever. Once those feelings faded, I craved another hit.

I begged Joel for another show, and he put us second on an upcoming bill. Once again, the demon called Making Up for Lost Time seduced me into pushing the guys as hard as I did before. Even though I knew it was wrong, I couldn't stop.

It didn't take long for the guys' phones to start blowing up during practice. Their women were pissed that their men were spending so much time away from them. I worried about becoming the least favorite person among my bandmates' partners. I took that as a wake-up call for me to back off a bit.

At our second show, we played every bit as hard and heavy as we did the first time. Too bad the crowd was different. The other bands on the bill were kind of lame, and their people just milled around in the pit. We couldn't get them excited about us no matter what we did.

I couldn't put all the blame on the crowd. We had to do more if we wanted to go over. The tunes we played at our second show were the same ones we rocked at our first gig. Some new songs might go a long way to improving our set.

I had a few ideas for new songs rolling around in my head. I wasn't the only one, either. The Kid brought some scorching riffs to practice one day, and I liked what I heard. I asked him if he wanted to turn them into Pure Spun Evil songs.

He said, "I thought you wrote all the songs."

"Things change," I replied.

Andy and Rikki were shocked too, and I knew why. I discouraged Klaus from writing songs, and it tore the band in half. A few months later, I was asking The Kid to collaborate with me on some new tunes. Nothing was shocking about it to me, though.

Andy, Rikki, and I had plenty of time to bond during the recording of the first CD. When we brought The Kid on board, it didn't take him long to integrate into the band. We were a band of brothers, and I had no problem with my brother writing songs with me. Andy and Rikki also added their magic to help us develop six new tunes.

We decided to cut a new CD before we booked another show.

Instead of recording at Andy's house, we bought time at Atlantis Recording Studio. The owner, Mike Matthews, is a super cool guy who played guitar in a local rock cover band. We knew he could capture the intensity of our live performance.

The friendship between the four of us showed during that recording. Everyone stepped up to help the other guy do his best.

155

Andy and I encouraged The Kid as he worked to lock in his guitar solos. Andy also was a huge help when he coached me through my vocals. Rikki was his usual funny self, keeping things light so the process was fun. The Kid was excited about the whole experience, which inspired all of us.

When it came time to finalize the raw recordings, Mike proved himself a wizard at the control board. It didn't take long for him to bring out our best in the mix, then produce a master. He provided 100 copies and did CD printing while Dave Kinder of Burton Printing produced our inserts.

Between Mike and Dave, we had 100 CDs printed, copied, packaged, and shrink-wrapped. We couldn't have asked for a better experience. With our new release finally finished, it was time for another gig at Metropolis.

When I went to book our third gig, I found out that Joel took one of his adventure vacations. I can't remember if he was hiking the Appalachian Trail or zip-lining through some third-world jungle. All I knew was that Joel was gone and Ingus Mat Burleson was booking the shows.

I didn't know Ingus, but he seemed cool about getting us on the bill. He was even kind enough to put us in the middle of the lineup of bands. That meant we wouldn't have to see a bunch of people show up 20 minutes after we got done playing.

By that time, people knew me as "the crazy guy who smashed the microphone into his head." The crowd loved it, especially when I drew blood. It became my trademark, or one of them anyway. Yes, it was derivative of GG Allin's performances, but I felt that I'd made it mine.

I decided to use my head-bashing to market our upcoming show. I sent out a mass email about the gig and the subject line that read, "If you want blood, you got it!" In the body copy, I shared a pic of me smashing my head at a past show and promised to do it again.

Ingus Mat responded about 10 minutes after I clicked "send."

He was freaking out about the whole thing, so I gave him a call. I told him I was known for the whole head-smashing thing during shows. He said he didn't want my blood and germs to infect Metropolis's microphones. I countered his objection with the fact that I used my microphone at all our gigs.

Ingus Mat changed gears and said that bleeding on stage would be a health code violation. He feared the health department storming in and shutting Metropolis down over my onstage antics. In no uncertain terms, he told me I couldn't do anything that would draw blood during our performance. That's not what I considered punk rock, but I promised him I'd tone it down a bit.

Was I pissed that he took that away from me? Sure, but I wasn't going to let my temper ruin things for my new band. I learned a lesson after Big Daddy gave me a lifetime ban from playing the Capitol. Besides, when Joel came home, I could go back to suffering for my art, and our audiences could, too.

Not a drop of my blood fell from my head that night. We had fun, but the crowd's intensity didn't come close to what we had during our debut performance at Metropolis. I did manage to fire up one of the club's security goons, though.

The new songs we added made our set longer. After we finished the second to the last song, I heard a strange noise in the floor monitor. I thought it was just some feedback, so I ignored it. I called out the next song, and the guys hesitated for a second, then jumped into it.

As soon as we finished, one of the security guards jumped onto the stage. He was glaring at me with eyes of fire, but I didn't know why.

He said, "Why'd you do that?"

"Do what?"

"Kept playing after I told you to stop."

"You didn't tell me to stop."

"Yes I did!" he said.

"When?"

"You should've heard it through the monitor."

"I didn't."

"Don't do that again."

He stormed off before I could reply, and it was probably all for the best. He had a good reason to be pissed. My mistake cut every other band's time short that night. I wouldn't be happy if someone did that to Pure Spun Evil.

While we had fun playing that night, we didn't quite recapture the magic and mayhem of our first show. I was getting tired of giving our all to apathetic crowds. They didn't get into our performance and, more importantly, they didn't buy CDs. There was only one thing left to do, and that was to take the show on the road.

20.
Evil on the Loose

Pure Spun Evil was too damn hardcore for Flint.

Those soft little scenesters were stuck in that '90s mentality, believing that "alternative rock" had to be safe. We were punk, and we liked to play rough. That meant we needed to play Detroit.

The Motor City was known for its tough take on punk rock. It's the birthplace of Iggy and the Stooges and Negative Approach, after all. I figured they would welcome us with open arms.

As a Flint punk, I'd only experienced the Detroit scene on two occasions. The first was when Lily and I saw the Jesus and Mary Chain at the Latin Quarter on March 16, 1990. The other time was when Frenchy and I saw Social Distortion at St. Andrew's Hall two years later. Both bands were national acts, but Detroit was happening on the local level, too.

I heard you could fit four or five Flint scenes into Detroit's and still come up 30 bands short. I believed it. There were a lot of clubs that hosted shows, and I wanted Pure Spun Evil to get its piece of the pie. Since Flint was the only scene I'd ever known, I'd need something to help me familiarize myself with what Detroit had to offer.

I found a 'zine called *Book Your Own Fucking Life*. It was a guide that listed every promoter in every venue across the country. It was put out by the folks at *MaximumRockNRoll*, the Bible of all things punk. I jumped right in and started emailing punk bars in and around Detroit.

Our first show was at a bar called The Labyrinth. It was in the basement of the Leland Hotel on Bagley Avenue in downtown Detroit. The pics on the website showed some big crowds there, so I booked a gig hoping we'd play to a full house.

When we got there on the night of our gig, everything about The

Labyrinth seemed perfect for us. A set of cold stone stairs led down into darkness. We descended until we came to a door that opened onto the bar. The inside featured a post-industrial décor that was a lot like Metropolis, only smaller.

The men's bathroom was the living embodiment of the punk rock esthetic. One of the urinals was plugged, and this left a good two inches of piss on the floor. We practically had to wade through that yellow river just to use the toilets. We might as well have stood in the doorway, whipped out our dicks, and pissed straight onto the floor.

We had bigger concerns than the bathroom. There weren't a lot of people at the bar. I asked Team Labyrinth about this and they broke the bad news. The Detroit Electronic Music Fest, aka DEMF, was happening that weekend. Most music fans would be tripping on Ecstasy and spinning glow sticks down the road.

There was no way that the Labyrinth squad didn't know this. They probably booked us hoping that we'd bring a crowd on a night that they knew they couldn't. Good thing we did... sort of.

A couple of The Kid's friends from college came down with him. Rikki's girlfriend was there, too. Even Brett Steel and his girlfriend drove all the way from Mackinac Island to see us. He won the title of most loyal Pure Spun Evil fan for that.

That was a start, but the handful of people we brought weren't enough to make for a good night. I mentioned this to the bar's promoter, and he told me that people from City Club would show up sometime during the night.

City Club was a happening nightclub around the corner from The Labyrinth. I'd heard about the place from some girls who used to hang out downtown. It basically was a nightclub for punks who wanted to dance to techno and new wave tunes. That gave me an idea.

We had some extra flyers for our show. I told The Kid to go to City Club and pass them out to people. Since he was the new guy in the band, he was eager to please. That wasn't why I picked him for "Operation City Club," though.

I specifically asked The Kid to do this because he was the best-looking guy in the band. His "Malibu Ken" handsomeness was a huge hit with the ladies. I'd seen it hundreds of times at Metropolis. By sending him to City Club, he'd encourage some women to come to The Labyrinth. And wherever the ladies went, some guys would surely follow.

159

The Kid got back and brought a bunch of people with him. I was glad to see that Operation City Club was a success. This got me psyched up to play The Labyrinth, and that's exactly what we did.

We ripped into our set like only we could do. By the time we blasted into our third song, I tightened my grip on the Sure SM58 microphone and planted both feet firmly on the stage. With a shout, I sent the mic's grated metal head speeding toward my forehead.

"Thump!"

The sound of the blow echoed inside my skull as stars danced behind my eyelids. I hit myself so hard that I almost stumbled off the stage. I shook my head, which helped me get my feet back underneath me. Instead of slowing down on the GG Allin routine, I slammed the mic into my forehead again.

"Thump! Thump! Thump!"

The crowd cheered on my self-destructive antics. That pushed me to do it more, and the pain stabbed my head like a white-hot knife. I felt something warm pour down the bridge of my nose. I reached up with my free hand and it came away coated in in blood. I wiped it on the white face of the Crimson Ghost on my Misfits T-shirt. It looked like it was bleeding.

We played our asses off that night. The Labyrinth's promoter paid us as well as he could, considering the size of the crowd. We also managed to sell some CDs, which was good. I thought we should play there again so we didn't lose the momentum from that performance. If we did, I'd make sure to pick a weekend when most music fans weren't somewhere else.

With our mission done for the night, all I could do was make that long drive home. My head throbbed for every mile of that journey. When I got home, I washed so much dried blood off my face that the water in my sink turned a brownish color.

I looked in the mirror at my bruised and lacerated forehead and wondered why I tortured myself like that. It wasn't just a tribute to GG Allin. I was acting out on my self-loathing because I was haunted by my past failures. That's why I punished myself.

Our next gig was at an all-ages coffee shop in Metro Detroit. It was called the Spastic Salamander, and its website advertised some well-attended live music shows. If half as many people in those pics came to see us, it would be the biggest crowd we ever had.

We all drove there separately like some kind of punk rock caravan. I was excited about the possibility to finally play to a room packed with Metro Detroit punks. When we got there, the place was nothing like it was on the website. Instead of having throngs of kids, the joint was practically a ghost town.

Long ago, we vowed to give it our all no matter who was in the crowd. That's exactly what we did at the Salamander. We took the stage and rocked that all ages coffee shop harder than it ever had been before. The 10 people in the crowd appreciated our performance; but, despite our inspiration and perspiration, we made zero dollars for our efforts.

After we loaded our gear, I said, "This sucks!"

"That's the nature of the beast," Rikki replied.

"What do you mean?"

"You get paid based on the number of people you bring."

"How do they know who's there to see each band?"

"They have someone outside who asks everyone who they came to see."

"Did they do that here?"

"Yeah."

"That's bullshit!" I said.

He told me it could have been worse. I asked how, and he said that some venues make bands pay a percentage to the sound guy. We didn't have anything like that in Flint, but Detroit was different. There was more competition, and that changes how bars and clubs do business.

The pay-to-play model was unfair to out-of-town bands looking to break into the Detroit scene.

For our next gig, I fixed my sights on the tiny town of Ithaca, Michigan.

Ithaca is about an hour northwest of Flint. While it wasn't exactly a hotbed of punk rock, it did have Rogue's Hollow. The place was a privately-owned-barn-turned-all-ages music venue that catered to punk and nu-metal. I thought it would be a great place to introduce Pure Spun Evil to kids we weren't reaching back home.

When we got there, the place was packed with kids. That was a good sign. The downside was that we had to go on first, which could be a death sentence to an out-of-town band like us. Most crowds don't warm up to the first band, especially if they've never heard it before.

We set up on the stage, which was a hayloft about 20 feet above the floor. From this unlikely performance space, we proceeded to blow the roof off the joint. The kids thrashed below us in a frenzy, which was a good sign. When we finished our 30-minute set, those same kids didn't want to have anything to do with us.

Our whole point for being there was to build our fan base. I could tell that wasn't going to happen, though. I figured the cold shoulder we got was due to our age. Andy, Rikki, and I were in our 30s, and I didn't trust anyone over 30 when I was those kids' age.

I suggested we get the hell out of there. As we started loading our gear, a bearded guy with camouflage shorts, suspenders, and a ZZ Top T-shirt asked us if we were leaving. He was the owner of the barn. Rikki whispered to me to ask the dude if we could get paid. It was the only way to salvage our investment in playing there.

I mentioned it to the guy, and he said they don't normally pay bands. Since he knew we drove a long way to get there, he gave us $40. It wasn't enough to cover our gas, but it was more than we would've made if I didn't say anything.

The four of us spent our gig money at a McDonald's outside of town. I told the guys I felt disappointed, and I took full responsibility. I was the one who booked the damned gig after all. They told me not to worry about it because it was all part of being in a band.

That was comforting, but I still wished we could have gotten more out of that gig.

I didn't need a guide to book our next gig.

Mount Pleasant was my second home when I was at Central Michigan University. I wanted to go back for a visit. The town had a small indie rock scene that was still going strong. I thought it would be fun and a bit nostalgic to perform there, too.

I called the promoter of a popular bar up there, and he wanted us to play the whole night. We didn't have enough material to do that, so I asked him if there was a local band who could split the bill. He said he could get Pennystock to open for us.

"You'll still need enough material to close the night," he added.

"We will," I replied.

I knew I lied the moment those words left my mouth. We didn't have that much material, and it wouldn't help us even if we did. Rikki had to be in Detroit for a work function the next day. Since he'd have to drive 153 miles to get there from Mount Pleasant, we'd have to cut our stage time short.

Rikki was a champ for doing it. He knew how important playing in Mt. Pleasant was to me, but I don't remember if I thanked him or not. If I didn't, it was a huge oversight on my part. I should have let him know how much I appreciated the sacrifices he made for that show to happen.

I felt guilty because I thought Rikki's sacrifices would be in vain. There was no way we could close that bar as I promised. I should have taken a pass on that gig, but I didn't. It was the demon named "Making Up For Lost Time" again. He seduced me into pushing forward with that gig.

On the night of our show, a bunch of vehicles filled my driveway. The Kid brought some of his fawning female admirers. There was a blonde, a brunette, even a redhead. Seriously! What were the odds that any guy could pull that off? Pretty high when that guy is The Zip Code Kid.

Andy brought his wife with him. His sister was going to CMU at the time, so she and her friends were going to be there, too. I invited Brett Steel, who never missed a gig, and he brought some friends. We led our traveling circus due north on I-75.

When we finally pulled into Mount Pleasant, it was just as I remembered it. After we loaded in, we sat through two agonizing sets from Pennystock. They were everything we expected from a nu-metal cover band of the early 2000s. To make it through their performance, Brett and his friends slammed one Long Island iced tea after another.

When we took the stage, Brett and his friends stopped slamming drinks and started slamming each other. The regulars didn't seem to appreciate that or our music. For college kids, they were a bunch of stiffs.

I tried to sell some CDs on our first break, but there were no takers. We had to cut it short because of Rikki's schedule. In a matter of minutes, we were back on stage, smashing through our second set. Despite our enthusiasm, we still got a sour vibe from the crowd. Even the promoter, a muscle-bound dude with multiple facial piercings, sneered at us.

I turned to the guys and said, "Let's show them who we are!"

163

We gave the rest of our set everything we had. Our intensity level had its desired effect on Brett and his friends. Chaos reigned supreme on the dance floor until Brett plunged head-first into a PA monitor. The Pumped-Up Promoter and his assistant ran over there in a panic while Brett stumbled to his feet and laughed.

I shouted, "This is punk rock, you lame fucks!"

We jumped into our last song and brought the show to a raging end. The guys held out the last note, and I shouted, "We're Pure Spun Evil, and you're a bunch of pussies!" The band pounded out the final note as all our friends shouted and cheered.

Since Rikki had to get going, everyone helped him load his gear. Once he was done, we loaded our equipment. After we finished, I went back into the bar to get paid. The Pumped-Up Promoter and his nerdy assistant cornered me in the kitchen.

"Whattya think you're doing?" the promoter snarled.

"Looking for you."

"Why?"

"To get paid," I replied.

Mr. Big Shot Promoter looked at his assistant, and they laughed. He told me he wasn't going to pay us for playing "half the night." I told him our drummer had a family emergency and had to leave. That was a lie, but he didn't know that.

The Pumped-Up Promoter said, "You're fuckin' up our night!"

"It's 12:45; there's not much of a night left."

"That's not the point!"

"What's your point then?"

He turned to his assistant and said, "Looks like we got a tough guy here."

"You're the one playing tough guy," I said.

As we argued, The Pumped-Up Promoter slowly inched his way toward me. So did his assistant. They stopped just outside my range, but they could cover the distance if they were motivated. I took a slight step backward with my right foot, which put me in a fighting stance.

In the middle of our standoff, Brett and his friends walked up behind me. Brett shouted, "Is there a problem here?" I looked at The Pumped-Up Promoter and said, "Well? Is there?"

"We're not paying you for your gig," he replied.

"That's bullshit," I said.

Brett and his friends shouted and called him a "thief." I told Mr.

Muscles that we brought the crowd that night, but he said Pennystock did. I called him a liar right to his face. If he ever needed a reason to do something, there it was.

Big Boy and his geeky assistant didn't make a move, but they didn't get out of my way, either. They were stuck in that place between fear and anger, and it made them freeze. I wasn't making a move, either, but I had a good reason for that. I knew how overzealous the cops in Mt. Pleasant are, and I didn't want to end up in the Isabella County Jail.

As all of this was happening, Andy pulled his car up outside the bar's open door. Out of nowhere, he laid on the horn. This caused The Pumped-Up Promoter to flinch and turn his head toward the door. That gave me the opening I needed.

I dropped into a three-point stance then charged forward. I smashed into the muscle-bound asshole's hulking frame and sent him crashing into some hanging pots and pans. I kept plowing forward to the freedom of the open door. In their overzealous charge, Brett and his friends sent the assistant sprawling to the floor, and one of them stepped on the guy's hand. That's the only way I could explain the assistant's bloodcurdling scream.

We piled into Brett's van, and he handed me the keys. I fired it up and got us out of there as quickly as I could. We managed to get out of Mt. Pleasant and Isabella County without seeing any flashing lights behind us. That alone was a small miracle.

By the time I pulled into my driveway, Brett was sober enough to drive himself home. I went to bed alone, tired, and upset with the way things turned out. The upside was that the police didn't call me the next day, or any other day after that. The Pumped-Up Promoter and his little friend didn't call the cops on us for steamrolling them.

So, our ill-fated Mt. Pleasant gig ended up having a highlight after all.

I thought long and hard about our out-of-town gigs. I'd noted what they did and didn't do for us, and it was a lop-sided list. With Christmas around the corner, the band would go on a break for a while. I had just enough time to book one more show in Flint. After our miserable experiences on the road, we needed a win.

I called Joel and asked him if he had a gig for us. He said he had two. One was at Metropolis, and the other was at Local 432, an all-ages club around the corner. We talked about playing there in the past, but I never followed through with it.

Joel said, "Can you do it?"

"Do the shows conflict?"

"No," he replied. "You'd go on at six o'clock at the Local, and about 10 at Metropolis."

Part of me wanted to tell him, "Thanks but no thanks." After what went down at The Spastic Salamander and Rogue's Hollow, it would be a waste of time. None of the kids at The Local would get into our band. But I wasn't the only one making decisions for Pure Spun Evil. That old demon Making Up For Lost Time had an equal say in everything.

The Local 432 was our first show that night. There were about 100 kids packed into the venue, which was a good sign. We tore into our songs no differently than any bar we'd ever played. The crowd seemed to be into it just like the kids at Rogue's Hollow.

I was feeling the vibe about halfway through our set. That inspired me to throw some CDs into the crowd. The problem was, I whipped one disc a little too hard. It took a wicked curve and sailed toward one kid's face like a ninja throwing star.

I watched in horror as it sailed toward his face in slow motion. I felt relieved when the kid caught it at the last possible moment. He must have seen it from the corner of his eye or something. I shouted "good catch" into the mic, and he nodded.

I was so glad it ended that way. If he would've gotten hurt, people would be saying, "Pure Spun Evil hates kids!" It would've become a huge thing, and I would never be able to live it one down.

After our set, I walked through the crowd to sell some CDs. Just like at Rogue's Hollow, the kids at the Local 432 suddenly didn't know we existed. I wasn't surprised. Again, Andy, Rikki, and I were old enough to be their dads. That made the whole thing awkward.

There was nothing left to do but pack up our gear and head to Metropolis. By the time we took the stage, we tore through our songs all over again. It was a lot like our other gigs there. Some people got into it, and others didn't.

Our gig was better than our out-of-town shows, but I still felt the urge to go home to lick my wounds. I decided to hang out at Metropolis instead. It would be the last time to be with the guys until after the holidays.

I sat there in silence while everyone else drank beer and had fun.

The empty feelings that used to gnaw at my insides came back with a vengeance. Pure Spun Evil was supposed to make those feelings go away.

Our "out-of- town-tour," if it could be called that, was more fizzle than sizzle. Some people liked us, but most people were indifferent. That was way worse than if they hated us as far as I was concerned. Hate implies some type of emotional investment. We could have turned some of that around in time. We didn't have a chance in hell of winning over those with no emotional connection to our sound.

I hated to admit it, but my fantasy of being in a punk band didn't match the reality. The whole thing seemed like a struggle where the rewards didn't match what we put into it. For the first time in over a decade, I remembered that my dad said my music was "a waste." I wondered if he was right.

Over the holidays, I'd take some time to figure it out.

21.
A Deep Dark Place

Christmas 2001 was weeks away, and I was miserable. It didn't take a genius to know why. The guys would be spending time with their loved ones while I'd be stuck at home with my dysfunctional parents. The holidays brought the worst in them.

Mom hated this time of the year because she couldn't be the center of attention. She did everything she could to ruin the day for Dad and me. If anyone in the house was happy or enjoying themselves, she made them a target. Dad and I wore Christmas-themed bullseyes on our chests every year.

She had an insidious way of instigating her holiday sabotage. She'd start by needling at the old man over every little thing. Once she knew he was inches away from exploding, she'd yell at me about something. When I snapped back at her, Dad would blow his stack. Like clockwork, he and I would start shouting at each other.

Mom immediately jumped on these opportunities. She'd assume a false moral stance in the midst of the chaos that she created. She'd scream and lecture us about how family needs to stay together during the holidays. We'd bark back at her, of course, and she'd start crying and run to her room. There, she would sleep for the next 12 hours. It was all part of her well-calculated plan.

As Mom slept off her responsibilities, Dad and I scrambled for our holiday meal. We'd usually eat at whatever restaurant was open, but we'd be too angry with each other to enjoy it. The two of us got stuck being the clowns in that ridiculous circus every year. Too bad we weren't smart enough to revolt against the ringleader.

All that drama made me want to spend Christmas alone. Taking a page out of my mom's book, I removed myself from my family equation. I got a case of beer and holed up in my apartment. Most of the time, I just sat in my darkened room. Drinking and listening to Tom

Waits' *Mule Variations* and Mike Ness's *Cheating at Solitaire* was better than anything that was going on at my parents' house.

On the second day of my self-imposed exile, I realized that being alone during the holidays sucked. With nothing but music to occupy my mind, boredom and self-loathing ravaged me like a pack of wolves. I needed something to distract me from myself, so I broke down and called Andy.

Out of everyone in the band, I was closest to him. When I had an idea for a song, I called Andy. If I was unsure about something, I called Andy. And if I needed someone to talk to, I called Andy. I came to rely on him so much that I started to call him "Dr. Harris." I never asked him if he was okay with any of this.

When "Dr. Harris" answered the phone, I asked him what he was doing. He said he was going to see his friend's band play at White's Bar in Saginaw. He asked me to come along, and I said, "Absolutely!" Anything to get out of the house where I was alone with my thoughts.

As I was getting ready to leave, I remembered that I promised my daughter that I'd call her. Since Andy was on his way, I knew I wouldn't have much time to talk, but I called anyway. I've always believed that a promise is a promise, even if I didn't have a perfect record of keeping them.

My ex-wife answered, and she had that tone in her voice. It was the same one I'd heard too many times during our marriage. I lit into her out of habit. She didn't have to listen to my tirade, but I was too proud and stupid to realize that. She slammed the phone down in my ear.

Five minutes later, her husband called. He tried to talk down to me like I was one of his kids. I went "Pure Spun Evil" on him, and he hung up on me too. I was so pissed that I called them back, but no one answered. They weren't going to let me talk to my daughter, and there was nothing I could do about it.

If I had half a brain cell in my thick skull, I should have kept my big mouth shut. Phone calls weren't part of our divorce agreement. That meant they didn't have to let me talk to my daughter, and they knew it. The whole experience left me feeling wounded and powerless.

I blamed my ex-wife and her husband for interfering with my relationship with my daughter. That triggered a tidal wave of adrenaline and cortisol to flood into my body. My blood burned a trail through my

169

veins, and my heart pounded like a war drum.

Just then, I heard a knock on the door.

I suddenly remembered that Andy was coming over. Good! I knew he'd understand the shit my ex-wife and her husband were putting me through. I told him to come in just like he'd done many times before. That poor, unsuspecting soul didn't know what he was walking into.

Andy barely shut the door behind him before I unleashed my emotional outburst. I told him about the phone call, what my ex-wife said, and what her husband tried to tell me. I then went on a tirade about how women have an unfair advantage in custody arrangements.

When I finished, I desperately searched his eyes for some sign of understanding. He stood there in silence as a growing sense of awkwardness filled the room. Finally, he pulled his hands up before him like a fence and said, "I know you're troubled by all this, but I didn't need to hear that."

His ice-cold response froze the once-burning anger that had possessed me. I stood there like a statue, too mortified to speak. Andy seized the moment and told me that he didn't appreciate me dumping my problems on him. He just came over to take me to the bar.

I knew he was right. That's why I hung my head in shame as he continued to tell me why what I just did wasn't cool. It felt like he was scolding me, and it cut me to the core. It was all the worst parts of Operation Dragon Fire, but this time it was coming from my friend and bandmate.

As I stood there, I felt more than shame. It was like I was reliving all the shame I've ever felt from every mistake I made. It was practically unbearable, but I stood there and listened to it all. After what seemed like an eternity, Andy said, "Well? You ready to go?"

I was in no shape to go anywhere that night, but I threw on my jacket and went with him anyway.

We drove along in silence, and I thought our uncomfortable discussion was over. Out of nowhere, he brought up the incident again. He reminded me about how inappropriate I was back at my place. As I quietly sat there in his car, the shame I felt quickly mutated into anger.

During the time I got to know him, Andy shared some personal things with me. I never asked him to do that, but I never scolded him for it, either. I tried to do what a friend was supposed to do, which was listen without passing judgment. While he was right about the way I bombarded him, I thought he was a hypocrite.

White's Bar wasn't the experience I wanted it to be. The band might have been good, but I was too distracted to notice. And after everything that was said, I didn't enjoy Andy's company that night, either. While I went to the bar with Andy to get away from my parents' house, I felt relieved after he brought me home.

I slipped back into the deep, dark place I'd been in all week.

Try as I might, I couldn't get that situation with Andy out of my mind. It triggered a nasty habit of mine. Whenever someone says something that pisses me off, I hyper-focus on one word they say. That word comes to embody all the shame the other person triggered in me, and the silent rage that follows it.

The word that stuck in my mind was "troubled."

Andy said that to me when he corrected me that night. I obsessed over it, and dark thoughts clouded my mind and heart. What the hell did he know about being troubled? His wife didn't leave him and not let him talk to his kids.

I had all of that to deal with, and I didn't have a friend to talk to about it. Now that's troubling!

I turned to music to help me process my emotions. I strummed some chords on my acoustic guitar, and a chorus eventually came together. After I played it a couple of times, I scribbled the words in my notepad. It didn't take long for my up-tempo alt-country song to come together. I called it "Troubled Man."

Nobody knows you when you're sitting in the county jail
Nobody wants to post your bail
Nobody offers a helping hand
They all just say you're a troubled man

Once I got busted
and the police took me in
The judge said "What you done boy,
is a sin"
Trouble is as trouble does
and I'm a troubled man
Soon I found out
my troubles just began

171

I called my family,
I called all my friends
The people who I thought
would be there 'til the end
I asked for some money
to help in my defense
I didn't get a dime
from those so-called friends, because...

Nobody knows you when you're sitting in the county jail
Nobody wants to post your bail
Nobody offers a helping hand
They just say you're a troubled man

Everyone ignored me
When I needed them the most
They saw right through me
Like I was a ghost
When I really needed help,
They gave me some advice
They all I said I needed help
Ain't that nice?

So, I'm sitting in this tiny room
I'm sitting in this cell
I can only tell you
it's a living hell
Locked up in this little cage
For something I didn't do
You should be glad that
it isn't you, because...

Nobody knows you
When you're sitting in the county jail
Nobody wants to post your bail
Nobody offers a helping hand
They just say you're a troubled man
Troubled man
Troubled man

If I wanted to do anything with that song, I'd have to play it for Andy at some point. Would he realize that he inspired it? At first, I thought he wouldn't. Then again, Andy is one of the most observant and intuitive people I know. If he remembered what he said that night, he'd probably figure it out.

If he ended up recognizing it, he'd have to do it on his own. I sure as hell wasn't going to tell him.

I continued to dig deeper into country, blues, and American roots music. Those old tunes had some things in common with punk. It was that emotional rawness that couldn't be denied, and the I, IV, V chord progression.

The more I immersed myself in that genre, the more songs I was able to cobble together. What they lacked in musical complexity, they made up for in heart and attitude. I described my new sound as, "The Ramones' tour bus crashes into Waylon Jennings' pickup truck at the liquor store."

I wanted to build a band around these new songs. I had just the name for it, too. It would be "The Last Outlaws." The name conjured up the imagery and romanticism of the infamous American gunfighters. I was a sucker for *The Old West* series from Time-Life Books. I remembered the commercial that said John Wesley Hardin once shot a man "just for snoring too loud."

I was so excited about my new songs and direction that I almost called Andy. I stopped myself, though. I knew we needed a little space after "The White's Bar Incident." While I held firm to that resolution, he ended up calling me about a week later.

Andy said. "I haven't heard from you in a while."

"I've been busy."

After a slight pause, he said, "Is everything okay?"

Was everything okay? That sounded like a loaded question. I wondered if he was probing me to see if I was upset over what he said that night. I wasn't angry with him, but I still was "troubled" about the whole thing. I couldn't tell him that, though.

I said, "Actually, I've been meaning to call you."

"Oh yeah?"

"Yeah. I wrote some new songs that I want you to hear…"

"…That's cool!"

"When you have some time, of course," I said. "No rush."

He told me that he was taking a drive up to Caseville. It's a vacation town in Michigan's thumb area, and Andy's family had a cabin up there. He asked me if I wanted to come along. When I waffled, he said it would be the perfect time to talk about my new songs.

I said, "Good point."

"I'll swing by in 20 minutes," he replied.

On the way to Caseville, I described my songs to Andy. He asked me if I wanted it to be a side project or something more. I said if it was a band, I'd call it The Last Outlaws. Before I did that, I wanted to play the songs for him and the guys.

"Why don't you come over and record them?" he asked.

"Would that be okay?"

"Of course!" he said.

He kept driving up Colwood Road until we came to an area called Kilmanagh. It wasn't a town, exactly. It was more like an intersection with a few derelict buildings. He pulled up in front of an old, decrepit two-story structure that looked like a saloon from the Old West.

"What's this?" I said.

Andy said it was all that remained of the old Woldt Brothers general store. In front of the building was an old gas pump that last saw use during the 1950s. It was tall, thin, and coated in rust. Halfway up the pump was a sign that read, "For use as a motor fuel only. Contains lead. (Tetraethyl)." The top was decorated with a yellow and red logo that read "Super Shell."

I was awestruck by that old pump's stillness and faded beauty. I told Andy it would make for some good background photos if I recorded my alt-country songs. He took a few pictures of me in front of it with his digital camera.

We hopped back into the car and drove another 15 miles into Caseville. In all the time I knew Andy, he always seemed calm, cool, and collected. A different side of him emerged when we entered that town. His eyes lit up, and he turned into an animated tour guide as he showed me his family's cabin and some other sights.

On our way home, I had a different outlook on "The White's Bar Incident." While Andy's words hurt me that night, the trip to Caseville felt like a peace offering. Even if he didn't mean it that way, it still

174

helped bring me back from the darkness that surrounded me. The magic of Caseville had something to do with that.

My new musical direction was also a huge help. The deeper I got into alt-country, the more I wanted to play that instead of hardcore punk. All the anger and rage of Pure Spun Evil burned me out. The Last Outlaws could help me express the more vulnerable side of my emotional core.

When it came time to record my new songs, Andy and I knocked them out in no time. He recorded me singing and strumming my acoustic guitar, then added a basic drum track to each tune. We weren't looking to make country music gold. We just needed something to give Rikki and The Kid an idea of my new sound.

Rikki liked it right away. His brilliant marketing mind seized upon the money-making opportunities of my new, audience-friendly sound. It meant that we could play rock and country bars, he said. He was definitely on board.

The Kid wasn't crazy about my change in musical direction. As a Metallica fan, country was never his thing. Since he was moving to California soon, he gave me his blessing. He also promised to come up with some lead guitar parts when we recorded these songs for good.

A CD, even if it only had five songs, would be great to have. We could give a copy to prospective guitarists and say, "Learn these tunes." I figured we'd record them at Andy's house, but he suggested we cut our disc at Downtown Digital in Saginaw.

If we did that, we'd be playing in the big leagues. Downtown Digital was owned by Michigan rock legend, Dick Wagner. (He recorded with everyone from Lou Reed to Alice Cooper and more.) It would be an honor just to stand in the mixing booth where Dick's gold records hung on the wall.

I was dying to record the CD at Downtown Digital, but I was concerned about the money. Sure, we'd made some cash from our gigs and CD sales, but we didn't have enough to record there. That's where Andy stepped up to the plate. He knew a guy who worked there, which meant that we could get a discount that made the whole thing possible.

We recorded and mixed the CD in roughly four days. Not long after that, The Kid prepared to leave for California. Our new country band played the going away party his parents threw for him. It involved lots of alcohol and words of advice from each member of the band.

The next day, The Kid packed up his minivan and drove west toward the setting sun. It was sad to see him go. He became as much of a friend to me as a bandmate. I understood why he wanted to move, though. Many people were leaving Flint around the same time for the same reason.

With The Kid gone, the decision to end Pure Spun Evil was an easy one to make. Turning our punk band into an alt-country group worked for me, Andy, and Rikki. It broadened my musical horizons and improved my songwriting. For them, it was an end to angry lyrics, bloody foreheads, and jockstrap-clad performances.

So, The Last Outlaws was a thing. We had a name, a CD, and a direction, but we still needed a lead guitarist. My gut told me that someone would come along, but I had no idea who that person would be.

22.
A Fantastic Find

I thought switching from punk rock to alt-country was a smart move. But where the hell would I find a guitarist who could play complex fills and solos, and wanted to play in an original band? As fate would have it, we didn't have to search for such a person because he came to us instead.

Rikki had a friend who worked with a guy named Andrew Partridge. This Andrew guy played guitar, and he was a huge rockabilly and country fan. Rikki reached out to Andrew, and the guy responded, saying that he was looking to join a band. At that point, Rikki turned it over to me.

I waited a day before I emailed Andrew because I didn't want to look desperate. I sent him a message about what The Last Outlaws were about. Andrew emailed me back about five minutes later. In his message, he thanked me for considering him, and he asked how long we'd been together. He also asked me to describe the band's sound, and why our old guitarist left the group.

I explained how The Last Outlaws grew out of our old punk group, and why we were looking for a new guitarist. I also thought it was best to be honest about my goals for the band:

> 1. We'd play some cover tunes, but the group's
> focus was my original songs.
>
> 2. We just recorded a CD with our old guitarist,
> and we planned to sell it at gigs.
>
> 3. We'd record another CD at some point.

Moments after I clicked "send," Yahoo notified me that I had a new email. Sure enough, it was from Andrew. He asked if I wanted to meet rather than trade emails all night. I told him we could get together at my apartment, and he agreed to stop by the following night.

On the day of our meeting, I barely had enough time to walk through the door when I heard a knock on it. I opened it and saw him standing there. He had long, scraggly brown hair and a pudgy face creased with lines around his mouth and across his forehead. I thought he looked like Alastor "Mad Eye" Moody from the Harry Potter movies, minus the googly eyepiece.

"Andrew?" I said.

"Hey, J.P."

I shook his hand then invited him inside. He handed me a six-pack of Pabst Blue Ribbon as he walked through the door. Back then, all Flint rockabilly cats drank PBR. I'm ashamed to admit it, but I got caught up in all that posturing, too.

Andrew and I talked about our musical influences. I was pleased to see that he liked many of the same classic country musicians I did. He was also into some that I hadn't heard of, like Webb Wilder and Danny Gatton. He said he'd make me a mixtape.

Andrew also had a thing for the local rockabilly groups. His eyes took on an ethereal glow as he waxed poetic about Dixie Hustler and The Swingin' Demons. According to him, these groups were "fantastic." When he said it, he emphasized the middle syllable, which made it sound like "fan-TAS-tic."

It's cool when musicians support their local scene. "Mr. Fantastic" took it too far, though. I didn't know if he really worshiped those guys, or just wanted to sound like a hip scenester. Either way, he came across as silly because some of the guys he admired were douchebags. I was sure they felt the same about me.

So, was Mr. Fantastic the guitarist I was looking for? On the one hand, it was cool to meet someone who was into the same kind of music that I was. On the other hand, there was just something off-putting about him. I couldn't quite put my finger on what it exactly was, but it was there.

The more we talked, the more I realized what bothered me about him. It was an underlying anger that simmered beneath the the false kindness he displayed in my apartment. I got the feeling that he didn't like talking to me, but he was trying his best to act like he did.

Based on those first impressions, I thought Mr. Fantastic wasn't right for the band. I hadn't heard him play a single note, but I wanted to take a hard pass on him right then. If I did, I knew the guys would say. It would be something like, "You're being paranoid and judgmental," or "You didn't give him a chance."

So, my gut screamed that Mr. Fantastic would be trouble. On the other hand, we needed a country guitarist, and they weren't easy to find. The best thing to do was to ask him questions to see if he really wanted to join The Last Outlaws or not.

I said, "So, you can probably tell we're not like your average bar band."

"That's okay," he replied.

"But is it something you wanna be a part of?"

"Absolutely!" he said.

"And you're okay with playing originals?"

"Why wouldn't I be?" he said.

"I had to ask," I replied.

"Look," he said. "I just wanna play good music with cool people and have some fun."

"Well, that sounds like us," I replied.

Despite my reservations, I invited Andrew Partridge, aka "Mr. Fantastic," to our next practice. If he was half as good as Rikki's friend said he was, he might be who we were looking for. I hoped so because that would be the shortcut I needed to start playing shows again.

On the day of his audition, Mr. Fantastic was the first to show up. He hauled his gear inside and got set up. Once he finished, I asked him if he had a chance to listen to our CD.

"Yeah," he replied. "I like what you were trying to do with it."

That sounded like one of those backhanded compliments I used to get at Pure Spun Evil gigs. There was always some old, washed-up musician who tried to "give me some advice." What that really meant was that they'd take their shots at me because they were jealous I was on stage and they weren't. I didn't know Mr. Fantastic well enough to be sure that's what he was doing.

"So, you had time to work with it?" I asked.

"Yeah," he replied. "I spent the whole night practicing to it in my basement."

"Well, that's good," I said.

"Not really," he replied.

"What?"

He said, "Your old guitarist was so bad that I had a hard time concentrating on my parts."

Okay. I didn't just imagine that. He disrespected The Kid, and I didn't like it. Just then, Andy and Rikki walked through the door, so I introduced them to Mr. Fantastic. Everyone shook hands.

After they got settled in, Andy did some scales runs on his bass while I strummed a chord in the same key. Rikki effortlessly banged out some complex drum rolls on his set. Mr. Fantastic stopped dead in his tracks and stared wide-eyed at Rikki.

"What's wrong?" Rikki asked.

"Dude... you're good!" Mr. Fantastic said.

"Thanks."

"I mean it," he said. "Your playing is fantastic!"

He went on and on about Rikki's skills until things got awkward. After nearly five minutes of that one-sided love fest, I said we should get down to business. We started with "Troubled Man."

For his first time jamming with us, Mr. Fantastic did a decent job. His fills and solos were complex and nuanced, which gave the song an authentic country music feel. When we finished, he asked me if I liked what he did.

"I do," I said.

"You sure?"

"Absolutely," I replied.

As we kept jamming, Mr. Fantastic brought that same approach to all my songs. At the end of each tune, he asked me if I liked what he did... twice. It was like he didn't believe me the first time I told him he did a good job. I thought it was odd because I wasn't sure if he was fishing for compliments or he was insecure.

When we took a break, I pulled Rikki and Andy aside and asked them what they thought about him. We agreed that he was a bit odd, but his talent level was exactly what we needed. Even though I still had some reservations about him, I offered Mr. Fantastic the position, and he accepted.

I hoped I wouldn't regret that decision.

23.
Troubled Band

With Mr. Fantastic in the band, I got to see our new guitarist at least two hours a week.

In his early days in The Last Outlaws, he seemed happy, fun, and friendly... on the surface. I sensed his anger bubbling just beneath the fake smiles and friendly tones. His mask would slip with little comments he'd slide in here and there. He usually did that before Andy and Rikki showed up.

The anger he'd been suppressing had finally burst to the surface one day. We were talking about how confusing it can get when a couple of coworkers have the same first name. For example, Mr. Fantastic had more than a few Jims at his job. Andy had a couple of Roberts at his job.

I worked in a small office, so we didn't have that problem. I did say that we have two Andys in the band. Mr. Fantastic's body became as stiff as a board.

"It's Andrew!" he snapped.

"Is that what you prefer?" I asked.

"Yes!" he said.

"Okay..."

"...If you call me Andy again, I won't be happy!"

Mr. Fantastic glared at me with pure malevolence. I knew the guys were watching to see how I'd respond. I didn't know what to say because the whole thing caught me off guard. He went from zero to 60 in 1.2 seconds.

Before I could say anything, Mr. Fantastic asked me if he could leave his amp in my apartment. I told him he could, and he said, "Thanks." It was like that whole "Andy thing" didn't just happen. It was strange, to say the least.

After the guys left, I thought about that brief but weird exchange with our new guitarist. It seemed like Mr. Fantastic could explode out of nowhere over things that, at least to me, weren't a big deal. While I wasn't sure about the things he said when I met him, what happened at practice was a genuine red flag.

One day, Mr. Fantastic had a "great" idea. He said we should make his basement our regular practice space.

I got the strange feeling that this was a power play on his part. It was all in the way he suggested it. His tone and body language suggested that he wasn't going to take "no" for an answer. I said I appreciated the offer but I wanted to keep rehearsing at my place. He sulked all through practice.

Mr. Fantastic's next big idea had to do with the CD we recorded with The Kid. He asked me if I planned to sell them at our gigs, and I said I did. He told me that was "stupid," and I asked him what the hell he meant by that.

"Your old guitarist isn't up to my level," he said.

"Is that so?"

"Yeah. And I don't want people thinking that's me."

I reminded him that The Kid's name and picture were in the liner notes. Frankly, I shouldn't have to say anything because he knew we'd be selling that CD. I made that clear to him from the start, and he agreed to it. Besides, I sure as hell wasn't going to throw away 100 CDs that we already paid for.

As we practiced, Mr. Fantastic shad this intense scowl. It was like all of the pent-up anger inside of him suddenly showed on his face. When Rikki saw it, he stopped drumming and said, "What the hell is wrong with you?" That shook Mr. Fantastic out of it.

"What?" Mr. Fantastic replied.

"Why do you have that look on your face?" Rikki asked.

"What look?"

"You look pissed," Rikki said.

"Everyone always thinks that, but I'm not," Mr. Fantastic said. "I'm just aloof."

I told Rikki and Andy that Mr. Fantastic's contrived grievances were starting to piss me off. Rikki said I should take that up with Mr. Fantastic during a band meeting. It was the Klaus and Falcon thing all over again, as far as I was concerned. I nixed the idea.

"I think you should," Rikki replied.

"This is an outlaw country band, not a group therapy session."

Rikki didn't appreciate my proclamation. The way he abruptly left my apartment was my first clue. I turned to Andy and asked him what he thought. He put his hands like a fence and said, "It's your band, I just play in it." He drew a firm boundary line just like he did on the night of the White's Bar Incident.

As I saw it, Mr. Fantastic wanted to control my band. Under normal circumstances, I would have kicked him out. The problem was that original outlaw country was a niche genre in Flint, and Mr. Fantastic was a specialist. We literally might never find someone who could replace him.

After a couple months of solid practicing, The Last Outlaws was ready for its first live show.

I thought The Loft would be a good place to play because of its small, intimate setting. It was also centrally located in Buckham Alley, right next to Metropolis. Rodney Ott, the owner of the bar, already hosted some local rockabilly bands there. I thought it would be easy to get us in there.

One night, I popped into The Loft to talk to Rodney. He was working behind the bar, as usual. I handed him our promo kit and said we'd like to play there. He was skeptical because he didn't know me well enough to know if I could bring a crowd. It was a business decision and I got that, but I didn't like it.

While we talked, Joel Rash strolled into the bar. As luck would have it, he sat down next to me and asked me what was up. I told him I was trying to get Rodney to book The Last Outlaws. Joel told him that my bands always drew a crowd.

Rodney said, "Oh yeah?"

"Yeah," I replied. "And we'll bring people who don't normally come here."

"Okay," Rodney said.

We shook hands to seal the deal. I was glad that Joel was there to give me instant credibility with Rodney. While it got me the gig, I still had to prove myself. I made a promise to draw a crowd, and Rodney would hold me to that. If we didn't pack his bar, we'd never get another chance to play there.

Everyone in the group was excited about the show. Even Mr. Fantastic smiled. Well, one corner of his mouth turned up a little bit, which was about as close to happiness as I was going to get with him. At least it was something.

On the night of our show, I packed my gear into my car and headed to The Loft. As I walked up Buckham Alley, I heard music emanating from the bar. It sounded like one guy crooning and strumming an acoustic guitar.

My suspicions were confirmed when I walked inside. Some dude was playing on the stage. He was bald, with a long, scraggly chin beard. Who the hell is he? And what the hell is he doing on the stage we're going to play?

I spotted Rikki, so I asked him if he knew the guy on stage. Rikki told me that he was Mr. Fantastic's friend. Apparently, our new guitarist took it upon himself to book this guy to "open" for us.

I asked Rikki why Mr. Fantastic would do something like that without checking with us first. Instead of answering, he nodded toward the bar. I turned to see Mr. Fantastic walking toward us.

I said, "Good. I can get to the bottom of this right now."

"What do you think of my friend?" Mr. Fantastic asked.

"I wish I would've known he was playing here before the night of our gig," I replied.

"It was a last-minute thing..."

"...You should've checked with us first."

"But you gotta admit he's good."

"I'm sure he's fantastic, but that's not the point," I said.

"What is the point then?"

"That's something we decide on as a band," I said.

"Okay..."

"...And we can't pay him for this."

"I know."

"Fine," I said.

"Fine!" he replied.

I took a seat at the bar and listened to Chin Beard finish his little one-man show. I didn't want to get in the habit of promoting other musicians because the favor wasn't always returned. Once he played his last song, we set up, tuned, and jumped into it.

184

When Rikki put together our setlist, he got downright obsessive about it. He agonized over choosing and arranging our first set with some country and rock covers. We plowed our way through them, and the crowd got into it.

When it was time to play our originals, the bar was hopping. We ripped into "Troubled Man" and my other songs, and everyone had a blast. Well, everyone except for Mr. Fantastic. He had that nasty scowl on his face the whole time he was on stage.

At the end of the night, Rodney handed me an envelope that made good on his end. Andy, Rikki, and I saved our cuts for future recording sessions. I paid Mr. Fantastic his share because it was better to have him as a hired gun than a member with equal creative input.

Rikki called me because he had something to discuss. I asked him what it was, and he said he noticed something at our gig. There weren't many people in the bar between 9 and 10 PM, so they missed our first set. How could we get more people to show up for our opening numbers at our next show?

I said, "That's a damn good question."

Rikki wanted to offer drink specials on cans of Pabst Blue Ribbon and shots of Jack Daniels from 9 to 10. He hoped this would inspire people to show up earlier. Once they got good and warmed up, they'd likely stay for our whole show.

I thought it was a great idea, but I'd have to run it by Rodney first. When I stopped into The Loft, he said he'd be happy to do it. He even said we were the first band to come to him with that kind of promotional idea. When I told Rikki about it, he said we should put it up for a vote.

"A vote?" I said.

"It'll make Andrew feel included," he said.

"Jesus Christ!"

"Hey!" he said. "You don't want this to turn into another Klaus and Falcon situation, do you?"

"No," I said.

"Then send out an email."

"Fine."

I didn't see what the big deal was, but I followed his advice. I was sure everyone would go for it, anyway. How could they not? It could bring more people to our gigs so we could make more money. Who didn't want that?

I sent an email out to the guys. I voted yes, and so did Rikki. Andy emailed us and said he was good with it, too. Mr. Fantastic's response arrived in my inbox. In it, he shared his opinion of Rikki's marketing plan:

> "As far as my vote goes, it's a NO, absolutely
> not. Paying people to like my band is the last
> thing I want to do. That's selling out and it goes
> against all my principles. If I'm outvoted, you
> can go ahead and do this, but if you do, you'll
> have to find another guitar player."

When I read that, I blew my stack.

I grabbed the phone and punched in Rikki's number. When he answered, I asked him what he thought I should do. He said we shouldn't do the drink promotion. I asked him why, and he said because we couldn't afford to lose Mr. Fantastic. I ranted and raved until I ran out of steam.

He said, "I'm surprised you're so upset about this."

"I'm surprised you're not," I said.

"Why?"

"Dude!" I said. "It was your idea."

"So..."

"...So, it's a good idea, but he's being a dick about it!"

"It's no big deal," he replied.

"I disagree!"

Rikki was unmoved by my concerns. To him, it was just one idea that got voted down. Nothing I said would make him see the big picture. At that point, the only thing I could do was warn him about the long-term dangers of Mr. Fantastic's controlling nature.

He said, "C'mon!"

"I'm serious!" I replied.

Rikki didn't see how Mr. Fantastic's response threatened the "democracy" of the band. I said that by caving to Mr. Fantastic's demands, we sent the message that his vote was the only one that mattered. Rikki didn't get it, so I said that Mr. Fantastic would threaten to quit whenever he got outvoted on anything. If we caved in to his demands, what was the point of even having a vote?

"We're literally handing him control of the band," I added.

"I think you're overreacting," Rikki replied.

Rikki didn't believe me, and that bothered me. I'd seen this kind of thing before and knew that it always ends badly.

24.
Troubled Band, Part Two

Things with Mr. Fantastic kept getting worse. His mood at practices was like a dark cloud that cast its gloom throughout my apartment. That wasn't the worst of it, though. Not by a long shot.

His habit of sniping comments increased. He criticized the quality of my guitar, my guitar skills, and just about every other little thing. He was smart about it too. He always managed to get his digs in without Andy and Rikki hearing him.

I didn't always sit there and let him put me down. He and I had our fair share of arguments. When this happened, Rikki usually intervened and told me to calm down. He never said anything like that to Mr. Fantastic, which pissed me off.

Going forward, I started to internalize my frustrations with our guitarist. It caused me to develop a nasty habit. Every time he escalated his attacks on me, I ran to Rikki. Andy already told me that he didn't want to have anything to do with Mr. Fantastic and his drama.

Rikki went in the other direction. He volunteered to be Mr. Fantastic's "handler." That meant Mr. Fantastic and I would go through Rikki instead of communicating with each other. Rikki would do his best to mitigate any disagreements between us for the sake of the band. It had to be better than me blowing my stack and losing our guitarist.

It sounded like a good idea, but I was concerned about one thing. Would this policy strengthen the bonds of friendship between Rikki and Mr. Fantastic?

I wanted to increase the band's reach, and that meant stepping outside of Flint's downtown music scene. I booked a show at Sylvia Jo's Wagon Wheel, which was Genesee County's best country-western bar. I was sure our throwback outlaw country sound meant we'd fit in there.

Sylvia Jo Burrow was Flint country music royalty. During her time in Nashville, she recorded songs and worked with some of the biggest names in country music. When she came back home, she opened her rough and rowdy bar on Richfield Road. I wanted the bragging rights of having played there.

Our debut performance got off to a rough start, thanks to Mr. Fantastic. He blew the intro on our opening number, "Broken-Hearted and Incarcerated." The rest of us kept playing in hopes that he'd catch up, which he finally did. We were able to finish the song without any more mistakes.

The infamous "Fantastic Fuck-Up" was the least of our worries. We had bigger issues with the crowd. Most of the regulars wanted to line dance to the latest country tunes. Our brand of outlaw country originals kept them glued to their seats, and not in a good way.

Before the end of our set, some of the regulars shouted for us to get off the stage. We didn't budge until we played our last song. By that point, I was over the Wagon Wheel. During my Pure Spun Evil days, I learned that booking is a hit-or-miss process. The challenge was remembering that wisdom when the crowd turns on you.

Mr. Fantastic took the crowd's rejection much harder than I did. He was really upset about it and blamed himself. That small flub he made gnawed at him like a tapeworm in his belly. He said that's why the crowd turned against us, but I told him it wasn't his fault. That made him more upset.

He stomped off to the bar with a friend of his who came out to see us. I listened as Mr. Fantastic grumbled to the guy about our set. I only caught snippets of their conversation, but I heard him blame our poor performance onto me. That was funny because, earlier that night, he was just as excited about playing there as I was.

As Mr. Fantastic continued to blame me for everything, I saw a familiar face. It was Andy, and he was sitting at the bar, right next to Mr. Fantastic. I wanted to get him alone so I could ask him if he heard what our guitarist was saying. As luck would have it, Andy got up and came over to my table.

I whispered, "What's that asshole bitching about?"

"How should I know?" Andy snarled. "I'm not his babysitter!"

His comment blasted me like an atom bomb and opened all my emotional scars. Shame filled my wounds, and I was stunned and speechless. Even if I could have come up with a response, I didn't have the chance. After lashing out at me, Andy got up from the table and walked away.

It didn't take long for rage to replace my shame. I didn't know why Andy felt the need to be so nasty with me over that. I didn't expect him to "babysit" Mr. Fantastic. I just wanted to know what the dude was saying about me. I only asked Andy because he happened to be sitting next to Mr. Fantastic.

Once I finally cooled down, I knew where I went wrong. Andy made it crystal clear that he didn't want to deal with any Mr. Fantastic drama. In my rush to learn what our guitarist was saying, I tried to drag Andy into the middle of it. It probably looked like I disregarded his wishes, but I wasn't. It was a simple case of forgetfulness.

I started feeling claustrophobic and needed to get out of the bar. I saw Rikki taking his drums out, so I followed him. Once we reached his car, I told him all about what Mr. Fantastic said to his friend. Rikki didn't seem to care about it.

I said, "So, it's okay that he blames me for his failures?"

"Calm down!" he replied.

"Why?"

"He might hear you."

"We're the only ones out here," I said.

"He could walk out any minute."

"Fine!" I said, lowering my voice. "But we still got a problem."

"What did he say again?"

Oh my God! Did I really have to repeat the whole thing? I guess I did, so I started from the top. When I got done, Rikki just stood there looking at me.

"Well?" I asked.

"Well, what?"

"Fuck this!" I said.

I turned my back on Rikki. As I did, he shouted, "Wait a minute!" It was too late because I was already storming back to the bar.

Mr. Fantastic desperately wanted to play Rube's Bar, which wasn't a shock.

It was one of his favorite hangouts, and he had a lot of friends there. Too bad it wasn't the popular college bar that it used to be in the '80s. By that time, it had degenerated into a past-its-prime dive smack

190

dab in the City of Flint. I was skeptical about our country band playing there, but Rikki talked me into book the gig.

On the night of our show, Mr. Fantastic was the first one to come to my apartment. He loaded his gear and left without any harsh words or nasty glares. That alone was a victory. By the time Rikki showed up, I was excited about our gig. That made me chatty. I blabbed away so much that I didn't notice the clipped, one-word answers he was giving me.

With the last of his drum set in his hands, he went to leave. I patted him on the back and said, "We're gonna kick ass tonight!" Rikki pulled his shoulder out from under my hand and growled, "Get your fucking hands off me!" He then stormed out the door and hopped into his car.

That hit-and-run attack left me wondering what I did to deserve it. I wracked my brain, but I couldn't figure out why. I was in a good mood and excited about our show, but that was no reason to bite my head off. What the fuck was his problem?

When Andy showed up, he took one look at me and asked me what was wrong. He could always tell when something was bothering me. I told him what happened with Rikki. When I got done, I said that I had half a mind to call it quits after our show.

"You don't mean that," he said.

"I do if he's gonna do things like that!" I replied.

"He does shoot from the hip," Andy replied.

"And I got hit with his bullets for no reason!"

Andy laughed, then said, "Don't let it get to you."

"How can I not?"

"Honestly, he's probably forgotten about it already."

Andy talked me down off the ledge that night. When I got to Rube's, Rikki acted like the whole thing that went down at my place never even happened. That helped me put the ugly incident out of my head so I could focus on our show.

I booked our next gig at The Loft so we could start drawing real crowds again.

People were packed into the ground floor of the bar. The second-floor landing also had a group of guys sitting there. I recognized them right away. It was the Pomade Brigade, the backing band for local singer/songwriter Billy Rocca, aka "Dad Glasses."

I called him "Dad Glasses" because he wore a pair of thick, horn-rimmed glasses from the 1950s. He complimented this look with a greased-up pompadour and Sailor Jerry tattoos. To complement his cliched retro-greaser image, he made sure to be seen with a can of Pabst Blue Ribbon in his hand.

When I was playing in Pure Spun Evil, Dad Glasses didn't know I existed. When I started The Last Outlaws, it ignited a weird, one-sided musical rivalry between us. He started acting strange and stand-offish whenever I saw him downtown.

So, the guys at The Loft were his bandmates. I figured they were there to check us out, then forgot all about them. I only remembered they were they when they came down from the landing and stood in front of the stage.

The four of them folded their arms across their sunken chests and glared at me while I played. They thought they were tough because they lived on Oak Street. It was a somewhat sketchy neighborhood on the outskirts of downtown Flint. Too bad I couldn't muster any fear for a group of kids who were about as intimidating as Weezer's kid brothers.

As silly as they were, I couldn't let them think they had me spooked. I pushed the base of my mic stand onto the floor and took a few steps forward. I was singing about six inches from their smug little faces. Our battle of wills didn't last long. They broke formation and shuffled back to their table.

I went back to playing, and we brought the show to a rousing close. I considered it a success, despite the brief and ridiculous interruption. I didn't see the guys from the Pomade Brigade again until I went to give Mr. Fantastic his cut. That's when I found our guitarist chatting away with one of those guys like they were old friends.

As they were talking, both of them raised a knee, tapped the bottom of their beer bottle onto it, then clinked their bottles together. The downtown scene had a ton of silly in-group things, but the "Pomade *Prost*" was the worst. I'd seen enough at that point and walked up to Mr. Fantastic. His little Pomade pal scampered away like the coward he was, and I handed Fantastic his money.

I found Rikki and told him that we needed to talk. I asked him if he saw the Pomade guys surround the stage and he told me that he did. I then mentioned that Mr. Fantastic was talking to one of them after the gig. Rikki agreed that this fraternizing was a serious issue.

I said, "I'm glad you agree."

"If you want to get to the bottom of it, you should have a band meeting," Rikki replied.

"I'm not ready for that," I said.

Rikki called me one day and said we needed to talk. My initial reply was, "What's Mr. Fantastic's problem them time?" Rikki told me that Mr. Fantastic thought the shows I was booking didn't do anything for us as a band. I asked Rikki what that was supposed to mean, and he said he didn't know.

I said, "Well, that's interesting."

"What do you want to do about it?" Rikki asked.

"I thought that was your job?"

"I said I'd run interference..."

"...Right."

"And that's why you're talking to me instead of him," he said.

"Okay," I said. "I got an idea."

"What's that?"

I said, "Let him book our next gig."

"Really?"

"Yeah," I said.

"Why?"

"You'll see," I replied.

I was eager to see how Mr. Fantastic would manage to book a show that "did something for us." I had a hunch he'd have us play Rube's or some other dive bar. The place would be empty, except for a few of his friends, and we wouldn't make a lot of money. O hoped that would finally show Rikki what a loud-mouthed fraud our guitarist really was.

Mr. Fantastic booked a gig at a house party on "Devil's Night." That's what us Michiganders call the day before Halloween. Kids celebrate this unofficial holiday by waxing windows, throwing toilet paper into trees, and setting abandoned buildings on fire. I couldn't help but wonder if that was some kind of omen.

I made the 50-mile drive to the party with Andy. Most of our time was spent driving down dark, winding country roads. When we finally got to the house, Mr. Fantastic told us that we'd be playing in the barn behind the house. It was a long haul to get our gear back there.

After we loaded in, the three of us waited for Rikki to show up.

After about 15 minutes, he called Andy's cell phone and asked for directions. I used to call Andy the "human compass" because of his geographic knowledge. I swear, he could find his home from anywhere just by using the stars to navigate himself. He talked Rikki in from wherever he was on the road.

As soon as Rikki got there, he barreled straight for Mr. Fantastic. Once the two were face to face, Rikki lit into him. There was some back and forth that I couldn't hear. I did hear one thing, though. It was Rikki shouting, "Next time, give better directions!"

I leaned toward Andy and said, "Looks like the honeymoon is over."

The owner of the house came out and led the four of us to the barn. Once we got there, he pulled the covers off an elaborate PA system with high-quality mixers and monitors. We plugged in and the dude took his time to dial in our settings. Once he was satisfied, he told us we could start whenever we were ready.

As we went into our first number, the host left to be with his guests. Instead of coming into the barn to hear us play, the party stayed outside on that cold, drizzly night. The only ones who supported The Last Outlaws was a group of cats that lived in the barn. Those faithful feline fans stayed with us to our last note.

At the end of it all, I wondered why the hell we bothered to play there. We didn't get so much as a "thank you," let alone any money or CD sales. As far as I was concerned, the gig was a huge failure. Before I said anything, I wanted to make sure I wasn't the only one who felt this way.

I asked Rikki what he thought about our experience. He told me he planned to talk to Mr. Fantastic about it. I asked him to call me afterward and tell me what Mr. Fantastic had to say. Rikki told me that he would do that.

True to his word, Rikki called me the next day. He told me Mr. Fantastic's reason for booking that party. The guy who owned the house was one of the best sound guys in Genesee County. Mr. Fantastic told Rikki that playing there would "get us in good" with the guy. I missed must have missed that memo.

I said, "So, he used us to suck up to people in the scene?"

"Yeah," Rikki replied.

"That's a load of bullshit!"

"He says it was the best show we've ever played."

194

"How so?" I asked.

"Sound quality."

"Sound quality?" I asked.

"We never sounded better, apparently," Rikki replied.

"So, we froze our asses off so we could play through a fancy PA system?"

"Pretty much."

"Well, I have a message for him," I said.

"What's that?"

I said, "Tell that asshole that I'm booking shows again!"

25.
A Case for Dismissal

Mr. Fantastic glared at me the minute I walked into The Loft. The day before, he sent me an email that said, "We need to talk." Experience taught me that whenever someone says that, it's never good. The look on his face added to my suspicions.

I wanted to turn around and leave, but I sat down and ordered a beer instead. We made some small talk as I waited for my drink to arrive. Rodney Ott set the frosty class on the bar in front of me, and I took a drink. I then asked Mr. Fantastic what he wanted to discuss.

Mr. Fantstic said, "I like playing in this band, but I have some things I need to address."

I noticed that he opened with a compliment, then followed it with the word "but." In that case, "but" was a contrast signal word, which indicates a change in thought. In other words, the nice thing he said before the word "but" would be discounted by what came after it.

He brought out our last show. It was in the cafe section of Border's Books and Music. We played there a couple of weeks after his failed Devil's Night gig. Border's didn't pay us, so we only worked for tips. I was expecting him to have a problem with that.

He said, "Do you remember what you did with your guitar case that night?"

"My guitar case?" I asked.

"Yeah."

"What did I do with it?"

"You put it right in front of my amp!" he said.

"Oh, yeah. That was when I broke a string…"

"…I don't care why it happened!" he snapped.

I was shocked by how abrupt he was, and I needed a moment to gather my wits. Mr. Fantastic didn't give it to me. He continued to condemn me for the outrageous sin of leaving my guitar case on the floor "right in front of him." What I remembered was setting my guitar case on the floor about five feet from where he was playing.

I said, "You called me out here to talk about a guitar case?"

"Yes!" he said. "And you better take this seriously."

"Oh really?" I said.

Mr. Fantastic's face became pinched, and an ominous storm brewed within his eyes. He leaned toward me until he hovered just on the edge of my personal space. He'd done things like that to try to intimidate me before, but he'd never gotten that close. It was creepy.

He said, "Can you please not do that again?"

"Okay…"

"…You just don't get it, do you?" he hissed.

"Get what?"

"Pull your head outta your ass or I'm quitting!"

"Hold on!" I said.

"No!" he replied. "You need to hear this…"

"…Okay."

"If I quit, you won't have a band." he replied.

The fear factory inside my mind suddenly kicked into production mode. It manufactured a massive load of adrenaline and cortisol, then dumped that toxic brew into my bloodstream. I felt my heart start pounding inside my chest, and I went into panic mode.

"It not just the guitar case," he continued.

"What is it then?"

"Your inability to see that you did anything wrong. It's just so…"

He paused, and the moment crackled with an intensity that he cultivated for effect. Wanting to end the uncomfortable silence, I filled in his sentence with the word "insensitive." The moment the words left my mouth, I regretted giving him ammunition to use against me?

He said, "Try rude and inconsiderate."

"Wow!"

"Did that surprise you?"

"Yeah," I replied.

"Well, I'm not pulling any punches!"

Mr. Fantastic continued to lecture me. He said he didn't mind playing in my band, but the only problem he had was with me. According to him, I was a "selfish, egotistical asshole." Since he was a "professional musician," he shouldn't have to deal with my bad attitude.

I said, "I don't exactly agree with your perspective…"

197

"...And I don't deserve to have guitar cases thrown at me!"

"I didn't throw it..." I said.

"...Interrupt me again, and that's the last time you'll ever see me!"

I froze, not knowing what to say.

"Well?" he asked.

"Well, what?"

"Don't you have anything to say for yourself?" he asked.

"I didn't know that this was such a big deal."

"It is!"

"I see that," I replied.

As he glared at me, I recognized the look on his face. It was the same one my parents gave me whenever I disappointed them. Mr. Fantastic wanted something from me, and I knew exactly what it was. Even though he didn't deserve what I was about to do, habit and conditioning took control of my panicked mind.

"I'm sorry I set my guitar case down in front of you," I said.

"Is that all?"

Just like my parents, my apology wasn't enough for him. Nothing short of my complete humiliation would satisfy his raging blood-lust. Fortunately, Mom and Dad did a great job of preparing me for that very moment.

I said, "I'll try harder to be more aware of how my actions affect others."

"See?" he said. "That wasn't so hard, was it?"

A smile spread across his face, but his eyes smoldered with pure hatred. It was a disturbing sight, and I didn't know how to react to it. I just sat there, speechless and in shame. That was my default position since the start of that bizarre meeting.

Mr. Fantastic ordered us some beers. As I sat there, he told me about all the "great ideas" he had for the band. I didn't hear a word he said because I was fighting the silent rage that flooded my brain. Mr. Fantastic said rude things to me before, but they were never so blatantly disrespectful as they were that night.

Something else angered me about that meeting. It was the fact that I apologized when I wasn't wrong to someone who didn't deserve it. I had a habit of doing that to maintain the many dysfunctional relationships I'd had in my life. That habit didn't do me any favors with Mr. Fantastic.

What bothered me most was how I reacted to him raising his voice to me. It took me back to when I was a kid, sitting through one of my parents' Operation Dragon Fire missions. I just froze up and didn't know what to do. That gave Mr. Fantastic the upper hand in the whole thing, and he knew it.

I left the bar that night with a strange feeling in my stomach. It felt like a knife was cutting its way out of my body. I'd never really liked Mr. Fantastic, but after that meeting, I hated him. The worst part about it was that I hated myself even more because of how I reacted to the whole thing.

I called Rikki and spilled all the gory details from my meeting. He waited until I finished, then told me that I could have avoided the situation. I asked him how, and like a broken record from years ago, he said I should have had a band meeting.

"Since you didn't, his issues festered," Rikki added.

"I won't argue with you there," I replied.

"It was only a matter of time before this blew up in your face."

"So, it's all my fault then?" I asked.

"Pretty much," he replied.

"Wow!"

"Well?" he said. "I'm not gonna sugar-coat it."

"Now you sound like him."

A thought suddenly flashed through my mind. What if Rikki was in on the whole thing? He didn't seem surprised about the meeting with Mr. Fantastic. I'll bet Rikki was talking to him about it all along. If that was true, he knew I was going to get ambushed, and he let me walk right into it.

I cut my call with Rikki short and called Andy. Out of anyone, I knew he'd understand. I told him about my meeting with Mr. Fantastic and said I couldn't believe he was so pissed over something so trivial.

Andy said, "That meeting wasn't about a guitar case."

"What do you mean?"

"He was shit-testing you."

"Shit-testing?" I said.

"It's something people do to see how much they can get away with."

"Explain."

"You said he's been doing little things to provoke you since he joined the band, right?"

"Yeah," I said.

"Those were little shit tests to see how'd you react…"

"…And I ignored them."

"Right," Andy said. "That's why he felt confident to push you as hard as he did tonight."

"What happens now?" I asked.

"Knowing him, he'll probably think he runs the band."

"He was acting like that at the bar."

"Yeah, that's gonna be a problem."

"Damn!" I said. "All this could've been avoided if I would've just stood up to him."

"If you did, he would've quit."

"Yeah," I replied. "After making all those threats, he'd have to quit, or he'd look weak."

"Now you're getting it."

I booked a show at The Loft before the "Infamous Guitar Case Incident" went down. That meant I'd have more practices with Mr. Fantastic. I was so upset with him that I didn't know how I could play nice. I didn't even want to be in the same room with the guy.

On the night of our practice, I sat on my couch, staring at my guitar. I didn't get up to tune it until about five minutes before the guys were supposed to show up. As I was turning the pegs, I heard a knock on the door.

"It's open!" I shouted.

Mr. Fantastic boldly strode inside my apartment like a conquering hero. He said "hello," and I mumbled an unenthusiastic response over my shoulder. I didn't bother to look at him. That added to the tension that sparked and crackled in the room like a downed power line.

He said, "Do you have a problem with me?"

The volume and sharp tone of his voice echoed inside my apartment. It also rang inside my ears. I jumped to my feet and shouted, "Yeah, I have a fucking problem with you!"

I finally had my chance to blast him with every grievance I had since he joined the band. In the blink of an eye, he snatched his guitar case and said something about leaving. That particular threat had lost all its teeth with me, and I promptly told him to get the fuck out.

"Fine!" he said.

"Fine!" I replied.

He stormed toward the door just as Rikki was walking through it. Rikki asked him what was wrong, and Mr. Fantastic gave him a highly fictionalized account of what happened. In his narrative, he was the innocent victim of my ruthless nature and explosive temper. I wasn't shocked to hear him frame it that way.

"I told you to get the fuck out!" I bellowed.

He turned to Rikki and said, "See what I mean?"

"Now!" I yelled.

Mr. Fantastic scampered through the door like a frightened dog. It made me feel like an angry parent scolding a misbehaving child. I found that odd. It was the opposite of how he made me feel at the bar. I didn't have time to explore that, though. Mr. Fantastic was giving Rikki a pleading look over his shoulder as he retreated.

"He can't help you now!" I shouted.

Rikki told him to wait outside for a minute. It made me look powerless as the leader of the band. I asked Rikki what the hell was he doing, and he told me that he had to salvage things.

"There's nothing to salvage," I replied.

"We have a show!"

"Then I'll cancel it!" I said.

"Just wait a minute."

Rikki went outside to talk to Mr. Fantastic. From the other side of the door, I heard that prick call me an "egotistical asshole." Then he had the nerve to ask Rikki to quit The Last Outlaws and form a band with him. I wasn't going to tolerate that level of disrespect at my house.

I barged outside and unleashed all my anger on Mr. Fantastic. I don't remember everything I said, but the words "low-life piece of shit" came out of my mouth. As I tore into him, a car pulled into the driveway. It was Andy, and he was late for practice.

Out of the corner of my eye, I saw Andy get out of his car and started walking toward us. When he got close enough to hear me shouting, he turned on his heel and quickly walked back to his car. I snapped my head back to Mr. Fantastic and saw that his eyes were welling up with tears. Wow! The grown-ass man who tried to be so gruff and intimidating was actually about to cry!

"Now I'm the one who's not pulling punches!" I shouted.

He mumbled something that I couldn't hear, so I told him to speak up. He said something about it "not being worth it," but I wasn't going to let it go. I told him if he had something to say, he should say it to my face. He swallowed and mustered up enough courage to say, "Everyone in this band should have a voice."

I balled up my fist just as Rikki grabbed me in a bearhug. He hoisted me off my feet then sat me down on the porch. As upset as I was, I knew that Rikki did Mr. Fantastic and me a favor. That would have gotten ugly and not ended well for him or me.

Rikki said, "You should probably go."

Mr. Fantastic said, "I don't wanna be here, anyway."

"You're not wanted here!" I shouted.

I watched our former guitarist slump off to his car like the defeated man he was.

Andy and Rikki joined me inside for an emergency band meeting.

Rikki's response to the situation was pretty much what I expected. He was mad at me for blowing up on Mr. Fantastic. He seemed to think that the band couldn't make it without that asshole. We couldn't resolve the issue because Rikki and I were too entrenched in our positions.

I turned to Andy, hoping he'd be the voice of reason. That was a risky move because I knew how he felt about the whole Mr. Fantastic thing. Putting him on the spot like that was an invasion of his boundaries. That could make him lash out at me like he was a trapped animal, but the situation was too important for him to ignore.

"What do you think?" I said.

"When all this started, I said I didn't want to get involved," Andy replied.

"That's true..."

"...But even though I wasn't on the field, I watched the game from the bleachers."

"What did you see?"

Andy said he was surprised it took that long for things to explode. I asked him what he meant, and he said he knew Mr. Fantastic had been pushing my buttons for a while. He even mentioned a few of those instances. The detail in his recollections told me that he had been paying attention.

I said, "I just don't get why he constantly fucked with me like that.

"In my opinion, he has some narcissistic tendencies," Andy replied.

I'd heard that term in a college psychology class, but I didn't remember the details. I thought a narcissist was someone who was in love with themselves or something like that. I asked Andy why he didn't say anything about that before, and he told me that he did.

"When?" I said.

"When I said that he makes grandiose statements."

"What does that mean?"

"That's a narcissistic trait," Andy replied.

"How was I supposed to know that?"

Andy shrugged his shoulders. I wished he would have told me all of that sooner. It might have given me a heads up about our guitarist. Then again, it might not have made a difference at all. I was so desperate to keep the band together that I probably would have thought I could have worked around Mr. Fantastic's eccentricities.

Everything would have ended the same way, which was bad news for The Last Outlaws.

I was so intrigued by the topic of narcissism that I looked it up on the internet. A bunch of results came up, and I spent hours reading everything I could about it. I discovered that grandiosity was one of its biggest traits. The other aspects of narcissism were just as bad:

1. An exaggerated sense of self-importance.

2. A sense of entitlement and deep need for constant admiration.

3. An expectation to be recognized as superior, even without the actual achievements.

4. Fantasies about success, power, and the perfect mate.

5. A belief that they're special and should only assoc-iate with other special people.

6. Harassing and bullying anyone they think is "below" them.

7. Taking advantage of other people.

8. An inability to recognize other people's needs or feelings.

9. Being jealous of other people.

10. Being arrogant, haughty, and boastful.

Wow! In my opinion, that described Mr. Fantastic to a T. The rock star posturing, tossing his hair, and strumming the guitar with exaggerated sweeping motions were all very grandiose. And then there was the way he acted around other local musicians. It was like he was in an elite club with them or something.

Yes, those traits were straight off the list, but did that make him a "narcissist?" Well, that depends on how you define the term. Is a "narcissist" someone with narcissistic tendencies? Or does the term refer to someone who's been professionally diagnosed with narcissistic personality disorder?

I'm not a licensed psychologist or psychiatrist. Far from it, really. Even if I was, some mental health professionals have a hard time diagnosing narcissistic personality disorder. That's because it's believed that every person has some narcissistic tendencies. It only becomes a problem when someone develops unhealthy levels of those thinking patterns. And even then, that doesn't guarantee they meet the criteria for narcissistic personality disorder.

In my opinion, it's enough to say that Mr. Fantastic displayed narcissistic tendencies. I just wished I would have known that before he joined the band. Then again, maybe I did pick up on those signs on a sub-conscious level. It was the way I noticed the strange vibe he had when we met for the first time.

There was something else I'd learned about narcissistic tendencies that, in my opinion, applied to Mr. Fantastic. It was the nature of how he related to me in the band. People with unhealthy levels of narcissism tend to cycle through a three-stage process in their personal relationships.

The beginning phase is called the "idealizing" period. That's when the person with narcissistic tendencies showers their target with compliments, aka "love bombing." They also tend to move too fast in the relationship. Back then, he was very complimentary to me and enthusiastic about joining my band.

Phase two is the "devalue" stage. It happens when the person with narcissistic tendencies stops being the fawning admirer. Those warm, bubbly feelings transform into moody, agitated, and irritable behavior. During this phase, the person with unhealthy levels of narcissism will lash out at the other person. I don't have to be a licensed therapist to say that Mr. Fantastic did that to me.

The "discard stage" is the last stage. That's where the person with narcissistic tendencies unceremoniously ditches their lover, friend, or business partner. To make matters worse, they make a point of hurting and humiliating the other person as much as they can. This stage never happened because I discarded Mr. Fantastic before he could discard me.

I thought that I'd heard the last of him after I fired him. The day after I kicked him out of the band, I got an email from him. The subject line read "The Last Outlaws." When I opened it, I saw a horrible picture of a stream of piss cascading down upon our band's sticker. That sticker was conveniently placed at the bottom of a urinal, of course.

In addition to the "selfie," Mr. Fantastic shared his uncensored thoughts about me:

> "The Last Outlaws won't be playing at The Loft or anywhere else for that matter. I can't in good conscience continue to lend my talents to a band led by such an egotistical asshole. Many of you who know me know how much of a struggle it's been for me to be a part of this project. I'm glad it's finally over. My only regret is that the other members let themselves to be abused by that ego-maniac. I tried to get them to leave that no-talent hack and do something where they'd be appreciated. They'll be happier when they do. I know I am."

So, Mr. Fantastic took one last desperate shot at hurting my feelings. I didn't care about anything he had to say at that point. What annoyed me was his implication that I couldn't find anyone to replace him.

Challenge accepted, motherfucker!

26.
The Definition of Insanity

I'd like to say that I replaced Mr. Fantastic, but it was Andy who pulled it off.

He knew a guy who knew a guy who played guitar for a classic rock cover band. That guitarist, Ernest Simpson, wanted to make more money for his upcoming wedding. He hoped that joining The Last Outlaws would be a good side hustle.

I emailed Ernest and did my usual interview-a-potential-band-member thing. He told me that all he wanted to do was play what I wanted him to play and collect his cut at the end of the night. I told him to audition with us at our next practice.

While I was excited about auditioning Ernest, I wasn't prepared for who came walking through the door. Ernest was a tall, heavyset guy with a bowl cut and glasses. The strangest thing about him was his voice. No matter what Ernest said, it sounded sad. He could say, "I just won the lottery," and it would still sound like the sad, "wah-wah" trombone effect from '70s game shows.

While Ernest's personality was dull and bland, his guitar skills were the opposite. He was an old school rock 'n roll shredder who filled his solos with every note in the scale. His style lacked the subtlety and nuance that Mr. Fantastic had, but at the end of Ernest's audition, I had a feeling he might work out.

I said, "We could use your skills in The Last Outlaws."

"Okay," he replied, in that sad tone of his.

Suck on that, Mr. Fantastic!

I thought Ernest was the unicorn we'd been looking for. Then I met his girlfriend, Rachel. She was a militant feminist with a blue Mohawk, combat boots, and baby doll dresses. She also wore the pants in that relationship.

Rachel wasn't shy about sharing her opinions. When we met, she lectured me about the racist, patriarchal, and misogynistic history of country music. I did my best to ignore her, but that only encouraged her to be more obnoxious and aggressive.

The more shows I booked, the more I had to put up with Rachel. It was getting harder to ignore her. Everything came to the boiling point one night after a gig. We were all hanging out at an all-night diner, and everyone was laughing and having a good time. Well, everyone except Rachel.

She told me a story about some dude who tried to hit on her online. At first, she thought the guy just wanted to be friends; but, after a while, he wanted something more. When she told him that she had a fiancée, he threatened to kill her and Ernest.

I said, "Do you think he'd try something at one of our gigs?"

"I don't know," she replied.

"Well, send me a picture of him so we know who to look out for."

"Only if you promise to smash his face," she said.

"I will if he shows up and makes a scene."

"Good!" she replied.

If Rachel stopped there, she would have had my sympathy. I know there are some weird guys out there, and it doesn't take much for them go into stalker-mode. But she didn't stop with her story. She described her experience as an example of "toxic masculinity."

"What's that?" I asked.

"It's something all men have," she said. "It's why rape culture exists!"

"Really?" I asked.

"Yes, really," she said, in a mocking tone.

"Okay..."

"...The fact that you'd even question me is proof that you're complicit in the problem!"

I said, "Not all men are like that."

"Yes, you are!" she said.

"Nope."

"You better learn to listen if you want to keep living in this world!" she snapped.

Andy flashed me a look. It was a silent plea for me to let it go. Too late. I'd been listening to Rachel's bullshit for over a month, and I'd had enough. To counter her narrative, I told her about some of the psycho things my ex-girlfriends did after we broke up. As I told Rachel about those acts of revenge, she glared at me with fire in her eyes.

"So, we bring this on themselves?" she said. "Is that it?"

"That's not what I'm saying," I replied.

"What your point, then?"

"Some people don't have the skills they need to process rejection," I replied.

I thought I hit the nail on the head. I addressed the issue outside the lens of Rachel's last gender theory course. My moment of triumph was short-lived, though. As far as she was concerned, I'd just attacked her.

She said, "When someone says something about a crazy girlfriend, do you point out that men are crazy too?"

"I don't have to…"

"…Why not?"

"Because when someone tells me a crazy ex-girlfriend story, they don't say that all women are bad."

Rachel didn't have an answer for that, so she went ballistic. She started swearing at me, and Ernest joined in by calling me a "sexist pig." After I told them to "fuck off," Andy led me away from the table. As we did, Rikki stayed behind to talk to Rachel and Ernest.

I said, "Why the hell is he even talking to them?"

"He's trying to save your band!" Andy hissed.

I could tell that Andy wasn't happy with me. Although he kept his political beliefs to himself, I suspected that he might stand to the left of where I was. More to the point, he had friends in common with Ernest and Rachel, so an ugly incident like that one could have reflected poorly on him.

To me, what happened was an issue of boundaries. Rachel's boundaries were very important to her, but she thought nothing about trampling over my boundaries. With that attitude, she was a disaster waiting to happen. It definitely happened that night.

Rikki was able to keep Ernest from quitting, but I wasn't sure that was a good thing. There was no way I could gamble my band's future on a guy with a fiancé like that. Even if I behaved like a saint, that wouldn't stop her from going at me the way she did from the beginning. Sooner or later, Ernest would quit or get fired.

I came up with a plan, and it was a simple one. I was going to bust my ass to book as many shows as I could while Ernest was still in the band. That would help keep The Last Outlaws alive in the scene. While we were out playing, I would start searching for a new guitarist.

The only thing I didn't know was how long Rachel would allow Ernest to stick around.

I booked a gig at The Machine Shop, which had the potential to be huge for us.

The place used to be a dive bar and pool hall on Dort Highway. Kevin and Craig Zink bought it in March 2002 and they revamped the place. They rechristened it as "Flint's premier live music destination," and it lived up to that reputation.

Everyone was excited about our gig at The Shop. The bar consistently had a big turnout every weekend. The bands were a big part of it, but so was the vibe. It was like a hard rock nightclub that was every bit as cool as some of the big Detroit clubs.

Days before our gig, Rikki gave me a call. He told me not to freak out if Mr. Fantastic showed up at our gig. I asked Rikki if he was still talking to Mr. Fantastic, but that was a rhetorical question. I obviously knew the answer.

"He reached out to me," Rikki said.

"What for?"

"I think he wants back in the band," Rikki replied.

"Of course he does," I said.

"Why do you say that?"

"Because no other band would have him."

Rikki loved his reputation for shooting straight from the hip. That's why I thought he would appreciate my uncensored opinion of Mr. Fantastic. I got the feeling that he didn't. I suppose I'd shared my thoughts a bit too much when Mr. Fantastic was in the band.

True to Rikki's word, Mr. Fantastic slithered into The Machine Shop the night of our gig. He was humbled when he saw that we went on without him. I was happy to see him so miserable. He slunk out of the bar shortly after our set, but I knew I hadn't heard the last of him.

Rikki called me the next day and cut right to the chase. He was hot to get Mr. Fantastic back in the band. His main selling point was that Mr. Fantastic's style was a better fit for us than Ernest's playing. He was right, but I think the way Mr. Fantastic constantly flattered Rikki had

209

something to do with it, too. I honestly couldn't blame him for that.

The Last Outlaws was the J.P. Ribner show. So was Pure Spun Evil. Rikki helped make both of those things happen, but he rarely got a chance to shine being trapped behind those drums. Maybe the praise he got from Mr. Fantastic helped fill the void that my need for attention created.

Rikki said, "So? What are you gonna do?"

"I'm not sure I wanna bring him back."

"Why not?"

"That would be like going back to my crazy ex-girlfriend," I replied

"What do you mean?"

"Things will be great in the beginning, but the honeymoon phase won't last."

"You think things are any better with Ernest?" he asked.

"No," I said.

"Sometimes you have to choose between the lesser of two evils."

To prove his point, he brought up "The Infamous Diner Incident." He focused on how offended Ernest and Rachel were over what I said. I told him that the whole thing was ridiculous, and he said it wouldn't have happened with Mr. Fantastic.

"No," I replied. "He'd just have a meltdown over drink specials."

My clever reply knocked Rikki back on his heels. Too bad it didn't get me out of the jam I was in. If I really had to choose between Ernest and Mr. Fantastic, I'd have to think about it. I'd already made a lot of hasty decisions since I started my bands. Those choices didn't always work out, and I wanted to break that cycle.

Since it was an important issue, I sought Andy's counsel. I told him I didn't have time for his I-don't-want-to-get-involved nonsense; I just needed an answer. He said, "okay," so I asked him if he'd rather have Ernest or Mr. Fantastic. He said that Rikki "had some good points."

That was a slick way of answering my question, and I knew why he wanted Ernest gone. Andy was so mortified by what I said to Rachel at the diner, and it created some tension between us. He just wanted to distance himself from the whole stinking aftermath of that night. Sending Ernest packing was the best way to do that.

I thought I was immune to peer pressure. As it turned out, my desire to please my bandmates was strong enough to make me go against my better judgment.

In the end, I decided to take Mr. Fantastic back. I justified this by saying that it would save me the time of finding and training someone to replace him. The thought of facing more downtime, especially after not playing music for a decade, was my biggest fear. I called Rikki and told him that I'd take our old guitarist back on one condition.

"What's that?" Rikki asked.

"He has to apologize to me."

"That's fair."

Rikki said he'd call Mr. Fantastic, then call me back. When my phone rang, Rikki said that I should reach out to Mr. Fantastic. I said "okay," but that didn't mean that I agreed to do what Rikki said. I was just acknowledging that I heard him. Since Mr. Fantastic was the one who acted like an asshole, he'd have to call me. I knew he would if I held out long enough.

Mr. Fantastic called me the next day. After some small talk, he asked me if I spoke to Rikki. I told him that I did, so he cut to the chase. He said he was sorry for everything that happened. His excuse was that he was going through some personal stuff, and he "might have" taken it out on the band.

"You took it out on me," I said.

"I'm sorry you feel that way," he replied.

I saw what he did there. He thought he was cute with that non-apology apology. He wasn't taking any responsibility for all the nasty shit he said and did. I wanted to tell him to go fuck himself, but I'd already let Ernest go. That made it easier for me to put the good of the band before my ego. I welcomed Mr. Fantastic back, and he thanked me.

I've heard that the definition of insanity is doing the same thing over and over and expecting different results. I hoped that what I just did would be the exception to that rule.

27.
Ego Tripping

With Mr. Fantastic back in the band, I thought we should record a new CD. That would go a long way to making him feel a part of the band again.

To keep our costs down, Andy volunteered to record it. We jumped right into it by laying down the drums, bass, vocals, and rhythm guitar tracks. The next step was to lock down Mr. Fantastic's lead guitar parts. Rikki said I shouldn't be there when that went down because the argument between us was still fresh. I agreed.

When Andy cut me a copy of the progress, I was expecting something great from Mr. Fantastic. I was disappointed with what I heard. He did a decent job on the fills, but his solos felt uninspired and uninspiring. I'd heard him do better during practice, so I had no idea what happened on the CD.

I resigned myself to the fact that our CD wasn't going to be as good as could have been. It was still decent enough to put out there, so we rolled forward with it. In the meantime, I planned to book as many shows as we could to help finance the production.

At our next practice, Mr. Fantastic asked me if I listened to his guitar parts on the CD. I told him that I did, and he asked me what I thought of his guitar parts. I said he did a good job, which was true, but I didn't say he did a great job. If he was expecting me to say that, he was going to be disappointed.

He said, "Well, I bet it's good to finally have a guitarist who knows what he's doing."

"I need to hear the final copy before I form an opinion," I replied.

He got that angry scowl again, but I didn't care. He took a shot at The Kid, which I didn't appreciate. That was one reason why I refused to give him the validation he craved. I also didn't want to heap praise upon someone who phoned in his guitar solos.

After practice, I told Andy and Rikki about my conversation with Mr. Fantastic. They didn't seem too concerned about it. I got the impression that they were sick of me running to them over every little thing Mr. Fantastic said or did. It felt like they didn't have my back.

The deeper we got into recording the CD, the more problems Mr. Fantastic had.

Rikki told me that Mr. Fantastic complained about everything from the shows I booked to the amount of money he made at gigs. He also railed on and on about my alleged "egomania" while being oblivious to what I considered were some textbook narcissistic traits.

At practices, he hardly talked to anybody. He also had that angry scowl on his face the whole time. He gave me the impression that he wanted to be anywhere but my apartment, practicing the songs I wrote. He didn't even enjoy the cover songs we played, even though they were from some of his favorite bands.

The effects of Mr. Fantastic's constant complaining had everyone stressed. I wanted to tear into him, but I couldn't because he would've quit the band. Rikki was under pressure trying to keep Mr. Fantastic appeased. And there was Mr. Fantastic, pouring salt in every open wound we had, which there were many.

Even Andy, who didn't want any drama, felt it, too. He started to distance himself from the band and me. He was always the last one to show up for practice, and he hardly spoke a word while he was there. He just went through the motions with a blank look on his face. I hated to see him like that.

Since I couldn't address my issues with Mr. Fantastic, I took my frustrations out on Andy. In addition to him being distant, I never got over that "babysitter" comment he made at Sylvia Joe's. I got my revenge by lashing out at him in a very passive-aggressive way.

I focused on something that was uniquely him. It was his habit of going on tangents whenever he told a story. When he'd start to drift, he'd always say "but anyway" to bring himself back on point. It was the perfect personality trait for me to weaponize against him.

In conversations and band emails, I went out of my way to tell long stories. At the height of those word mountains, I'd say "but anyway," then wrap it up. I said it like I was joking, and even Andy thought it was funny… at first. I kept doing it until it aggravated him, then pushed it far beyond that.

I knew that I was being vicious, and it wasn't helping matters, but I wouldn't stop.

The stress caused by Mr. Fantastic affected my relationship with Rikki. Being Mr. Fantastic's handler made him go from a happy-go-lucky joker to someone who simmered with anger. It seemed like Rikki was ready to lash out at me over the smallest of things.

We almost came to blows one day over some cover songs. The tune that caused the problem was "The Weight" by The Band. It was that damn three-part backing vocal arrangement on the choruses. Trying to sing it that way would be next to impossible, so I suggested the guys just sing along with me.

"No!" Rikki said. "We're doing it exactly the way The Band did it."

"Why?" I asked.

"It's the defining part of the song."

"But we might not be able to hit it."

"We're doing it the way I said we're doing it," he growled.

"We'll see," I replied.

We breezed through the first verse, but the shit hit the fan when we got to the chorus. It was the part where the guys had to sing "you put the load right on me" a half step behind me. Our first try was a complete failure.

Rikki pushed us to do it again, and we failed that time, too. After about 50 more disastrous takes, "The Weight" was living up to its name. Since we were no closer to nailing it down, I said we should drop the song.

Rikki's face turned beet red, and his hands started to shake. I thought he was going to jump over his drums and go for my throat. It was lucky for both of us that Andy stepped in and said the song just wasn't working out. Rikki agreed, but I could tell he wasn't happy about it.

We got into it again after a charity gig at the Buell Lake Patio Bar & Grill. Rikki put our setlist together, and he spent hours making sure the ending note of each song lined up with the beginning note of the next tune. He printed up a copy for each of us at the gig, and I taped mine to the stage beneath me.

As if by fate, the bar's air conditioner crapped out the day before the show. It was like a sauna inside that place, and I was sweating like a pig halfway through our set. Right before our last song, a drop of sweat rolled into my right eye, and it stung like an angry hornet.

I looked down at the setlist and could barely make out the words. I read what I thought was our closing number and called it out on the mic. Rikki shouted something, but I couldn't make out what he said. I turned around, but he was already doing the count off. The four of us came in on the one and closed our set.

Despite the setbacks, I thought our gig was okay. There weren't a lot of people in the bar, and the lack of air conditioning had something to do with that. Everyone was in high spirits though, and we even managed to sell a couple of our old CDs.

While I was loading my gear, I saw Rikki walking toward me from the other side of the parking lot. He was moving rather quickly. When he got closer, the look on his face had all the subtlety of a rodeo bull just out of the chute.

"What the hell did you do up there?" he snarled.

"What?" I said.

"You skipped a song!"

"Which one?"

"The second to the last."

"Oh! I got sweat in my eye and…

"…I don't wanna hear it!"

"Can I finish a fuckin' sentence?" I shouted.

"No!" he bellowed. "And if you can't be professional, you have no business leading this band!"

He stormed off before I could say another word. Out of everything that happened between us, that pissed me off the most. I mean, it was bad enough that he yelled at me because I accidentally skipped a song. He made things worse when he refused to hear my side of the story.

The closer we got to finishing the CD, the more agitated Mr. Fantastic got. I didn't expect that energy to affect Rikki, but it did.

One day, Andy called me with some bad news. He said that Rikki refused to record a drum track for "Ballad of an Outlaw." It was the last song on our upcoming CD, and I didn't understand why he wouldn't do that. He always drummed to it when we played it live.

215

Andy said that Rikki told him the song "didn't need a drum part," and that was that. There was some dead air between us, and I knew what was up. He wanted a drum track on that song, and he wanted me to mention it to Rikki. That wasn't an unreasonable request since I was the leader of the band. It was my job to address the issue.

I said I'd give Rikki a call, and Andy said, "Good luck." I wondered if that was an omen. I hadn't spoken to Rikki since he yelled at me over the setlist at Buell Lake. Still, I had to address the issue with him.

When I got Rikki on the phone, I asked him why he wouldn't drum on "Ballad of an Outlaw." He said the song didn't need it. I asked him why he felt that way, and he said, "It just doesn't." I reminded him that he drummed along with it every time we played it live.

He said, "I'm not gonna budge on this."

"Okay," I said. "We'll use an electronic drum track then."

"Do that and I'll quit the band!" he snarled.

"So, you won't put a drum track down, but you'll quit if I use an electronic track?"

"That's right!" he said.

"That's stupid," I replied.

"What are you gonna do about it?"

"So, that's how it's going to be?"

"Yup!"

Rikki hung up on me, and a scalding wave of anger surged up my throat. That was the second time he blew up at me in a little over a week. Why was he being such a dick? Oh, I know. Mr. Fantastic is back in the band, and he's rubbing off on Rikki.

Threatening to quit in order to get his way was straight out of Mr. Fantastic's playbook. I was mad at Rikki for that, but I was also pissed at Andy. I wondered if he set up that confrontation between Rikki and me. I didn't have any proof of that, but I couldn't shake my suspicions.

Since I let Mr. Fantastic back into the band, my relationships with Rikki and Andy were disintegrating right in front of me. Worst of all, I felt helpless to stop it.

It had been months since we laid our tracks down, and I hadn't heard anything about our CD. I put in a call to Andy about it, but he hadn't called me back. In the meantime, Rikki called me and asked me if I was going to be at home.

216

"Yeah, I'll be around," I said.

"Good," he replied. "I'll be over in a minute."

"What's up?"

"I have something to show you," he replied.

My conversation with Rikki put me on high alert, but all I could do was wait for him. When he showed up, he handed me a piece of paper. It was an email from Mr. Fantastic to Rikki. He sent it that day, which was right before Rikki was leaving for a two-week work retreat.

I read what our guitarist had to say about me:

> "I'm sending you this cuz I've had it with our so-called singer. He's a no-talent asshole with a bad case of LSD, and he's running the band into the ground. I have my principles and I can't just sit back and stay quiet anymore.
>
> "Dude, you're the most talented drummer I ever known. Your skills are fantastic, but they're being wasted playing for that raging egomaniac. We could do SO much better if we started a band of our own. Think about it. A band founded on REAL MUSICAL TALENT! We could play whatever we want without that immature, childish loser holding us back. With your skills alone, we could get all the best musicians in the scene to join!
>
> "That's about all I have to say about this mess. The last thing I want to do is give that no-talent dipshit the attention he so desperately craves. Not my intent and I don't care to stick around for a pissing contest with someone who's so childish. All I can say is I hope you decide to leave. If you do, I'm here for anything you wanna do."

So, according to Mr. Fantastic, I was an "egotistical asshole" with "lead singer disease," aka "LSD." Those were some nasty things to say, but it wasn't a surprise. I was more upset by how comfortable he felt sharing that with Rikki. If I needed a reason to kick Mr. Fantastic out of the band again, Rikki just handed the smoking gun.

Rikki said, "Promise me something…"

"…What?"

"That you won't act on this; no phone calls, no emails, nothing."

"Why not?"

"Because I don't want you going off half-cocked," he replied.

"But I have everything I need right here in black and white!"

"I know you feel that way now, but you don't want to do something you'll regret," he said.

"Oh, I won't regret it!"

"Just promise me you won't do anything until I get back."

"But I wanna solve it now!" I said.

"I know," Rikki replied. "But it's better to wait."

"That's bullshit!"

"No. It's important that you just calm down…

"…Would you be calm if he said this shit about you?"

"He would never say that about me," Rikki said.

"Then telling me to stay calm is easy for you to say!"

"We'll get into all this when I come back," Rikki said. "Until then, I need you to promise me you won't contact him."

"What if he reaches out to me?" I asked.

"Don't answer the call or reply in any way."

I could tell by the look on his face that he was serious about this. He was right, too. No good would come from me talking to Mr. Fantastic when I was so riled up. If I did, it would be worse than the night I blew up on him. I promised Rikki that I'd keep quiet for the next two weeks, but I wasn't happy about it.

I obsessed over every nasty word in Mr. Fantastic's email. What bothered me the most was that he called "egotistical." I was worried that Andy and Rikki thought I was. It wouldn't surprise me if they did because, deep down inside, I knew it was true.

My parents told me that I was a loser so much that I believed it was true. The only time I ever felt any self-worth was when I had a microphone in my hand. That's why being in a band was so important to me. It made me feel powerful, and that power went straight to my head.

I knew I'd made this mistake because I'd did it during my Audacity days. I ended up destroying my relationships with Dan and Lily, and they were the two people I cared about the most. It was happening again with The Last Outlaws, and I was pushing Andy and Rikki away.

Instead of embracing that revelation, I wanted someone to tell me it wasn't true. A little outside validation would have immunized me from the ugly truth swimming in my subconscious like a sea serpent. Since I was feeling so pathetic and needy, I naturally called Andy.

When he answered the phone, I told him about Mr. Fantastic's email. He said Rikki already filled him in about it. I asked him if he thought I was a "raging egomaniac." All he had to do was say something, anything, to make me feel better, but he didn't. All he said was that I should wait for Rikki to get back.

My memory flashed back to the time Andy and I went to White's Bar. Like a needy child, I practically begged him for some much-needed validation. He didn't respond the way I wanted him to, and that filled my mind and heart with dark emotions. Once again, those thoughts pounded inside me like raging storm clouds.

I was sure that I was losing my band and that had me spinning out of control. If I had a shred of insight, I would have seen that. I also would have realized that the power to solve this problem had been inside me all along. All I had to do was fire Mr. Fantastic and adjust the direction of the band.

Too bad I didn't do that.

I convinced myself that Mr. Fantastic had turned Rikki and Andy against me. It wouldn't be long before all three of them quit the band. That would leave me looking like a fool just like I did when David Bierman and Handsome Dan quit Audacity. To keep that from happening, I had to get rid of them before they got rid of me.

I was about to make a huge decision. It was one that most people would take time to weigh the pros and cons before making such a decision. Not me. I wanted to be free from the stress and anxiety that gnawed at me since Mr. Fantastic rejoined the band. Pulling the plug on The Last Outlaws was the easiest way to do that.

I didn't want the guys to see how hurt I was. They would just use that to make fun of me. I decided to distance myself from them by ending things in the coldest, most impersonal way possible. I sent them all an email that read:

219

"From this moment forward, The Last Outlaws
is no more. Come get your equipment from my
apartment as soon as possible."

I clicked "send" and a warm wave of relief washed over me. I
dumped them before they could dump me. That made me the winner.

Each member of the band took the news in a different way. When
Mr. Fantastic got his gear, he was the happiest I'd ever seen him. And
why wouldn't he be? Thanks to me, he was free to pursue Rikki for
whatever half-assed musical project he had in mind.

Andy, on the other hand, asked me to drop his gear off at his
house. It seemed like a power play on his part, but I wanted to wash my
hands of the whole thing. I was happy to drive his gear over to him,
mostly because he lived close to me.

When I got to Andy's house, he didn't seem happy or sad. He said
he understood why I did what I did, and he didn't hold it against me.
He even hugged me before I left, which wasn't like him at all. I drove
away wondering who was that guy? And what did he do with the Andy
Harris I knew?

Rikki was the one who took the news the hardest. He thought he
deserved more than an email that basically said, "Come get your shit." I
understood where he was coming from, and I tried to apologize to him.
He wouldn't have it. Maybe that's why he held out so long before he
finally got his drums.

For the first time since I'd moved back home, my living room was
empty. It seemed so lonely and barren without all the guys' gear in it. I
said, "It had to be done." My voice echoed in that lifeless space.

While I was talking to empty rooms, Rikki and Mr. Fantastic were
making music together. Mr. Fantastic joined a band called "Megahertz
Affection," and he asked Rikki to come on board. That hardly surprised
me since Mr. Fantastic was Rikki's one-man cheerleading squad.

When I looked back on it, I realized that I walked head-first into the
trap Mr. Fantastic set for me. When he couldn't woo Rikki into quitting
The Last Outlaws, he kept prodding me until I finally snapped. That
made me look like the crazy one, and I didn't need any help with that.
My actions left Rikki ripe for the pickings.

I wrestled with the idea of checking out Megahertz Affection's website. The better part of me urged me to avoid it. My anger and jealousy argued against taking the high road, and the lesser part of my nature won the argument. When I clicked onto the site, one line in the band's bio jumped out at me:

> "Rick Rokowski and Andrew Partridge worked
> together in a now-defunct alt-country project."

I was sure that Mr. Fantastic did that. He knew I'd check out their page, so he took the opportunity to rub my nose in his victory. It pissed me off, but I was smart enough to stop myself from leaving this message in the website's comment section:

> "I'd rather be a defunct alt-country band
> than a de-funked power-pop group."

I'm glad I didn't leave that stupid comment. It would have made me look petty and resentful, which I was. I didn't want the world to know it, though. It still burned to know that Mr. Fantastic played me like that.

In the end, I had the last laugh. Someone close to the band told me about Mr. Fantastic's misadventures in his new band. In the beginning, he was head-over-heels in love with Megahertz Affection. Once he got comfortable, he complained about gigs and recordings, and threatened to quit the band a few times.

Things came to a boiling point one night just before a gig. More than 100 people were at the bar, which made it the biggest show the band had played to that point. For reasons no one could understand, Mr. Fantastic didn't want to play it.

In the parking lot of the bar, Mr. Fantastic started whining to Rikki about the gig. He said, "What is this show going to do for us?" Rikki tried talking to him about it, and Mr. Fantastic got nasty with Rikki. That was a big mistake on his part!

Rikki told Mr. Fantastic to play the show or get the fuck out of the band. Mr. Fantastic allegedly said, "You can't fire me because I quit!" I thought that was hilarious, but not surprising. It was just Mr. Fantastic being Mr. Fantastic.

There was an irony to this whole thing. When Mr. Fantastic acted up in The Last Outlaws, Rikki defended his actions. In Megahertz

Affection, Rikki finally saw what it was like to be the target of Mr. Fantastic's seething animosity. It was no surprise to me that Rikki reacted the way that he did when Mr. Fantastic came for him.

In the end, I thought it was sad that things ended the way they did for Rikki and Mr. Fantastic. Just kidding. Hearing that Rikki kicked him out of Megahertz Affection was fucking hilarious!

A burning thirst for knowledge pushed me to revisit the subject of narcissism.

I researched it for the first time after I kicked Mr. Fantastic out of the band. When I read about narcissism, it felt oddly familiar to me outside of my experiences with Mr. Fantastic. When I read about it again, I realized where I'd seen those unhealthy personality traits.

Narcissism had surrounded me my entire life.

I always knew something was wrong with my parents, but I couldn't define it. Learning about narcissism gave me the language and knowledge to put their destructive behavior into context. My entire childhood was a case study of narcissistic abuse. It was almost like the authors of the books I read had written my life story.

Mom and Dad were possessed by a group of demons. Those infernal legions turned my life into the seventh layer of Hell. Verbal, emotional, and physical abuse were regular parts of my upbringing. That's why I nicknamed my childhood home "Trauma Central."

My parents' cruelty conditioned me to always feel ashamed. It became easy for other people to trigger those toxic emotions inside of me. Whenever they did, the flashback was so overwhelming that I would do anything to escape it. That's why I was so averse to conflict as a bandleader.

I realized that my parents were the ones who ruined my bands. It was all in how they raised me. Knowing this sent me into a highly emotional state. I wrote a song, which is what I tend to do when that happens. It was 100 percent hardcore punk.

"Trauma Central"

My inner child is wounded and scarred
Beaten, battered, bloodied and marred
I'm still trying to break these bars

222

At Trauma Central

That Hell house was my childhood home
Where the wounds stab straight to the bone
The only safe space was to be alone
At Trauma Central

Hello Mom, it's your pride and joy
Your infantilized baby boy!
Hello Dad, whattya say?
It's your loser son who you pushed away

My inner child is wounded and scarred
Beaten, battered, bloodied and marred
I'm still trying to break these bars
At Trauma Central

Swallow the pain until I choke
Protect the lie, that one sick joke
This haunting is ancestral
Crush my soul, destroy my dreams
Then they feast upon my tortured screams
The demons here at Trauma Central
At Trauma Central

PART THREE

2004-PRESENT

28.
Mr. Wonderful
Goes to Nastyville

I crashed and burned after I broke up The Last Outlaws. I'm talking total flameout. The first couple of months after it ended felt like torture because I still yearned to be performing in front of a crowd.

To stay on track, I dove headfirst into everything I'd been neglecting. I buckled down at my job. I also invested in a 401K and started going to the gym. When things eventually came into focus, I decided to get my love life back on track.

When I was younger, I tried to make whoever I dated the next Mrs. Ribner. That was desperate on my part, and it always ended in disaster. To make up for my shabby romantic record, I dated as many women as I could without getting too serious. It was the only way I'd find what I really wanted.

It only took me nearly two years and many dates to find the one.

In March 2008, I met a woman named Rosemary Kondraciuk. Her alluring blue eyes and golden hair caught my eye. She's Polish, and I'm part-Polish too, so I thought that was cool. The hot blond from Detroit also had the quickest wit I'd ever seen, and her intelligence was off the charts.

There was only one thing about Rose that took some getting used to. As a Taurus, she lived up to the bullish qualities of that zodiac sign. In other words, she was brutally blunt. In our first few arguments, I felt like an unlucky rodeo rider who'd been thrown and trampled.

In the heat of the moment, I didn't appreciate her brutal honesty. After calming down and thinking about what she said, I had an immense amount of respect for her. That's because I realized that her unique brand of unfiltered truth was what I needed.

Rose didn't say the things she said to hurt me. She was painfully honest with me because I needed to hear it to become the best version of myself. And she didn't want me to achieve that for what it might do for her. Rose saw that I was suffering from my dysfunctional upbringing. She was the first person who cared about me enough to help me overcome that.

It didn't take long for me to know that this tough-talking Taurus was the one for me.

My life did a 180 after Rose and I became serious. Instead of bumming around dive bars in Flint, I spent my weekends with her. It was a nice change.

My addiction to music reared its ugly head just when I got comfortable with our new routine. That little monkey on my back started digging its nails into my flesh while it chattered in my ear. It was too loud to ignore, so I tried to negotiate with it. The monkey only wanted one thing, though.

I had to give that annoying little primate a reality check. I couldn't do music anymore because Andy and Rikki weren't going to help me. That didn't silence the monkey's horrifying shrieks. The noise got so bad that I told Rose that I wished I could record another CD.

"Then do it," she replied.

"I don't know…"

"…Why not?"

"Because I'd be setting myself up for disappointment."

"If you have that mindset, you will," she replied.

I couldn't argue with her logic, so I told her I'd think about it. It was my best attempt to put the monkey's demands on the back burner. That didn't stop it from yammering, but I managed to muffle its cries enough so I could focus on other things.

Life went on until our routine was interrupted late one Saturday morning. Rose came into the room and said, "I think I'm pregnant, and my ex-husband is coming over." In my half-awake state, I combined both of those sentences in my mind. I jumped up and shouted, "What the fuck?" She realized how that sounded and assured me that those two things weren't connected.

That was a small relief, but it put an end to my sleep-in day.

After her ex-husband left with his kids, Rose and I talked about the first part of what she said. She'd been throwing up the last few days, but at 40, she thought getting pregnant was no longer possible. When she vomited again one morning, her mom said, "You're pregnant." A package of pregnancy tests proved that mother knows best.

I said, "Well, I'm glad I didn't record anything."

"Why?" Rose replied.

"Because we're gonna need every dime when the baby comes."

Rose said it was the perfect time to record. I was still living in Flint, and I had a few extra dollars in my pocket. Once the baby was born and we bought a house, I might not be able to record for a while. That encouragement pushed me to pursue my crazy dream one more time.

By then, I shifted my focus back to punk. There was only one person I wanted to work with, and that was Andy Harris. I didn't think he'd want to record me again, though. I said this to Rose, and she asked me why.

I said, "He'll probably say 'no.'"

"Will that kill you?"

"No…"

"…Then what's the problem?"

"Nothing, I guess."

"Okay then," she said.

"I'll give him a call," I replied.

I couldn't believe I was reaching out to Andy. Would he be okay with it? Or would he go cold on me? It was the not knowing that made me nervous.

Since I didn't know how Andy would react, I sent him an email. I worked up the courage to type something along the lines of, "Hey. How's it going?" If he was going to shoot me down, it would be easier to deal with that way.

I clicked "send," and Andy responded in a positive manner. That turned into a short conversation where we got caught up on each other's lives. After a while, he said I should give him a call, so I did. About 10 minutes into our conversation, he asked me if I had a music project in the works.

I said, "You saw that one coming a mile away, didn't you?"

"Let's just say I know you," he replied.

I described my project as "harnessing the power and fury of Pure Spun Evil without all the anger and rage." He said it sounded good, then asked me if I had anyone to record it. I told him I had some money saved up for some studio time.

He said, "I wouldn't charge you to record it."

"But you deserve to get paid for your time," I said.

"You have a kid on the way…"

"…Yeah, but still."

"Seriously," he said. "I don't mind."

"I'd love to work with you, but I'd feel bad if I didn't pay you."

"Maybe you can get me the student version of the software I need to record you."

"How much is that?" I asked.

"I think it's like $75."

"Okay!" I replied.

It wasn't like me to turn down free studio time, but I had a reason for wanting to pay him. Over the years, he and I started a few projects that never got finished. I didn't want that to happen again. I thought that if I paid him, he'd have the incentive to see my project through to the end.

Andy asked me who I wanted on guitar and bass. I told him I'd like him to play bass, and I mentioned a couple of guys we knew for guitar. He said he could probably get at least one of them on board.

He asked me who I wanted to play drums. I said programming some drum tracks would be the easiest way to get that done. He didn't like that idea, which wasn't a surprise. Even though he programmed drum tracks for his techno songs, I knew he preferred live drums for rock projects.

I said, "I don't know any drummers who want to work with me."

He said, "What about Rikki?"

"I haven't talked to him since… you know."

Andy said that he and Rikki kept in touch, which was an understatement. The two of them became close friends after I broke up The Last Outlaws. Andy said that the last time they talked, Rikki asked about me. Then he chuckled.

I said, "What's so funny?"

"Don't take this the wrong way…"

"…Take what?"

"When I talked to Rikki, he asked me if I'd talked to 'Mr. Wonderful' lately."

"Mr. Wonderful?" I asked. "What did he mean by that?"

"I think he was just goofing around."

I laughed then said, "Yeah, that sounds like him."

I might have played it off to Andy, but I was offended by Rikki's comment. It was way too similar to "Mr. Fantastic." Was Rikki suggesting that I had the same narcissistic tendencies that I suspected our old guitarist of having? It sure felt like it.

Andy said, "So? You gonna give him a call?"

"Maybe…"

"You should," he said.

"Okay," I said. "It will be good to work with him again."

"That's what I was thinking," Andy added.

I didn't have any anxiety about reaching out to Rikki. Yes, he called me "Mr. Wonderful," but he still asked about me. He probably missed jamming with me as much as I missed jamming with him. Plus, my call with Andy went well, so I figured Rikki and I would be fine.

He wasn't surprised to hear from me. I did catch him off guard when I introduced myself as "Mr. Wonderful" though. We laughed about it then Rikki cut to the chase. He said he'd play drums on my project, but he needed to get some things off his chest.

"What's that?" I asked.

"It's about the way you broke up the band," he replied.

"What about it?"

"What the hell were you thinking?"

"Honestly, I don't know…"

"…I told you to wait two weeks," he continued. "Two weeks, then we could deal with the issue together."

"I know…"

"…Then the next thing I know, I get an email that says the band is done."

Rikki was really going in on me, but I didn't argue with him. When I detonated the band, I was only thinking about my feelings. He showed me how my decision affected other people, namely him. When he finished, all I could say was, "I'm sorry." To his credit, he accepted my apology.

He asked me if there was anything I needed to discuss. I didn't bother to mention that I was upset about him joining a band with Mr. Fantastic. He already knew how I felt about that. I had something more

230

important to discuss.

I said, "Why did you blow up at me for no reason?"

"What do you mean?"

I reminded him of the times he exploded out of nowhere. I vividly remembered those incidents, so I had plenty of details to share with him. I also explained how it sucked to be on the receiving end of that, especially since I didn't know where his anger came from.

He said, "That was all your fault."

"What?"

"If I yelled at you, you must've done something that pissed me off."

"Seriously?" I said.

"That's right," he replied. "And if you piss me off on this project, I'll do it again."

"I'm sorry you feel that way," I said.

"Look," he said. "I'm doing you a favor here..."

"Okay..."

"...So, you're gonna have to deal with the way I do things."

I should have pushed back on that because Rikki was wrong. If I did say something that pissed him off back then, he should have told me right away. Blowing up at me days or weeks after the incident didn't solve anything. It just made me feel like I was the victim of another one of his outbursts over trivial things.

As strongly as I felt about that, I swallowed my anger and my pride and said nothing. It was all for the sake of getting my songs recorded.

It felt good to be working with Andy again.

We put down some rough guitar, bass, and vocal tracks for each of my songs. This would give the guys something to work with. When Andy came back with the other musicians' parts, I was blown away. I couldn't believe how fast, hard, and powerful those tunes were.

With everything in place, it was time for me to drop my final vocal tracks. It took the better part of a few nights, and Andy coaxed my best performance out of me. I was excited about how everything was coming along. After we finished, he and I discussed the project as he walked me to the door.

I said, "I can't wait to get this out there!"

"I wanted to talk to you about that," he replied.

"What's up?"

"I think some of the songs need to be re-recorded."

"Why?"

"I'm not happy with them."

"But they sound great," I said.

"I think I could do better."

I started freaking out, but I managed to keep it to myself. I didn't think there was anything wrong with the songs. They just needed to be mixed and mastered. I told him that we'd talk about it later.

My thoughts started racing as I drove home that night. Somewhere between Andy's house and mine, I convinced myself that he was trying to sabotage my project. It was his way of getting back at me for breaking up the band.

When I got home, I called Rose in a panic. She told me to stop freaking out over something that probably was a misunderstanding. She then urged me to call Andy and discuss it with him before my paranoia made things worse. I came up with a less-confrontational solution.

I decided not to call or email Andy for a while. If the project was important to him, he'd reach out to me. A couple of weeks went by, and I hadn't heard from him. At that point, I became even more convinced that he had no intention of finishing my project.

That weekend, Rose came to Flint, and we checked out a new bar/restaurant. As soon as we sat down, someone shouted my name from across the room. I turned my head to see Rikki walking toward us. When he got to our table, he asked me how the project was going.

I said, "Talk to Andy."

Rikki said, "He told me to talk to you."

"The ball is in his court at this point," I replied.

Rikki paused like he didn't know what to say to me. He recovered quickly and told me I should call Andy. My response was cold and noncommittal, and he picked up on it. After he walked back to his table, Rose asked me why I didn't tell him about my conversation with Andy.

I said, "It doesn't matter."

"What do you mean?"

"They're best friends," I replied. "Who's he gonna believe?"

"It seems like he's excited about the project, though," she said.

"That could all be an act..."

"...An act?"

"Yeah! To set me up."

"You sound insane!"

"Andy saying he wants to start over from scratch is insane."

"Then tell Rikki about it!"

"My credibility is shot with those two," I said.

"If that was true, they wouldn't be working on your project," she said.

"If Andy is trying to sabotage me, I don't wanna look like the idiot who didn't see it coming."

"I think you're making a mistake."

"Rikki will tell Andy that he saw me," I said. "If Andy is serious about this project, he'll call."

The one thing she and I agreed on was that we should have dinner somewhere else. The restaurant's menu didn't have anything that looked good, and I was upset. With Rikki sitting about 20 feet away, I didn't want him to hear anything else I might have said that night.

I was sure that Andy was screwing me over. I hadn't heard from him in weeks; no phone call or email. I was proud of myself for not feeling needy and calling him a million times like I used to do. While I was patting myself on the back, I realized that I paid him $75 for a project that never happened.

Since I didn't have a CD of finished songs, I needed to get my money back. I emailed Andy a message that read, "Do you want to send my refund through the mail? Or should I come pick it up?" He responded about 20 minutes later with, "What refund?" That told me all I needed to know.

I didn't respond to Andy. I called Rose instead and told her that Andy just used me to get the money for that software. She said I had no way of knowing that, but I disagreed. I was sure that he was going to use that program I bought to record his real friends' music projects.

Rose said, "You sound like a crazy conspiracy theorist."

"You don't know him like I do."

"You're gonna do what you wanna do no matter what I say," she said.

"I already did," I replied.

"I know," she said. "That's the problem."

Even though he wasn't there, I heard my dad's words ringing in my ear. He was telling me for the thousandth time that my music was a waste. I heard it over and over again. That triggered the shame/rage

233

cycle that had dominated my life.

I was upset with Andy, but I was furious with myself for being so gullible. To keep from going crazy, I searched for something positive from the experience. All I could say was that if it took losing $75 to learn that people can't be trusted, I got off cheap.

I said this to anyone who would listen, and I was blind to how crazy I looked when I did.

My punk project died on the vine, but I still wanted to record a CD.

I had another idea, but it meant going back to outlaw country. That was something I didn't want to do, but time wasn't on my side. I needed to get something done right away, and all the rock musicians I knew were friends with Andy and Rikki. Like it or not, I had to do outlaw country if I wanted to do anything at all.

My idea was to record some dirty country songs and call the project "Nastyville." I wish I'd thought of that name, but I got it from a Nashville local. I was in "Music City" on a work trip, and I went to a party store to grab some Pabst Blue Ribbon. Too bad the brew wasn't in the cooler.

I said, "The country music capital of the world doesn't have any PBR?"

Someone said, "This here's Nastyville!"

He pronounced it "nah-shtee-veel." I peeked over the rack of potato chips and saw a dude in his 20s. He had a wild and untamed patch of greasy brown hair and a tracheotomy hole in his throat. Rather than cover up that gaping chasm in his neck, he had a ring of fire tattooed around it.

"There's no PBR?" I asked.

"They're too good for that in Nastyville," he replied.

I knew what he was getting at. What Nashville gained in money it lost in its soul. While that might be, I got a kick out of his nickname for the city. Although he didn't know it, that dude with the flaming tracheotomy hole gave me the perfect name for my country music project.

My idea was hardly groundbreaking. Dirty country songs had been around for decades. There was Garry Lee and Showdown's "Rodeo Song," and August Campbell's "I-95 The Asshole Song," just to name a few. My only claim to fame was that no one else was doing it in Flint.

So, I had a vision, a name, and some money in the bank. The latter was particularly useful since recording with Andy was no longer an option. I did the only thing I could do, which was to call Mike Mathews at Atlantis Recording Studio. He was happy to do the job.

I found some talented local musicians to help me make it happen. The first person I recruited was a drummer. His name is Lance Dey, but I call him "The Local Legend." He's been drumming for Flint punk bands for decades and is practically an icon in the scene.

I rounded out the Nastyville rhythm section with a bassist named Dennis Perkins. He played for Bullhonky Deluxe, the hottest country band in Flint at that time. Even though he was very busy, he made the time to help me out. Best of all, he didn't charge me a dime for his services.

The last member of my team was a guy named Wiz Feinberg. He was one of only a few steel guitar players in the Flint area. He worked as a hired gun for any band that wanted his pedal steel skills and could afford his rates. I was more than happy to pay him to have that authentic country slide picking on my songs.

The first one to join me in the studio was The Local Legend. My acoustic guitar parts and his drums would lay the foundation for Dennis and Wiz to build on. I wish I could say that his studio time went off without an issue, but The Local Legend managed to put a hitch in the project's giddyap.

Before our studio date, he came over to my apartment and practiced the songs. As we did, I saw why he was such a popular drummer. After we got done, he said he charges $5 an hour for his studio time. I thought that price was more than fair, and we sealed the deal with a handshake.

Once we were in the studio, he knocked out all six songs in one or two takes. When I went to pay him, he stood there with his hand out toward me, palm up. I peeled off the amount that corresponded with his rate multiplied by his time in the studio. He counted it then told me I was short.

"What do you mean?" I asked.

"I charge for practice time, too."

I felt blindsided and I was tempted to react in anger. I wasn't mad about the money, though. His rate was so low that the practice time only added $15 to the bill. I was pissed that he wasn't upfront about charging for practice, too.

I also didn't like the way he brought it up. It was like he wanted to make me look bad in front of Mike or something. At least that's how it seemed in the heat of the moment.

I said, "You should've told me that ahead of time."

"Yeah. Okay."

"I'm serious," I replied.

The Local Legend just stood there with his hand out like a wicked imp. I shook my head then forked over the cash, including his last-minute practice fee. At that point, our business was done so I left him alone to lug his entire drum set up the steep flight of stairs.

I had 100 copies of *Welcome to Nastyville*, and I was determined to sell them all.

When I tried, I ran face-first into the same problem that many indie artists experience. Too many people expected me to give them my CD instead of them paying for one. I spent too much on this disc to turn it into a freebie. I did manage to sell about 35 copies, though.

I ran into another problem while selling my discs. Too many people told me that they liked my punk stuff, but they weren't into country music. That sucked because I wasn't close to my break-even point. At the very least, I wanted to earn back the money I spent on the project.

I never had these problems selling CDs at our shows. That's when it hit me. If I didn't want this investment to be a huge waste, I'd have to put a band together. Without Andy and Rikki, that wasn't going to be easy.

29.
Plans Aborted

To build The Nastyville Band, I hung a musicians-wanted flyer in music stores around Flint. Since it was 2008, I also posted ads on BandMix.com and CraigsList.com. I hated that approach because it was like ringing the dinner bell for every deadbeat, loser, and weirdo in the music scene.

The first person who called me was a bass player nicknamed "Speck." He told me that he listened to my songs online and described my style as, "Real outlaw country, not that pussy sellout shit those asshole country bands play." That was rather flattering, so I shot him a reply. He responded the next day:

> "Yo, I deleated my facebook and myspace and
> hardly check my email. Holla on the tele.
> Peace."

I called Speck and went straight to his voicemail. I left him a message but never heard back from him. The whole thing could have ended right there, but I was desperate to build a band. I called him three days later and went to his voicemail again.

Just when I was ready to give up on him, he reached out to me over email. That was odd because he wanted me to "holla on the tele." I figured he was at work and couldn't call me. Whatever the case was, Speck's message was short and sweet:

> "Hey man, we got some phone tag happinin. I can
> hook those tunes up we just gotta hook up...lol. I'll
> call again this eavnin."

While that sounded promising, he never called me back. Because

237

of that, I thought of Speck as "The Phantom." He was a hazy, flickering shadow in the corner of the eye. When I turned my head to get a better look, he'd disappear. While that made a good ghost story, it wouldn't help me build my band.

Since I didn't hear from him in a couple of weeks, I wrote The Phantom off. That was exactly the time when he returned to haunt my inbox. He told me that the uncertainty of the Obama economy cost him his job, and he had to move out of state. I wished him the best of luck and scratched him off my list.

Just when The Phantom disappeared like a whisper on a summer breeze, he came back yet again. When I got home from work one day, his message was waiting in my inbox. He told me that he decided to stay in the Flint area after all and said I should hit him up about my project.

Against my better judgment, I gave him a call. All the hope I had in having The Phantom play in my band evaporated when my call went straight to voicemail. I didn't bother to leave him a message. It was up to him to call me back.

True to the nickname I gave him, The Phantom ghosted me. I never heard from him again, and I no longer cared.

I was shocked when Lance Dey, aka "The Local Legend," called me about my project. I hadn't spoken to him since that day at the studio. I was willing to keep an open mind, though. It wasn't like I had a line of drummers beating down my door.

We met at a bar that was halfway for both of us. He was fashionably late because he's The Local Legend, of course. I gave him a copy of *Welcome to Nastyville*, and he didn't' seem impressed. He'd been playing on tapes and CDs since the 1980s, so I didn't expect him to be starstruck over my six-song EP.

He said, "Did you find a drummer yet?"

"No," I replied. "Do you know somebody who wants the gig?"

"Yeah," he said. "Me!"

"Aren't you in a band right now?"

He told me that situation "fell through." I asked how much he expected to make per gig, and what nights he could jam. He expected no more than a fourth of what the band got paid, assuming there would be four members. As far as practices, he said he was available in the evenings.

"How about this Thursday?" I asked.

"What time?"

"Seven..."

"No problem," he said.

"Cool," I replied. "But there's just one thing..."

"...What?"

"I can't pay you for practice."

He laughed, then said he doesn't charge for practice. It was like that awkward situation at the studio never happened. While I thought that was weird, I was glad to hear that practices weren't going to cost me. It would've been hard for The Local Legend to collect anyway since he didn't bother to show up that night.

I sent him an email, messaged him on Facebook, and even left a voicemail on his phone. The Local Legend never replied. I found that funny because he bragged about being a "professional musician." That night, he pulled a no-call/no-show, which screamed "rookie move."

I eventually found out why he stood me up. A guitarist from a local country-rock band told me that they recruited him for their project. His audition with them was the same night as my practice. Once a mercenary, always a mercenary, I guess.

I got a real blast from the past when Charles Watkins, aka "Chaz the Spaz" called me. Yes, the same Chaz the Spaz who sided with Wally when he broke up Death Symbol. I hadn't spoken to him since high school; but now, he wanted to be in The Nastyville Band.

People who say I hold on to grudges are wrong. I latch on to them with the locking jaws of a pit bull and refuse to let go. Despite the intensity of my feelings, I agreed to meet him at the bar to hear him out. It was against my better judgment.

Since I hadn't seen Chaz since high school, I didn't know what to expect. That night, he was wearing a studded leather jacket, torn jeans, and an Exploited T-shirt that was very punk rock circa 1986. While his fashion sense hadn't changed since high school, he looked like Hunter S. Thompson on the bad end of a week-long bender.

I took a seat next to Chaz at the bar, and he caught me up on his life after high school. He'd moved to Peoria, Illinois, and shared a house with a group of local crust-punks. He and his friends partied with all the big acts that came through the area. All of his tales started with how

239

much he drank that night, and they ended with him humiliating himself as a result.

He eventually came around to the reason he asked me to meet him at the bar. He wanted to play bass for my band. I told him that I didn't know he liked country, which caused him to launch into the sordid tale about the night he met Hank Williams III in Bloomington.

Chaz said, "His tour manager kept pouring me beers, man."

"Oh yeah?" I said.

"Yeah," he replied. "And I got so drunk, I ended up puking all over Hank's boots."

"What happened then?"

"They threw me off the bus!"

"Yeah," I said. "I can see that."

"I passed out behind a dumpster, and my friends drove 40 minutes to pick me up in the morning."

"Sounds like you had some good friends," I said.

"Those Peoria crust-punks were the most generous people I've ever known!" he replied.

"Cool."

"But to make a long story short, I'd like to play bass for you," he said.

My mind ran through the pros and cons of working with Chaz. The pros were simple: he played bass. The cons were a more exhaustive list based on the person I knew in high school. But was he still the same person who screwed me over 22 years ago?

Finally, I said, "I can squeeze you in for an audition."

We transitioned into more small talk. Most of it centered on the state of the Flint music scene. We agreed that the younger generation wasn't punk, and most of the new bands sucked. Out of nowhere, he said that he heard that Rose and I were expecting.

I said, "Yeah. In March."

"What do you think about abortion?"

"What?"

"What's your opinion on abortion?"

"Why'd you ask me that?"

Chaz puffed up his chest and proudly proclaimed that he's very pro-abortion. He tried to justify his statement by saying, "Death is just a part of life, man." His campaign speech didn't stop there. He went on to say that aborting a fetus is like pulling out an ingrown hair.

240

I said, "Are you serious?"

"My girlfriend's uterus has been scraped more times than a car window in winter," he replied.

Back in high school, Chaz never knew when to shut the fuck up. He clearly hadn't matured over the past two decades. Why else would he go on a rant about abortion when he knew I had a child on the way? Then I realized that he was shit-testing me.

I said, "You can forget about that audition."

"Huh?"

I got up from the barstool and headed for the door. From behind me, he shouted, "So that's how it's going to be?" Hopefully, the slamming of the door behind me gave him the closure he needed. It worked for me.

Just when I thought there was no one left in the Flint scene, I got a call from a rockabilly bassist. The guy's name is Gary Truss, and his band opened for The Last Outlaws at a show in Metro Detroit. He said that band broke up and he wanted to do something with me.

It would be great to jam with Gary, but he played rockabilly and I played outlaw country. Both genres have some things in common, but they have their differences too. The biggest one is how the bass guitar is played. Rockabilly basslines run up and down a blues scale while outlaw country uses the classic two-step.

"It's not a problem at all," he replied.

"So, you don't mind playing a country bass?

"No," he said.

We made plans for me to stop by on a Thursday night. It was a long drive because he lived in the northernmost part of Saginaw County. If it resulted in me picking him up as my bass player, my time and gas money would have been a good investment.

We went through many of my songs, and Gary nailed them. He used a standard, two-step bass part with plenty of fills between the chord changes. It was exactly what the songs needed. Once we finished, he asked me if we could go through them one more time.

On our second run, Gary used rockabilly runs. I didn't say anything at first because I wanted to hear how it sounded. After three or four tunes, I could tell it wasn't working. I stopped and asked him why he decided to change things up like that.

He said that the country style was "pussy bass," and I should switch to rockabilly. Then he started to tell me all the changes I needed to make to become the rockabilly player he wanted me to be. That was a lot different than when he said he was okay with playing outlaw country. "Gary Goosechase" picked up on my disappointment.

He said, "Thanks for contacting me about your project, but I won't have the time to do this."

"I wish you would've figured that out before you called me," I replied.

"It's late and I have to work in the morning," he replied.

"Whatever," I said.

Some guy named Robert Cullen gave me a call one day. He played drums for Whistlin' Dixie, which was a band he was in with his dad and brother. Robert said he was looking for something more long-term, and he said my project "sounded interesting."

I vetted him with the usual questions about availability, expectations, and if he was cool with playing originals. His answers checked out no better or worse than anyone else who answered my ad, so I asked him to stop by.

When Tom showed up, he had his father Jim with him. I thought it was weird that a dude in his 30s would bring his dad to an audition. The only thing I could figure was that the old man was there for moral support. Since I'd already gone that far, I figured I might as well see it through.

As we played my originals, Robert's dad stood there with his arms folded across his chest. I felt his cold blue eyes scrutinizing me from across the room. When Robert and I finished, it was Papa Jim who did all the talking.

He said, "We need someone to fill in on rhythm guitar and I think you'd be good for that."

"I got my own thing going," I replied.

The old man pulled a piece of paper and handed it to me. It was a list of cover songs that Whistlin' Dixie played. He asked me how many of them I could learn in a week. I looked over at Robert, who just sat there with a stupid look on his face, so returned my gaze to Papa Jim. At that point, there was only one thing I wanted to say to those two.

"Get the fuck out of my house."

My attempts to recruit my band from Flint-area musicians was an epic failure. I didn't see a solution, and I shared my feelings with Rose because she was my rock.

She said, "Since you're moving down here, you should find some musicians in this area."

She was right. Flint was my past. Trying to recruit a band from there was like looking at mile markers in my rear-view mirror. I needed to focus on what was in front of me, and that was the life we were building in Metro Detroit.

I immediately put the Rose Kondraciuk plan into full effect. I changed my musicians-wanted flyer and online ads to reflect my future zip code and hung them in Metro Detroit guitar shops. I also used BandMix.com and CraigsList.com.

The first call I got was from a guy who introduced himself as "Tim Holland, just like the country." He was a hair metal guy from the '80s, and he said that my flyer "spoke to him." He had the time to be in a working band because a back injury forced him into early retirement. I emailed him the files of my songs, and we made plans to get together.

That weekend, I hauled my gear to Tim's house and set up in his basement. He'd been listening to my songs for a week, so he was familiar with them. When we jammed, his hard-hitting style was a lot like Rikki's, so it felt like I was picking up where I left off.

I said, "I'll have to find a lead guitarist and bassist so we can start playing out."

"I'll be here," he replied.

I got an email from a bassist named Nick Bellender. He checked off all the boxes as far as musical style and experience were concerned. He also said he was cool with playing originals. My only concern was that he lived in Port Huron, but he said he didn't mind the drive.

I asked Nick if he could jam with us that Saturday. He told me to send him a setlist, so I put together some outlaw country songs. I also added a few rock tunes like "Dead Flowers" by the Rolling Stones, and "Used to Love Her" by Guns N' Roses. I sent him the list, and he responded right away:

"i gotta be honest up front... although i am not
the main singer/song-writer/frontman, i have a

243

strong vision of my own, and want to be true to
it. Songs like "i used to love her" and "dead flowers", although great in their own right, are not
on my radar. personally, i'd like to do several
hank sr. tunes, and a good variety of outlaw,
50's-60's obscure and not so obscure country,
etc. especially in a competitive market... i believe a band has to go for, and project an image...and stick with it. (which it seem like you
are trying to do)... bar crowd, or not. once you
go off the rails, (the crowds expectations change)
and you're in a category with every other country
and classic rock, etc. band and just fall into the
abyss. Dont wanna sound like i'm hard to get
along with... i'm just the opposite... but, like
you, i know what i want and what i wanna do...
(even if i'm just the lowly stand up bass guy) lol.
Having regurgitated all that...see you saturday."

Son of a bitch! Nick hadn't even auditioned yet, and he was already
trying to tell me how to run my band. And the false humility of his
"lowly-stand-up-bass-guy" bullshit was equally disgusting. My response
was swift and to the point:

"I appreciate your honesty regarding your vision
for your musical career. That said, as the frontman
(and bank account) for this project, I cannot allow
someone else's vision to overshadow my own. Most
country bars want paint-by-the- numbers, modern
country that their patrons can dance to. They're not
particularly interested in bands with original songs,
and/or those that are limited to the golden oldies.
My focus is my original music, which is absolutely,
unequivocally outlaw country. These go over in rock
bars where the crowd is also familiar with popular
outlaw country tunes. The rock covers in the setlist
appeal to these crowds. My vision, while not compromised, must also be tempered with the wisdom
of what I know is gonna work. The songs in my set-

list have been proven time and time again in bar after
bar. Having said that, I'll see ya Saturday."

"Nagging Nick" was a no-show, and I wasn't surprised. He flexed
his muscles, but I put him in check. There was no way he could jam
with us after that because his ego wouldn't have allowed it. To save his
wounded pride, he disappeared without even so much as a whimper.
What else could he do?

I shared the bad news with Tim. He did his best to seem upbeat,
but I could tell he was disappointed. Like me, he wanted to put a band
together so we could start playing shows. He said we should take a
break and come at it again next weekend.

"I don't want to lose the momentum we've built," I said.

"Don't worry," he replied. "I'm not going anywhere."

On the day we were scheduled to practice, I loaded my gear and
drove to Tim's house. When he answered the door, I could tell that
something wasn't right. He seemed upset and on the verge of tears.

I said, "Is everything okay?"

"I'm really sorry, but I can't do this anymore," he said.

"Why?" I asked.

"I got some bad news from my doctor…"

"…Your back?"

"Yeah," he said. "I have to get steel rods put in!"

"Sorry to hear that, man."

"And the worst part about it is that I can never play drums again!"

"Oh my God!"

"Yeah," he replied. "And I want you to know that it's not you…"

"…I get that."

"I really liked working with you."

"Thanks," I replied.

I shook his hand and wished him the best. When I lugged my gear
back to the truck, Tim followed me outside. He continued to apologize
to me, and I told him I understood; his health had to come first. He
wouldn't let up with the apologies, which made me wonder if he was
trying to convince himself instead of me.

Tim and I stayed connected on Facebook, and I was glad we did.
One day, he messaged me an invite to a gig at the Token Lounge in

245

Westland. He was drumming for a hair metal cover band. It turns out that the only problem he had with his backbone is that he lacked one when it came to telling me he didn't want to jam with me anymore.

I clicked the "message" button and typed, "Congratulations on your miraculous recovery!" The only reply I got was discovering that he had blocked me.

Finding the right people for my band turned out to be a circle jerk without a happy ending.

After my initial anger wore off, I crashed head-first into a deep depression. Even though I thought I took all the rights steps, I couldn't put a band together in two counties. All I succeeded in doing was attracting a group of circus freaks.

Music scenes are filled with those types of players. Some have the dream but not the drive, while others have egos that exceed their talent. Worst of all are the passive-aggressive losers. Those are the idiots who don't have bands of their own, but they're very ambitious on other people's dime and time.

After having that string of bad luck, I thought it was best to take a break from the band thing for a while.

30.
A Rock and a Hard Place

In April 2010, the only thing I focused on was getting our condo.

I was excited about my upcoming life change. I naturally shared the news on Facebook, which is what most people do in these situations. My cousin read my post and asked me to meet him at The Loft that night. I thought it would be the perfect send-off of my downtown days.

When I got to the bar, some of my excitement drained from me. My old nemesis Billy Rocca, aka "Dad Glasses," was doing a solo performance. It was just him, his acoustic guitar, and harmonica playing all of his whiny, broken-hearted ballads. Instead of leaving, I made a beeline to my cousin's table.

I sat down between my cousin and his friend, Libby Fraumilch. I didn't know her personally, but I knew of her. She fancied herself as Flint rockabilly royalty, and she carried herself with a regal air. She also made it clear that she detested having to sit next to a mere commoner such as myself. It was as if I were nothing but a loathsome bug to be squashed beneath her pinup girl pumps.

As Dad Glasses played, I studied the faces of the crowd as they sang along with him. They adored him, and that didn't surprise me. He'd been a fixture in the scene since at least the '90s. Those kids grew up listening to him play at The Local 432. That's why his songs had such an impact on them.

It became obvious to me that Dad Glasses was a hometown hero. That was something that I could never be. I never kept a band together long enough to make the kind of impact that Dad Glasses did. That night, I realized that I was more than a little jealous of him for that.

Dad Glasses finished his set, and people started shouting ironic song requests. They were saying the typical things, such as "Slayer!" and "Skynyrd!" Just to be a dick, I shouted, "outlaw country!" Beside me, I heard Queen Libby say, "Western swing."

I turned to her and said, "Huh?"

"I prefer western swing," she replied.

She spoke to me with the scolding tone of a schoolteacher. She even tilted her nose up as she said it. As silly as it all was, Queen Libby's comment flipped a light switch in my brain. It changed my perspective on the whole rockabilly/alt-country thing.

That scene is split into many different sub-genres. There are rockabilly and psychobilly, as well as alt-country, outlaw country, and her majesty's beloved Western swing. Generally speaking, people only want to hear their favorite style and to hell with everything else.

Thanks to Queen Libby, I realized that starting The last Outlaws was a huge mistake. There weren't enough outlaw country fans in Michigan to sustain that band. My journey into outlaw country was just a phase, and it was time I phased out of it. My passion for writing and recording songs was reignited by punk rock, my first musical love.

Rose and I closed on our condo sometime in the spring. By summer, I was ready to start playing punk.

Since I didn't have enough money to record a CD, I thought I'd put a band together. I had to find some like-minded musicians to do that. I was looking for people who were down for playing original music and could practice once a week.

While scrolling through Facebook, I found that person. It was Matt "Falcon" Falconi, the quiet, brooding guy who played guitar in Pure Spun Evil for a minute. In his post, he said that Nick "Klaus" Sauermaische moved out of state. This left Falcon looking for a new project. He wanted people who were willing to put in the time and effort.

I didn't jump at that opportunity. I launched myself at it like a speeding rocket. I messaged Falcon and told him I wanted to put something together. He messaged me back and asked me to give him a call. I took a seat on the flat-topped boulder outside our house and dialed Falcon's number.

He repeated everything he said in his Facebook post. He also said that he wished he would have stayed in Pure Spun Evil longer because it was a lot of fun. I told him that it still could be. He told me he'd love to do a P.S.E. reunion, but he wanted to run it by Klaus.

That was the proverbial record-scratch moment where everything just stopped.

Why the hell did he want to call Klaus? The dude lived 17 hours away and had nothing to do with anything. While I didn't understand Falcon's need to do this, I didn't question it. I just asked him to call me back when he finished his call.

I was on pins and needles while I waited for that phone to ring. When it did, I snatched it up and said, "Hey, Falcon!" in an overly-enthusiastic tone. I cringed at how desperate I sounded, which was the first clue that my instincts were trying to tell me something.

Falcon said, "I can't jam with you, man."

"Why not?"

"Well…"

"What?"

"I don't know how to say this…"

"…Just say it," I replied.

"You like things a certain way…"

I asked him what he meant, and he said something about me being "hard to work with." That didn't surprise me. After everything that went down in Pure Spun Evil, I could see how he'd feel that way. Too bad the version of me he thought he knew was 15 years old. I didn't try to argue that point because he was the last person I should be begging to jam with me.

I said, "Well, I guess there isn't anything more to say."

"I guess not," he replied.

As I sat on that rock, my thoughts raced through my head. After sorting them out, I knew what I needed to do. It wasn't a snap decision, either. It was something that I'd been considering for a while, but I kept putting it off. I could no longer deny that its time had come.

I told Rose about my call with Falcon, and she picked up on the disappointment in my voice. When I got to the end of my sad story, I said, "It's time to call it quits."

"Are you serious?" she asked.

"Yeah," I replied. "I can't keep banging my head against the wall."

"It might be hard to hear this now, but you'll see that you made the right decision," she replied.

I knew she was right. I also knew how permanent my decision was. When I said I was done with music in the past, I was young enough to get back into it if I changed my mind. When I said "I'm done" after Falcon's phone, I was in my 40s. I was too old to take a few years off, and Father Time agreed with me. This time, I'd given up for good.

That was one of the hardest nights of my life. I tossed and turned in bed because it felt like I had a terrible, burning itch raging through my body. No amount of scratching or digging could make it go away, and that drove me crazy.

I needed to calm down, so I took deep breaths of air then let it out slowly. I did that over and over until that horrible itching feeling lessened. That's when I realized that the itching sensation distracted me from the unpleasant thoughts that intruded into my mind.

Now, I had to deal with those thoughts, which felt like a hoard of demons trying to drag me down to hell.

There is a name for what I was experiencing. Philosophers and scholars call it "The Dark Night of the Soul." They describe it as an "ego death," and my ego fought back every step of the way. It made all sorts of threats, bargains, and promises to get me to quit this spiritual journey. When I refused, my ego assaulted me with everything I'd been hiding from myself.

I got punched in the gut with the ugly truth about my Pure Spun Evil persona. At that time in my life, I was plagued with deep-rooted feelings of inadequacy and self-loathing. My anger numbed me to those uncomfortable thoughts, so I forged a false identity from that emotion. It made me feel dominant and important.

I wrapped myself in the cloak of my false self and ventured out into the world. Every inflammatory song I spewed was an indictment against a society I thought had done me wrong. During the Dark Night of the Soul, I realized that my circumstances were the result of the choices I'd made. My so-called stage act was just me blaming everyone else for my problems.

My ego then put me in a headlock and shoved my ridiculous outlaw country identity into my face.

The Last Outlaws was a manifestation of my neediness, alienation, and low self-esteem. I thought that ridiculous caricature would mask my shortcomings, but it didn't. Worse yet, I was the only one who couldn't see through that pathetic disguise. The self-pitying songs I wrote betrayed the fragility of my true self to anyone who was listening.

When those false versions of myself crumbled away, it revealed the truth about me. I destroyed every chance that life gave me to live my dreams. Even the few times when something wasn't my fault, I made things worse by the way I reacted. Those decisions slammed the nails into the coffin that holds my punk rock ambitions.

There was something ironic in coming to terms with all of that. I felt wounded and shamed, but I had nowhere to hide. That's because I didn't have a band anymore. That was always the way I fed my ego and numbed myself to the emotional pain of my harsh reality.

In the end, I was left with two choices: I could get bitter, or I could get better. Only time would tell which way I'd go.

31.
Caught in a Spotlight

I was furious that my singing days were gone for good. That triggered my darkest thoughts, and I descended into a mid-life crisis. I'd get up, go to work, then come home to watch the kids while Rose went to work. I felt trapped in those circumstances.

Facebook was my only escape. In typical middle-aged guy fashion, I spent countless hours chatting online with female friends. I lavished them with the attention that I denied my wife and kids. At night, Rose would go to bed alone while I kept doing what I was doing. I'd stumble to bed hours later, only to get back on that hellish hamster wheel in the morning.

My wife and kids suffered from my absence, but they suffered from my presence too. In my miserable state, I took my frustrations out on my family. Sometimes, I'd even start fights with Rose, so I had an excuse to remove myself from the family dynamic. I justified my behavior by saying that I put a roof over their heads. That was the same excuse my parents used for their abusive ways.

My egocentric train ride came to an end when Rose finally had enough. I pushed her too far one day, and she just snapped. My loving and patient wife called me out on my horrible behavior as only she can. Being put on blast like that made me feel like I was standing in the beam of a white-hot light. Its blinding glare shined through my paper-thin defenses and exposed all my flaws.

Rose's unique brand of "Spotlight Therapy" triggered my shame/rage reaction. In typical J.P. Ribner fashion, I made a last-ditch effort to save my wounded pride. The best I could come up with was saying that she was guilty of doing those things too.

She shouted, "You're a narcissist, just like your parents!"

That was Rose's most blinding blast of brutal honesty, and it devastated me. I'd always told myself that I wasn't like my parents. She made me see that was just my vanity talking. Rose was right when she said I was just like them. The shame I felt was practically crippling so, once again, I tried to salvage my pride.

I said, "You don't know that."

"That's right," she replied. "I'm not a licensed therapist..."

"...Exactly!"

"I'm just a mother who doesn't want her kids to grow up and write a song like 'I Was a Teenage Scapegoat!'"

The reality of the situation hit me like a sledgehammer because she put it in a way I could relate to. It also was a hell of a wake-up call. I always thought I was so special and unique because I recognized my parents' abusive behavior. I honestly thought that was enough to keep me from becoming just like them. Ironically, that was textbook narcissistic thinking.

Rose's words damn near killed me, but they opened my eyes to my narcissism. I think I always knew it was there, but I'd pushed that uncomfortable truth into the darkest parts of my mind. Leave it to my wife to shine her spotlight on it and make me confront the ugliest of truths.

After an argument like that, I expected Rose to cut and run. Every other woman I'd been with had done that... if I hadn't discarded them first. Rose stood by me and committed to helping me break the cycle of narcissism that haunted me all my life. Without her, I had no hope of undoing 40+ years of abuse and trauma.

Rose came up with strategies to help me battle my indoctrination into narcissism. One of her most effective ones is to remind me that I'm not a "Flint Ribner" anymore. That's usually enough to snap me out of the narcissistic rages that threaten to possess me.

If I need more help, her soul-scorching Spotlight Therapy sessions are always the perfect reality check.

The last time I researched narcissism, I became convinced that my parents ruined my band. After listening to Rose, I realized that I was lying to myself. The only one responsible for my failures was me. It was the same for everything else in my life.

Yes, my narcissism is a result of growing up in Trauma Central. There's no denying that. But blaming Mom and Dad for my problems was a cop-out. I was in my late 30s when I was in The Last Outlaws. If

I knew that I grew up in a dysfunctional home, I should have got the help I needed. I didn't, though.

So, what happened?

Well, the better part of my nature worked hard to create my opportunities in music. That was just the set up for my narcissism to come in and destroy it. To prove this to myself, I applied the symptoms of narcissism to my behavior when I was in bands. All I would need to have is five of the nine traits to be a candidate for narcissism:

1. Demeaning, bullying, and belittling others.

    If I tried to deny this, my former bandmates
    would call me out. As a teenager, I wrote a
    song about a girl who took a face dive into
    some bleachers. As an adult, I indiscriminately
    lashed out at everyone. There's a mean streak
    inside of me, and that's a horrible quality for
    anyone to have. I'm mortified this was my go-
    to behavior.

2. Exploiting people for personal gain.

    The Great Con Job of 1986 was just the beginning.
    When I wanted something, I took advantage of
    anyone I could. What worse is that I was proud
    of my deceitful and ruthless nature. These were
    the same qualities that I detested in other local
    musicians. Project much? (That's a rhetorical
    question.)

3. Fantasies about unlimited power and success.

    This was SO me. Having a band wasn't enough.
    I had to dominate the Flint and Detroit
    music scenes. The fact that I thought I could
    do that shows how deep my sickness was. The
    only thing I succeeded in doing was pushing away
    the people who cared about me. The irony there
    was that without them, I was powerless. I learned

254

that the hard way.

4. A need for constant admiration.

    I was an insecure kid who was emotionally and
    physically abused. Performing my music in
    front of a crowd was the only thing that gave me
    a sense of self-worth. I thrived on the attention
    and validation I got; it was like a drug. No wonder
    I was always so desperate to be in a band.

5. Intense jealousy and envy.

    I've always hated it when anyone accused me of
    being jealous because they were usually right. If
    I'm being honest, I hated the other bands in the
    scene because I envied their success. They were
    getting the attention that I wanted for myself.
    This made me feel insecure, and that brought
    out an ugly side of me. This prevented me
    from forming friendships and enjoying more
    opportunities in my local music scene.

So, it's clear that I'm a solid five out of nine for narcissistic traits. I
probably have the other four traits of narcissism, too. I won't go into it
here, though. There's only so much self-flagellation I can handle.

So, my days in music have come to an end. The crowds have gone
home, the stage lights have dimmed, and the ringing in my ears has
finally stopped. I never became the punk rock icon I dreamed of being.
I'm just the idiot who detonated his band, pushed his friends away, and
discovered that he's a narcissist.

That's not the future I dreamed about, but it's the one I made for
myself through the choices I made. I'm still learning to live with that.

One day, I found out that my dad's health took a turn for the worse.
That didn't come as a surprise. He'd been battling Parkinson's Disease
and Diabetes for a while.

He had to have hip replacement surgery. In his condition, that took a huge toll on his body. After the operation, he went to a rehabilitation center to heal. While he was there, he called and begged me to visit him. I told him I'd stop by after work.

I had no idea what I was walking into.

I worried about how I'd pass the time with him. My dad and I were never that close, so I didn't know what we'd talk about. We ended up making some small talk, and he asked me how Rose and the kids were doing. I told him everyone was doing fine.

Then, he said, "I know I wasn't a good father to you."

That caught me off guard. Before I had a chance to wrap my mind around it, Dad apologized for the mistakes he made when I was a kid. Then he told me that he was proud of me, whether I believed it or not. I felt dumbfounded because he never said things like that to me.

"I need to know that you forgive me," he said.

"C'mon, Dad," I replied.

"I'm serious," he said. "This is important to me."

"You really need to hear this right now?"

"Yes!"

The old man really put me on the spot, and I didn't know how to respond. He and I never discussed our feelings with each other. My mind scrambled to come up with something to say. I told him to stop worrying about me and focus on getting better and going home. That was the best I could come up with.

"That's not what I asked you," he said.

"Fine," I said. "I forgive you."

"You have no idea how much that means to me," he replied.

We shared a moment of uncomfortable silence, and I felt awkward. I really didn't know what to say after that awkward apology of his. I didn't have to say anything because Dad spoke up.

He said, "You probably don't know this, but I always wanted to play the violin."

"Why didn't you?"

"My parents couldn't afford it," he said.

If I was taken off guard by what he said earlier, that was more disorienting. The violin? What the hell did that have to do with anything? The whole thing made me feel uncomfortable, so I told him I had to get going.

He said, "We should spend some time together when I get out."

"Okay," I replied.

As I drove home, I started feeling resentful. I hated how Dad put me on the spot like that. I also felt weird about the way he apologized to me. He didn't address any of the horrible things he did to me over the years. He just said, "I'm sorry," like that would just cover everything. I didn't know how to process all that, so I called Rose.

I said, "What the hell was he talking about?"

"You want my honest opinion?"

"That's why I called."

"It sounds like he was saying goodbye," she said.

"What are you talking about?" I said. "He'll be home in a few days."

"He knows more about his health than you do," she replied.

"True," I replied. "But do you really think that's what it was?"

When she said that, my thoughts started racing. When I finally calmed down, I could see the wisdom in what she said. Dad hadn't been well for a long time. It would be hard for anyone to stay healthy with all that going on, especially someone who was 76.

I said, "Well, what about that stuff about the violin?"

"What do you think he meant?" she said.

"I don't know," I said.

"Think about it."

"Maybe he was saying sorry for all the shit he gave me about my music," I said.

"It's deeper than that."

"How so?"

"I think he was jealous of you," she said.

"Jealous?"

"Yeah," she replied.

"Why would he be jealous of me?"

"Because you did something that he was afraid to try."

When I thought about it, it made sense. My grandparents didn't have the money for violin lessons, but he could have played music later in life. He had the money and the time, so why didn't he try? Rose asked me what I thought about it.

"I don't know," I said.

"What's the one thing narcissists fear most?"

I said "shame," and that's when everything fell into place. The old man never tried to play the violin because he was afraid of failing. That fear contradicted the false image he created of himself. Those

257

uncomfortable feelings turned to anger, which he projected onto me because I had the guts to play music. That explained why he hated it so much.

I reminded Rose of all the things my dad did to crush my desire to play music. I wanted to do it so badly that I didn't let him stop me. All the things he did still humiliated me, though. That's why I knew I didn't really forgive him, even though I told him I did. His apology was too little too late.

She said, "Oh my God!"

"What?"

"Now you're being narcissistic."

"Bullshit!"

"You honestly expect him to give you a complete recounting of all the ways he hurt you?"

"No. Just one or two things," I replied.

"...He's a 76-year-old man who's probably on his deathbed!"

Once again, Rose was right. There was no way my dad could have covered everything he did to me in the state he was in. All he could do is apologize the best way he knew how, and he did. If I would have understood that at the time, we might have got the closure we both needed.

The whole thing was so ironic. Of all the times my dad said I let him down, the one time I really did was when he needed me the most.

I never had another heart-to-heart with my dad. When the pain of his Parkinson's Disease became unbearable, he decided to morphine drip his way out of this world. The problem was that he didn't tell anyone about this plan until after he set it into motion.

One day, a hospice worker called me out of the blue. Someone who I didn't know was telling me that my father didn't have long to live. I needed to come to Flint if I wanted to see my dad one last time. The whole thing was so surreal.

Rose and I packed the kids into the truck and headed to Flint. By the time we got there, Dad had slipped into a coma. The best I could do was say "I love you" to something that no longer resembled the man who raised me. His only response was a low, winding groan. I'll never know if he heard me or not.

I didn't like that he chose to go out without telling us, but I

258

understood why he did it. My Mom is a weak person who can't handle the truth about anything. The old man shielded her from reality for as long as I can remember. He protected her from his decision to die because she would have fallen apart if he told her beforehand.

She couldn't talk him out of anything once he slipped into a coma. That didn't stop her from trying, though. As he laid there, slipping away, she cried, wailed, and begged him to come back. He struggled in vain to force his eyes open each time she bleated, "Don't go, Johnny!"

I was disgusted by how selfish she was. Yes, it was hard to watch her husband die. I get that; but, at the end of the day, it was his choice. The least Mom could do was let him go in peace. That was too much to ask of her, though.

My chance of reconciling with my dad died with him on May 4, 2015. Yes, he'd done a lot of hurtful things to me, but he was still my dad. That's why I was upset that I screwed up the one opportunity I had to put things right between us. That small bit of resolution I got at the rehab center was all there would ever be.

Dad's death plunged me into a black hole of depression. I fought like hell to keep from sinking further into that dark abyss. I'm grateful that Rose threw me a lifeline, then helped pull me out of that pit. If it wasn't for her, I would've lost that battle.

The old man's death shattered Mom's fragile grip on her sanity. My parents aided and abetted each other in their sheer madness and shared personality disorders. Mom made excuses for Dad's anger and violence while he shielded her from much-needed criticism. With no one there to make excuses for her, Mom exposed her failings to the world. It was an ugly sight.

Now, she spends her money like a drunken sailor on shore leave for the short-term dopamine rush it gives her. The things she buys don't fill the hole inside herself, so these useless trinkets continue to fill up her house. It all adds to the growing collection of clutter that's taken over her home like an invading army.

The last time I visited her, her house looked like it was auditioning for a role on *Hoarders*. I begged her to let me throw away some of the most festering bits of trash, but she attacked me. That was my cue to get out of Trauma Central before things between us got worse.

As I drove home, I had a horrible vision of how things will probably end for my Mom. After not hearing from her for a while, I'll drive up to see her. When no one answers the door, I'll use my key to get inside. The stench of death will assault my senses the minute I open the door.

I'll know exactly what I'm walking into, but I'll have to do it. With my hand over my nose, I'll venture forth into the house. It won't be hard to find her; I'll just follow the smell.

I'll walk down the small flight of stairs that leads to the living room. That's where I'll find her. A cloud of flies will scatter to reveal a festering corpse. The worst image will be that of her beloved Boston Terrier, Shotzi, who will be feasting on the rotting remains of something that once was my mother.

I've certainly painted a disturbing picture of my mother's last days on earth, but it's inevitable. She's pushed away everyone who could help her. Now, she just sits alone in that house, unable to face her many demons. She'd rather bargain with them, instead.

I know from personal experience that it's a fool's bargain.

32.
Wasted Youth?

I've agonized over the question of whether I wasted my youth chasing after a dream that didn't come true.

My dad is part of the reason I think it might have been a waste. He must have told me that about 100 times. But I'm not my dad, and my dad isn't me. What I think about my experience is more important than his opinion.

So, how do I really feel about it? To answer that question, I'd have to find a way to measure something like this.

I could be like some of the entrepreneurs I've worked for and take a hard look at the numbers. To do that, I'd have to compare the time and money I invested in my music. Then I'd compare those expenses to what I got out of the experience, aka my rewards. The answer would determine if I achieved an optimal return on investment or R.O.I.

When I look at it that way, I didn't even come close to hitting the mark. There were no record deals, music videos, or major tours across the country. There weren't any movie roles, publishing deals, and iconic status achieved, either. I didn't even make a dent in my hometown scene.

If I only look at the numbers, the old man was right. My pursuit of punk rock was a bust, and I have very little to show for it. I can hear him now, shouting his famous phrase, "It's a waste!" Years after his death, those words are still echoing inside my head like a sound byte on an endless loop.

It's wrong to look at this as an entrepreneur, though. Some things can't be measured on a balance sheet, especially the things I've learned.

My misadventures in music were an exercise in self-discovery. That was the most important journey I'd ever taken. It stripped away the false images I created of myself and forced me to confront some of my biggest flaws. I wouldn't have learned anything about myself if I never picked up a microphone.

There's something I learned from my journey into punk rock. It was a valuable lesson in the importance of friendship.

There's still a punk scene in Flint, but it's a lot smaller than it was back in the day. Some of the people I knew are still playing in bands. I used to drive myself crazy wondering how they can do it while I can't. Thanks to my journey of self-discovery, I know why.

Those folks are still doing shows because they've mastered the one thing I couldn't, which is relationships. Yes, their talent and hard work also play a part, but being in a band is a relationship. Maintaining relationships has always been my biggest weakness, thanks to my narcissism.

I was fortunate to have worked with two of the greatest musicians and friends I've ever known. They were also two of my closest friends. Too bad I pushed them away when they disagreed with me and criticized my bad behavior.

When I talk about a "wasted youth," that's the biggest waste of all. It's also one of the hardest and most important lessons I've ever learned.

I miss Andy Harris, and I'm not too proud to say it.

He's a great guy who went out of his way to help me when I was down. Did I do anything to show him that I appreciated and deserved his kindness? No, I didn't. I chose to resent him because he established some boundaries with me.

One of the last times I talked to him, he told me something very profound. We were looking back on our Pure Spun Evil/The Last Outlaws days, and he said, "I think we all said things to each other that we probably shouldn't have." He's right, of course.

While I didn't argue with Andy about what he said, there is something I'd like to add to it. Yes, we all said some mean things to each other during that time. The bigger problem was my inability to handle what was said to me. I was the leader of the bands, after all. My terrible reactions did more damage than anything that was said to or about me.

There was another problem with our friendship dynamic, and the problem was all mine.

Andy did so much for me that I became dependent upon him. It

262

wasn't just recording my songs or playing in my band. He also validated my self-esteem, and I became addicted to that. Like a junkie craving a fix, I hounded him with my problems to get his attention and compliments.

Only now am I able to recognize the enormous burden I placed upon him. I turned myself inside-out and exposed myself as the demanding emotional toddler that I was. That meant Andy lost a friend and gained a child. He deserved better from me, but I just kept trying to drag him down into my emotional hell.

For both our sakes, I should have been my own therapist instead of putting so much pressure on him.

I could have been a better friend to Rick Rokowski, aka Rikki Roxx.

He was more than a friend and a bandmate, he also was a mentor to me. He freely shared his musical experience to help make me a better songwriter. Every song I wrote in Pure Spun Evil and The Last Outlaws bore his mark, and my work was better for it.

Rikki also was a motivational life coach. On more than one occasion, he gave me the kick in the ass I needed to get back in the game. I'll never forget the advice he emailed me when I was frustrated over not being able to master Doc Watson's fingerpicking style:

> "I recommend wiping the slate clean. Just clasp
> both hands and arms together and clear the entire
> table, throwing the past on the floor and digging
> deep to focus on what is truly you. THAT is a un-
> ique and profitable venture that you'll never regret,
> and one that knows no genre or boundaries."

Of all the things Rikki taught me, I ignored his most important lesson. I'm talking about the times he encouraged me to be more assertive with problematic bandmates. I wish I would have listened to him, both for the bands' sake, as well as for my personal development.

I also should have done a better job of working with Rikki during the few times we butted heads. I enacted the nuclear option instead, which destroyed all the good memories we created with Pure Spun Evil and The Last Outlaws. It also caused me to miss out on more than 10 years of friendship with him.

Rikki's wedding was another thing I missed. Andy didn't, though. He was one of Rikki's groomsmen. It would have been great to be there with them, just like when Rikki, The Kid, and I attended Andy's wedding. You only get one chance at moments like that, and I blew mine.

Because of my bad choices, I can only look back on that lost decade of our friendship through lenses tinted in a dark shade of regret.

The one person I can thank and apologize to is my wife, Rose.

We met after I destroyed The Last Outlaws. Since that was still an open wound, Rose listened to all my band stories. My victim game was strong back then, and I told her about all the "evil" things Andy and Rikki did to me. When I finished whining, she administered her trademark Spotlight Therapy. That gave me a more realistic perspective on everything.

Without her tough love, I would have never written this book. Or maybe I would have, but it would have been a lot different. There would be no honesty, self-discovery, or regrets. This book would be nothing more than page after page of me blaming everyone else for my failures. That would be more tragic than losing 100 bands.

Rose's help went beyond putting my band mistakes into perspective. She also made me aware of my narcissism, which was the real cause of most of my problems in life. She also helped me hone the tools I need to battle it. Without her keen insight and intervention, I would have ended up as nothing more than a carbon copy of my parents.

Her intervention saved me from suffering the horrible fate of passing on my parents' abuse and neglect to my kids. Because of that, I owe her a debt of gratitude that I can never repay. All I can do is keep trying to do my best for her and our kids, just like she wants me to.

They say that a smart person learns from his mistakes. They also say that a wise man learns from the mistakes of others. I've certainly learned a lot from my messy past, but I don't think that makes me smart. I still wish I wouldn't have screwed up so badly in the first place.

If learning from other people's mistakes makes you wiser, keep reading. I might be able to reach more people with my mistakes than I ever could through my music. But it's just my mistakes I'm sharing, it's the things I've learned from them. It's five points that I call my "life rules," and I hope they help someone. If not, then I've suffered for nothing.

1. Before you leave home, do some housecleaning.

Dysfunctional families make great sitcoms, but they're not funny in real life. If you've grown up in one of these homes, the trauma you've suffered has left deep scars. This can make you act out in ways that alienate friends, loved ones, and employers. If you don't get the help you need, you might end up alone. There's no reason to feel ashamed or embarrassed by your upbringing because it's not your fault. You're only to blame if you don't get the help you need as an adult.

2. You can be a pinball, or you can make a plan.

Do you want to achieve your dreams and goals? You should make a plan to achieve them. If you don't, you'll be like a pinball in a pinball machine. When life slams you hard, and it will, you will go bouncing and crashing all over the place. You and your dreams deserve better. That's why you have to make a plan for your life and stick to it. It's the best investment you can make in yourself. You deserve to succeed.

3. Be the friend you want others to be for you.

Seems simple, right? Unfortunately, it's easy to forget this take on "The Golden Rule." As humans, it's our nature to selfishly focus on all the things we expect from our friends. It's more difficult to be a good friend to the people in our lives, but it's worth the effort. Show your friends how much they mean to you through your actions, and you'll get the same from them.

4. Don't stand under dark clouds.

Dark clouds drop rain and lightning down on anyone who stands beneath them. Dark cloud-people
do the same by projecting their resentment, animosity,
and self-hate onto you. They can't be reasoned
with or appeased. You deserve to have the right
people in your life. So does the dark cloud, believe
it or not. They just have trouble letting go of bad
relationships because it's all the know. If a dark
cloud settles over your life, be the gentle wind that
sends them on their way. You'll be happier if you do.

5. You can't find self-worth outside of yourself.

Some people live their life seeking the approval
of others. No matter how much praise they con-
sume, they still feel empty because they don't val-
ue themselves. They pass through life like a black
hole, devouring compliments but never feeling satisfied. If this sounds familiar, it's time to seek
your own approval. You'll find it when you
learn to become less dependent on what other
people think of you. When you can finally dis-
cover your self-worth, you won't crave external
validation. Arriving at that understanding is the
hardest thing you'll ever do, but it's worth the
effort. You deserve to believe in yourself.

Now, I know what you're thinking. "Why should I take life advice
from someone who admits he's a narcissist?" Or maybe you're thinking,
"Why should I listen to a total screw up like you?" Those are good
questions, and I have an answer for both.

I've come by these life tips after a lifetime of mistakes and regrets.
I've learned from those mistakes, and fully recognize the dysfunctional
behavior patterns that caused them. Other people go to their graves
without ever having admitted they did something wrong. So, just

consider what I have to say. It might save you from doing something you'll probably regret.

There's one more thing I'd like to say about my "rules for life." I've come up with the list, but I haven't mastered this wisdom. I still make mistakes when I forget what I've learned, and let my emotions take over. Sometimes I have to kick myself in the ass because I should have known better. It happens.

There's really no end to the journey to being a better version of myself. It's an ongoing boot camp that makes me confront my shame, trauma, and narcissism every day. It's far from comfortable, but I'm not running from my pain anymore. These days, I accept the pain because those uncomfortable feelings are just weakness leaving my body and mind. I'm better off without it.

Now that's punk as fuck!

The End.

CPSIA information can be obtained
at www.ICGtesting.com
Printed in the USA
FSHW020500040521
81111FS